# THE BATTLE FOR ROOM SERVICE

Mark Lawson was born in London in 1962. His first work of fiction, *Bloody Margaret: Three Political Fantasies*, was published by Picador in 1991 (paperback 1992), to great critical acclaim, and was shortlisted in the First Book section of the 1992 Commonwealth Writers' Prize. He is currently writing a novel. *The Battle for Room Service: Journeys to All the Safe Places* is his first non-fiction book.

Since 1988, Mark Lawson has been chief feature writer for the *Independent Magazine*. He also writes a weekly column for the *Independent*. His first job in journalism was with the *Universe*, a weekly Catholic newspaper. Subsequently, he wrote as a free-lance for *The Times* and the *Sunday Times*, before joining the *Independent* in 1986 as TV critic and then parliamentary sketch-writer. From 1990–91, he was TV critic of the *Independent on Sunday*. He won a British Press Award in 1987; BP Arts Journalism Awards in 1989, 1990, and 1991; and Broadcast Journalism Awards in 1989 (critic) and 1990 (feature writer).

He has written and presented two television documentaries: *Byline – Vote For Ron* (BBC, 1990) and *J'Accuse – Coronation Street* (Channel 4, 1991). He appears regularly on TV and radio, including *Start The Week*, *The Late Show*, and *Behind The Headlines*. He lives in London.

ALSO BY MARK LAWSON IN PICADOR:

*Bloody Margaret*: Three Political Fantasies

MARK LAWSON

# THE BATTLE FOR FOR ROOM SERVICE

*Journeys to all the Safe Places*

PICADOR ORIGINAL

A Picador Original

First published 1993 by Picador
Pan Books Ltd

This edition published 2013 by Picador
an imprint of Pan Macmillan, a division of Macmillan Publishers Limited
Pan Macmillan, 20 New Wharf Road, London N1 9RR
Basingstoke and Oxford
Associated companies throughout the world
www.panmacmillan.com

Associated companies throughout the world

ISBN 978-1-4472-6667-9

A CIP catalogue record for this book is available from
the British Library

Typeset by Cambridge Composing (UK) Limited, Cambridge
Printed and bound by CPI Group (UK) Ltd, Croydon, CR0 4YY

To Frank and Teresa Lawson
My mother and father

With love and thanks

# CONTENTS

PROLOGUE

# WAR AND KINDRED RISKS

The Northern Ireland correspondent for a London newspaper once told me the intriguing story of the Belfast Tourist Board. This outfit sounds like the winner in a joky magazine competition to come up with the ultimate thankless profession – other contenders might be the Tel Aviv Bacon Marketing Board or the British Royal Marriage Guidance Council – but Belfast does, in fact, have a tourist body dedicated to convincing prospective visitors that they will not end up as, well, a tourist body.

The existence of this organization was a source of great amusement to my informant. His cynicism was perhaps justifiable, given the nature of his daily work. The flashier kind of word processors have something called *save-get* keys, allowing a frequently used phrase or formula to be stored and called up with a single stab. The Belfast correspondent was thinking of electronically memorizing the sentences 'The victim was a married man with — children' and 'The — later claimed responsibility in a phone call to a local newspaper', simply typing in the number of offspring and the initials of the killers later on. So you can understand why he was somewhat unpatriotic in his attitude to the Belfast Tourist Board. He would pass the time between reporting sectarian executions by imagining slogans to be used by the BTB in its advertising campaigns. One, I remember, ran: 'If you long to feel the soil of Ireland under your feet, come to Dublin. If you long to feel the soil of Ireland *over* your feet, come to Belfast.' An equally melodious piece of deceit was: 'Belfast – where the cares of daily existence will be taken away from you.'

But the journalist was perplexed not only by the mere existence of the Belfast Tourist Board but by its apparent success. Every January, the organization would issue a press release proudly announcing an upsurge in visitors in the previous year. Surprised

I

to see a rise claimed at the end of a period of more than common atrocities, he re-examined previous figures. The pattern was standard. The more bombings and shootings in any twelve months, the greater the tourist boom in the subsequent dozen.

Worried that he had discovered a phenomenon of ghoulish tourism – a more formalized equivalent of car-crash gawping – he asked the board for its methods of measurement. It transpired that they judged traveller traffic by (1) airline tickets (2) hotel capacity (3) car rental bookings. He realized the truth. Those holiday rushes consisted of out-of-town journalists, flying in to write 'BELFAST – TWINNED WITH HELL' pieces, after some particularly grim incident.

The moral of the above story is a simple one: that, in broad terms, the world divides into the tourist zones and the terrorist zones. It is inevitable that travel agents and tourist boards will try to haze the borders between them – as a resource which is theoretically renewable for ever, travellers make a significant difference to a nation's balance of payments as traditional industries fail – but these attempts should be treated with some scepticism.

It is true that a country may occasionally move from one zone to another, sometimes with uncomfortable rapidity. Most of the 1992 guidebooks had managed to pull Yugoslavia out of the sections detailing what to do in Europe. But some had not and their breathless recommendations – 'friendly people', 'quiet beaches', 'plentiful and cheap food' – stood as a warning of the fragility of lucrative tranquillity. Similarly, Beirut was once a resort mentioned in the same breath as Biarritz. I recently read that there is to be an attempt by the Lebanese to reinstate Beirut as a vacation place, but, unless they adopt criteria similar to those of the Belfast Tourist Board – counting the ordeal of the Western hostages as 1500 hotel nights, for example – it would seem a hard market to crack.

Certainly, you are unlikely to be find me on the first Lazy Lebanon Days Package tour. I have stuck – as both a journalist and a holidaymaker – to the tourist zones. It has always been my problem that I love travel but am touchy about where I end up. Wanderlust and cowardice make uneasy headfellows. I live under the Heathrow flightpath. In the window of the room in which I work, the 747s are briefly suspended, in miniature size, in the top quarter-pane of glass as they bank for landing. Wishing myself on each one, I then reconsider the desire in the light of the liveries. I particularly magic myself aboard the flights of Qantas and American.

But catering to such neuroses is now a profession. I read – in a business magazine, left appropriately enough as a compliment in a hotel room – that Control Risks, a 'security and crisis consultancy', divided the places of the world in to four categories for prospective travellers. These were:

> LEVEL ONE (Aware): The crime risk is insignificant. No terrorist groups are active and, although isolated incidents are possible, the security threat to travellers is minimal. Example: Singapore.
> LEVEL TWO (Vigilant): There are occasional demonstrations or terrorist incidents, but these provide no more than incidental threats to business travellers. There is little crime risk to travellers provided they exercise common-sense discretion. Example: South Korea.
> LEVEL THREE (Caution): There is a high crime rate or significant political unrest which could disrupt business travel at short notice. Terrorist attacks occasionally cause disruption. Example: Berlin.
> LEVEL FOUR (Danger): Conditions verge on war or civil war; law and order are in imminent danger of breaking down; or there is a terrorist campaign directly affecting business travellers. Travel should be postponed unless absolutely necessary. Example: Iraq.

I realize that the genre of travel writing is, these days, mostly practised on Level Four nations. If there is no political disturbance, then an equal danger must be found in the geography or wildlife of the terrain attempted. Level Three destinations may be accepted if the place concerned is probably merely in transition to four-star awfulness: i.e., at the time of writing, Berlin, New York, Los Angeles.

I am equally aware that the territories described in this book – New Zealand, Australia, Middle America, Alaska, Canada,

Luxembourg, Brussels, Switzerland, Milton Keynes, Disney-world, Expo '92 and Center Parcs – would, in the eyes of most people, not even merit a level one rating. It would be necessary to invent another:

> LEVEL ZERO (Nonchalance): There is almost no serious crime. Politically, one right-wing monetarist government is occasionally replaced by another, but this leads only to minor traffic hold-ups on polling day or during a royal visit or religious procession.

The genesis of this project – an attempted journey in to the heart of lightness of the modern world – should therefore be sketched in.

James Fenton, a long-time hero of mine and one of the bravest journalists of his generation, wrote in the introduction to his battle-scar memoirs *All the Wrong Places* of his hunger, from a young age, to put himself in the presence of danger. In the squirmiest scene of many in this work, hunger proves literally dangerous, when Fenton's hosts in Cambodia hand him a bowl of rice, on which, he notices as he lowers his fingers to eat, an army of ants is already feasting. Reluctant to give offence, he shovels down both the rice and the lice.

You have heroes for two reasons: in hope of emulation or in acknowledgement of the impossibility of following. My interest in Fenton was of the second kind. One of the most cowardly journalists of his or any other generation, I have, all my life, had a hunger to put myself in the presence of safety. Ants in the rice? A fly in the soup and I was checking the insurance policy. Thrilling as it was to read fearless reporting from the frontlines of the world, I always knew that fearful reporting from the backlines was more my cup of (weak) tea. Not only did I not cover the Gulf War, but, sent to America on an unrelated assignment during the conflict, I insisted on flying Swissair via Zurich because of the terrorist threat to Western airlines.

The process of coming out as a coward was a gradual one. Newspapers are collegiate places, more so since the vogue for

open-plan offices, and, occasionally, heading for my safe houses
of Arts or Books or Colour Magazine (quiet Western elections
my speciality), I would drop off in Foreign for a chat. There was
a distressingly messy map of the world – this was the beginning
of the post-1989 period when emergency place names and fron-
tiers were weekly scribbled in with felt-pen – and a wall of clocks
(Moscow, Delhi, Peking, they were labelled) up to a day either
way out of tock with ours.

The atmosphere was thrilling to a young reporter but – quite
unlike other juniors who made this pilgrimage – I was happy for
the thrill to stay vicarious. I knew that, if you picked up a phone
on one of these desks, there was a strong chance that the
interference on the line was bullets hitting it. One day, a correspondent stabling in London between assignments idly gave me a
tour of his wounds. There was his Vietnam knee, his Jakarta
forearm, his Tiananmen leg. I gulped. If I had wished to recipro-
cate, I could only have shown him the negligible discoloration
above one temple, where, in Washington DC one fateful morning, the door of the bathroom cabinet in the Hay-Adams hotel
had swung out suddenly and hit me on the head.

I seemed, however, to be my profession's only sufferer from
this condition. The journalist who sat opposite me went off to
discover Xanadu, succeeded, and wrote a gut-churning book
about the physical risks and discomfort involved. More recently,
I read a piece by another colleague who, having spent a decade as
a reporter in Brussels, had reluctantly left Belgium for Washington, but who remained, I assumed from my regular meetings
with him there, a fellow peace-zone specialist. Indeed, he talked
longingly of returning to Brussels, now that it was 'getting really
hot there', as a result of Europe's moves towards unity in 1992.
However, the piece I now read was headlined: 'For some reason
he didn't shoot me.' The gentle Belgian specialist had driven his
rental car into a black ghetto during the events in Los Angeles
which marked America's moves towards disunity in 1992.

One of my regrets about my wimp illness was that I would
clearly be unable to write a travel book. Just as there are handy
phrase books for travellers, there are also – the general public may
not realize – handy phrase books for travel writers. In the one that
I picked up second-hand – the names of the previous owners are

sadly not quite decipherable on the title page – I found the following suggested usages for different situations:

HEALTH AND PERSONAL SAFETY: 'Dulled perhaps by the lingering effects of the tsetse-fly fever, I never saw the snake, even though it was yards long and exotically marked, like a garden hose painted by Jackson Pollock. It was only when Paolo the scout pounced, splitting the serpent with his *speara* like a West 44th Street stall-holder slicing the bratwurst for the mustard squirt, that I was aware of the certain death on which I was about to tread. 'One bite, you die two minoot,' grinned Paolo, scooping the coiled, rent carcass into his rucksack. Later, it would be our lunch.'

TRANSPORTATION: 'My guess was that the ravine was four hundred metres deep. If there was any comfort in this, it was that the angry frothing of the sea against the rocks below sounded, from this height, like a child's whisper. If I was not to know its true volume, then I was dependent on the rope bridge which swung, like a summer garden hammock, but less substantial, between the two crumbling heights. Instinct told me that even the minimal luggage I had in my rucksack would dangerously influence the equation of man against thread. The bulkiest items were my paperback Proust and my last fresh water bottle. There was no pain as I watched the tin receptacle spin in the air, halt half-way against a rock, then drop to meet the sea, its fresh water swirling from the burst stopper to meet the brine beneath. What else could I do? If I were lucky, I might well find another clear stream between here and Orinoco. I knew that I should not discover another bookstall. Lighter, in both impedimenta and spirit, I rested a sandal on the first frayed lattice thatch of the bridge. There was a creak which would have been thought excessive from a castle door in a Hammer Horror movie . . .'

POLICE AND EMERGENCY SERVICES: 'Until the actual moment that the cell door closed, and the drunk with the gangrenous head wound swung his tequila bottle at me in friendly greeting, I was convinced that my arrest at the carnival had been a bureaucratic error, which would rapidly be rectified with smiles and a "Way you go, *gringo*." At three in the morning, when the drunk's mouth had stopped erupting but his bowels had taken over, I was again convinced that my release was near. A dapper man in pin-stripe and bowler hat clicked across the courtyard on well-stitched heels, scuttling the cockroaches with his solid tread. "*Ambassadore?*", I asked the drunk. He spat lavishly into the corner where his fly-buzzed slops bulked. "*Nada. Nada. Suspendatore*," he croaked. "'Ow you say, in English, hangerman . . ."'

I knew from these phrase books that it was a language I could never learn. Courage was what publishers wanted. But commissioning editors, comically unaware of my problem, took me out for pleasant lunches and then, over the *sambucca*, mooted going *there* on a camel, or *here* without a map, or up such and such a gulf with only two pairs of knickers and a tube of Polo mints as provisions, or into this particular city where the ruling military government was becoming promisingly unpopular.

I would politely point out that the only Fall I had witnessed (or would wish to) had been the collapse of the breakfast melons at the Sheraton Mirage on Queensland's Gold Coast. Furthermore, the only overseas conflict in which I had ever been involved was the battle for room service. I read Fenton's *All the Wrong Places*, I would tell them, and I *shook*. The only travel book I could ever write, I would conclude my sarcastic riff, would be *All the Safe Places*. My put-off was their synopsis. And so here we are.


My map would be that of the quiet world, tourist not terrorist, to adopt the earlier distinction. I made my selection of places through a combination of personal prejudice and outside nomination, criteria made clear in the individual chapters. My object was to visit those places most unlikely to be subject to bloody insurrection. P.J. O'Rourke called a book *Holidays in Hell*. This, perhaps, was *Holidays in Purgatory*. He had pioneered macho travel. Here was wimp tourism. The hidden heroes of this book are two Englishmen with the same surname. They are James Cook, who had the courage to discover the world, and Thomas

Cook, who made it possible for others to discover it without courage.

Throughout my journeys, the rule would be the same. All those places which the great travel writers ignored with a yawn would call me as Kashmir called them. The point was that you could not really imagine a newsreader saying 'An uneasy ceasefire holds on the streets of Auckland tonight.' Or: 'A state of emergency has been declared in Brussels, as United Nations observers abandoned a second attempt to enter the beleaguered city.' Or: 'Continued rioting is reported in Barrow, Alaska, where dog-teams hostile to the ruling Republican party are stoning the government igloos.'

In short, the qualifications were tranquillity, stability, and conventionally civilized values. I stress this, because the idea somehow got around in a few of the countries I visited that this project was an examination of the world's most boring countries. Untrue. If such judgements must be made, I prefer to follow the modern practice of linguistic sensitivity, or political correctness, and refer to these destinations as 'activity-challenged', 'differently interesting', or 'places of calm'.

But it was inevitable that the project would be subject to just such miscomprehension. For example, as the relevant chapter explains, it became necessary, in the section on New Zealand, to change the names of the local informants to protect them from threatened reprisals. Let me reiterate: the identities under which they appear here are not their real ones. It would therefore be futile for anyone in New Zealand with nothing better to do – a group which may very well be sizeable – to hunt among the sheep for 'Cousin Claire' or the others.

This phenomenon, however, is part of the culture of the quiet world. Editors of newspaper letters pages and producers of late-night radio phone-ins know that – when faced with the emergency of unfilled columns or a lifeless switchboard – they can rely on the law of territorial outrage. Instruct a journalist or a disc-jockey to suggest that a town or a part of a town – or, in a really serious drought of material, an entire nation – is dull, drab, or generally resident-unfriendly. The yelps of refutation from those who live there will provide you with days of correspondence or telephone calls.

Merely in the newspapers of the week in which I wrote this section, there were two examples of this residential defensiveness. 'Your writer seems to have it in for the Swiss,' complained one resentful correspondent, referring to an article on Helvetian obsessiveness, and going on to ask 'in which of the four languages spoken in that federation' the writer was proficient enough to have made the judgements complained of. On the Letters page of another publication, a writer objected to a sentence in a previous edition about 'one of those rare creatures, a famous Dane'. The relentless list of national figures is a particular risk of running down a small country in print. We have all seen the roll calls of great Canadians and celebrated Belgians clogging up correspondence columns because of similarly insolent punditry.

Here, then, came the register of Danish excellence: 'Søren Kierkegaard, Carl Nielsen, Hans Christian Anderson, Nils Bor, Asger Jorn, Karen Blixen, Victor Borge, Martin Hansen, Kim Larsen, Gabriel Axel, Dea Trier Morch.' I must say that my reaction to this catalogue was that you wouldn't much want to be stuck in a lift with any of them, except Anderson, and even he might start to pall the second time round on the Ugly Duckling. It also seemed to me that this list was perhaps the apotheosis of tedious-place special pleading, in actually including a celebrity called Bor. But the point is well made. Geographical loyalty is a powerful factor.

Yet the truth is that, for most of us, home is a compromise. The majority of people inhabit a particular region because of an accident of birth (our parents' dream home is, for an average of at least sixteen years, our own home-base), a necessity of relocation (the pursuit of work or love) or the simple logistics of the housing market and the mortgate system. We would ideally like to live in A (if we could afford to), B (if there was a company branch there), or C (if our partner's family ties were not five hundred miles away) or, increasingly in Britain, in A, B, or C if we could sell our bloody house in D. But, alas, for any of these reasons, D is where we are stuck. Yet call D dull in public and you will discover that each of the D-siders resides there apparently from choice. They live there because they love there.

Hence insults from elsewhere must be rebuffed. Many of the places featured in this book are victims of that racism which even political correctness still permits. Opinion-disinfectant, though splashed over most national generalizations, has not yet been applied to the beliefs that Canada, New Zealand, Belgium, and Switzerland are strikingly boring countries, populated by dullards. It remains OK to say these things in company. Although my itinerary was to some extent dictated by these sterotypes, I was going to weigh up the evidence. Perhaps Canada would dazzle, and Switzerland dizzy.

And I was also interested in what it was like to be born into, or to inhabit, territory of such notoriety. Stereotypes do not wound uniformly. In the Europe of the popular imagination, an Italian was assumed likely to seduce you and a Frenchman to cook you a memorable meal or to be inventively offensive in refusal, but a Belgian was expected to send you to sleep. In stereotypical North America, a resident of the United States was expected to be vulgar but fun, while it was reckoned that, on introduction to a Canadian, you would long to find a newly painted wall and monitor its progress.

There would be the ghost of a serious purpose on my journeys. Almost every evening during the period in which I was writing this book, the television news showed lines of rough coffins and makeshift biers ready for interment in the ground of what had once been the popular holiday resort of Yugoslavia. The supposed Chinese curse 'May you live in interesting times!' has entered common currency in the West. But who could watch such pictures without invoking on themselves the blessing: 'May you live in boring places!'

Even before it became part of my job to write about politics, I would always learn as much as possible about the government and political system of any country I visited. It was part of the weather for me, and therefore hangs around behind the travels recorded here. What intrigued me about the quiet world locations selected for this book was that they were the kinds of places in which, traditionally, the electorate had quietly left politicians to get on with the business of government, whether from satisfaction or apathy.

So I was interested in whether there was such a thing as a safe country in a way philosophically beyond the definition of one in which nothing much currently goes on. Could the Ayatollah

Khomenei have produced in the inhabitants of Timaru or Ottawa or Milton Keynes the reactions he won from those in Tehran? Lenin lived briefly in Zurich but, had he been Swiss, could he have led a revolution there? Do some nations have anaesthetic temperaments and environments which render them immune to demagoguery and revolution? Or is it just a matter of money luck, which, while it endures, dampens down unrest?

The research would be, in two senses, flying visits. Entire travel books had been written about Australia, Alaska, and Canada – although I know of no long volumes about New Zealand or Milton Keynes – and this book would attempt to do them all in one. Therefore, the intended effect would be something between tourism and journalism. The tourist and the journalist have much in common. Both are dropped in strange places and expected quickly to interpret them – though one is paid to do it and the other pays – before dashing somewhere else.

In many modern travel books, the author is, at this stage, flinching from foot-long inoculatory hypodermics at the tropical diseases clinic or training with the SAS in Hereford. All I had to do was check all the windows and doors very carefully, and catch a taxi to Heathrow. On the way, from habit, I checked my travel insurance documents. 'This policy does not cover you against war and kindred risks,' it warned. This was as it should be, for there were surely no places nor people less kin to those risks.

# PART ONE

# AUSTRALASIA

# CHAPTER ONE

# BEACH TOILET STILL SHUT

## *New Zealand*

It was the cockney in the Reactolite shades – savouring his last authentically greasy British breakfast for a fortnight or even more – who voiced the secret fears of all around him. He loudly struck the note which all the others waiting expectantly in the Sky Café, in Heathrow Airport's Terminal One, that morning towards the end of the year, were trying not to hear.

'If the market crashes while I'm gone, this'll go off anywhere, any*fuckin*where, in the world . . .'

He unclipped from the inside pocket of his traffic-light casual jacket a small grey plastic bleeper, like a doctor's. This one, though, would summon him only to fiscal intensive care units, where bleeping screens were wired to the heartbeat of the dollar, yen, and pound.

'Yeah? So it goes off on the beach, you're not going to be able to do fuckin' nuffin' abaht it, are you?' another member of his party objected. 'All you'll know is you can't afford anuvver fuckin' drink. Ask me, it'd be better not to know . . .'

'Nah. Satellite phone, I showed you, right? Damage limitation. Whole point of this gear is, these days, you can be there when you're not there . . .'

The exchange made you nostalgic for the time when all that holidaymakers worried about was whether the plane would crash. With economies so dodgy, you could land safely and still get back to find you had lost your life. It was the very end of 1991 – a year in which the West's celebrations over expelling Iraq from Kuwait had been wrecked by domestic economic collapse – and the atmosphere at Heathrow seemed near to hysteria.

Even in normal circumstances, everyone at a British airport

was euphoric. You never sensed the same release at a terminal in the USA. Americans routinely flew – weekended or visited relatives by plane, even commuted to work by air – and, when they took vacations, fled the summer sun in their cities. But, because of the British climate, a holiday was like getting out of jail.

And, these days, there was even more reason to feel liberation from the steely winter. You didn't need a degree in economics to guess that the concourse bustled with people going somewhere fun while they still had the money, or starting their early retirement with a break funded by a lump sum, or consoling themselves in even earlier retirement by spending a bit of the redundo in the sun. As desperate for business as everyone else, airlines were offering long-haul flights for the kind of money you expected to pay on a train.

Helped by one of these plunging prices, I had stretched to business class for the Australasia leg of the project. With fewer businesses around every time the FTSE, Dow, or Nikkei closed, the extra leg-room and bottomless wine bottles of business class were briefly in reach of the ordinary traveller, or at least of travel writers on a publisher's advance. So I had checked in three hours before the flight and, after breakfast in the Sky Café, reported to the Business Lounge, the sofa-bar-and-telly den which airlines run for those on more expensive tickets.

All around me, people were drinking wine and liquor, some-times double-fisted, barely an hour after breakfast time. They were not, I think, on the whole, alcoholics, but merely people conscious of how much these free drinks were costing them. Getting good value was a mantra of the time.

As research for my journey, I read the editions of New Zealand and Australian newspapers scattered around the lounge. In New Zealand, the Prime Minister, Jim Bolger, was apparently to be given an entry in the *Guinness Book of Records*, having recorded the world's lowest popularity rating for an elected leader (7 per cent) since polling began. Unemployment, business fail-ures, and manufacturing depression were blamed for the contempt he suffered. In Australia, the Prime Minister, Bob Hawke, was reported to be on the point of overthrow by his own party. His unpopularity was attributed to the country's financial situation. For refugees from a recession, there was not much getting away from it all that year. But at least I was flying from winter to spring, and towards the first – and perhaps most tantilizingly non-exotic – quarry of my project.

My search for the mystical city of Timaru began, like many great quests, with an accidental tip-off. Soon after meeting the woman to whom I am now married, I realized that the only seriously off-putting thing about her was an interest in New Zealand which – by normal British standards of an occasional giggle or continual ignorance towards the place – amounted to perversion. You would take her to some celebratedly picturesque location in the world and she would say, moistly: 'It reminds me of New Zealand!' Subsequently, when we shared a house, I would often open a door to find a New Zealander unexpectedly sleeping or eating there. When the subject of honeymoons came up, my fiancée's only dilemma was between the North Island and the South Island, Auckland or Christchurch.

All marriages hold secrets, and I felt it wrong to probe this cultural infidelity too deeply. I did learn, however, that she had never herself visited the country. Her Kiwiphile cast of mind was a product of friendship with a Christchurch girl, working in London as a nanny, whom my wife had encountered through some metropolitan yuppie network. I will give this friend the pseudonym of Jessica, for reasons of her personal security, a necessity which will become clear later in the book. Jessica returned to Christchurch, but my wife subsequently provided advice and shelter for her acquaintances and relatives who visited London. Indeed, her unofficial refugee programme for these New Zealanders apparently achieved such domestic recognition that it became standard airport form for anxious parents to press her name and address into the hands of their departing offspring. My wife had become a sort of Mother Theresa for Kiwis overseas.

Jessica stayed with us when she came back to Britain on vacation. One night, she went out to an event organized by her old London crowd.

'Good time?' I asked when she came back.

'Strewth, no! It was like going to a party in Timaru!'

'Like what . . .?'

'It's what we say back home. For a really dull time. Timaru is the most boring place in New Zealand . . .'

'But how . . .?'

I had nearly said, in an echo of the New York reaction to the death of President Coolidge, *But how can they tell?* It was clear that this phrase was the Antipodean equivalent of English declarations of non-enthusiasm like: 'It's about as exciting as a wet weekend in Wigan!' (Newark for Americans, Melbourne for Australians.) And yet the existence of a New Zealand version surprised me. The joke-location, the gag-town, surely depended on a perceived sharp contrast with the place in which the joke was made. Newark was amusing to New Yorkers because it was small cheese beside the Big Apple, Sydney residents thought Melbourne tight-arsed in comparison with their let-it-hang-out city.

However, at least from my prejudiced perspective, it seemed unlikely that a person living in any given place in New Zealand would be in a position to quip about elsewhere being less exciting. A British magazine used to run a weekly feature called *The Expert's Expert*, in which members of a profession elected one of their peers as the best. In the same way, if what Jessica said was correct, then Timaru, New Zealand, was the Dull Place's Dull Place. For someone planning a project such as this, the lure was unrefusable. Timaru promised to be the Mecca of the non-event, an oasis of stasis, the world centre of the early night.


The kind of travel writers who proceed by elephant or canoe tend to sneer at those who go by air. But planes are not without their pains. 'You can reach Australia in less than a day now!' people say in wonder, usually just after watching a television documentary about Captain Cook or Christopher Columbus. You can be reasonably sure that those expressing this sentiment have never spent twenty-five hours in a vacuum-sealed aluminium tube aimed at the Antipodes.

You nonchalantly ignore the safety demonstration, wondering why they still do the bit about life-jackets and inflatable rafts when no passenger plane in aviation history has successfully ditched in the ocean. It is presumably a confidence trick for twitchy flyers. You read the in-flight magazine, learning of Sir

Peter Ustinov's embarrassing flatulence at a luncheon with the Queen Mother. While listening to the first cycle of the 'Classical Favourites Selection' on the complimentary head-set, you pull the free-gift, complimentary one-size fluffy leisure socks over your own, discover that the one size appears to be Dustin Hoffman's, and reflect in passing why wearing two pairs of socks in the air should be thought automatically more comfortable than wearing one, these soft socks presumably being a complicated way of encouraging flyers to remove their shoes.

You choose between the complimentary Riesling, Chardonnay, and Shiraz. You realize that you have heard the words 'The ever popular Mozart, in his short and tortured life, produced . . .' before. The 'Classical Favourites Selection' is beginning its second cycle. You look up restlessly, but the helpful red line which charts your journey on a pull-down world map at the front of the cabin has barely left the British mainland for the Irish sea.

You shuffle the three novels which, you calculate, you should *at least* have got through before New Zealand. You manage fifty pages of the first, but your eyes are protesting, perhaps dried by the recycled air, maybe edged together by the sedative effect of the complimentary American Riesling, Chardonnay, or Shiraz. The red wine is served icy, not from a sommelier's mistake, but because of what room temperature is at 33,000 feet. The fold-out cinema screen comes down. There appears that actor with the moustache about whom, a few months earlier, you had thought, after seeing him in a not-bad late-night film, I wonder what he did after that? What he did after that, it appears, was to star in a movie about a baseball team which develops a new robot pitcher which upsets the opponents and, unfortunately, falls in love with the coach's wife. Sadly, the robot blows a gasket in the World Series play-offs, thus underlining the superiority of humans. The coach's wife goes back to him.

You chew your Pâté en Croute with Cumberland Sauce and choose between Fillet Steak with Horseradish Butter and Prawns with Tomato and Fetta in Filo Pastry. When the dish comes, you have to check the menu to see which you are eating. The man in the next seat – whose beefy forearms keep winning the game of elbow wrestling you play each time one of you leaves the seat – tells you about his daughter's university course, and gives a run-down of his views on the world's airports, citing Singapore as the most pleasant and well appointed. The red line on the cabin map now curves plumply across the Atlantic.

If this were a flight to New York, you would be looking for your shoes and completing immigration forms. But you are not going to New York. You are heading to New Zealand, still three New York flights further on. Meeting resistance from your novel, you drift into a Riesling, Shiraz, or Chardonnay doze, jerking awake to an announcement about turbulence and the importance of a fastened seat-belt, which yours already is. On the fold-down cinema screen, that actress who looks a little like Jane Fonda is appearing in a black comedy about a bank robbery. You fiddle with the dial on your complimentary head-set. 'The ever popular Mozart, in his short and tortured life, produced . . .'

You land at Los Angeles, where it is the late afternoon for Americans but the small hours of the next morning by your interior timepiece. There is five hours between flights. You take a cab out to Brentano's at Century City, in case of running out of books on the second leg of the flight. Back at the airport – American dusk, a London time when only babies are awake – you change planes and airlines, where the Maori stewardess offers a choice of complimentary New Zealand Riesling, Chardonnay, or Shiraz and a new in-flight magazine, in which you learn of Sir Peter Ustinov's embarrassing flatulence while dining with Dame Kiri Te Kanawa.

The captain announces that the approximate flying time to Christchurch from Los Angeles is thirteen hours and fifty-five minutes. (All long-haul flying times end in fifty-five, just as all prices end in ninety-nine, and for precisely the same reason, to prevent the consumers guessing the truth.) The airline magazine also features an article on how to enjoy (PR-speak for 'survive') a long-haul plane trip. 'Stand up as often as possible. This helps to guard against haemorrhoids and blood-clots.' This squirmy detail confirms that the 'enjoyment' of the flight offered is of a some-what negative kind. 'Drink as little alcohol as possible.' But what else is there to do up there?

You shuffle the now five books in your seat pocket, abandon the delicate English novel about the Second World War, seventy pages read, for the latest conspiracy theory about the Kennedy assassination, bought discount in Los Angeles. Somewhere between the grassy knoll and the Cuban with the umbrella despite the sun shining your body-clock punches you out for three hours. Waking shivering and sludge mouthed, you stare uncomprehendingly at the middle frames of a movie about a boy in a wheelchair who wants to be a baseball player. Staggering down the cabin to the latrines – is that ache around the thigh a haemorrhoid or blood-clot gathering bulk? – you discover a queue and a faecal smell drifting back.

Eventually admitted, you find the suction lavatory blocked with a wodge of paper, bright blue disinfectant fluid, and a more disturbing dull brown trickle. You struggle with the complimentary miniature toothpaste tube and brush. The toothpaste has a metal seal across the top. You blearily try to burst it on the serrated edge of the tap, but the tube shears off and nicks your thumb. You settle for brushing your mouth with probably recycled water. You try, with your eyes, to tell the next person waiting that the blockage was there when you took occupancy, for the protocol of jets' heads, of smells and messes, is a peculiar one. Unlike in other public conveniences, users are subsequently in proximity, vulnerable to the astonished sidelong glance, the accusatory mutter.

Seated again – at what, for your stomach, is breakfast time – you choose between Escalope of Chicken with Rambutan and Tamarind and Poached Salmon Trout in Basil Cream Sauce. Weren't salmon and trout two different things when you left the ground? The stewardess offers to leave a bottle of the Chardonnay with you. No, no, thank you, yes, all right, please. The man in the next seat tells you that there will be no economic recovery until the government stops taxing small businessmen like him so hard, lets go of their balls, gives them some incentive to invest. You have mysteriously started sneezing.

As the red line on the cabin map folds over Honolulu, you are sweating and coughing. You fiddle with your complimentary head-set, riding the channels for distractions. 'Mozart was only thirteen when he . . . *I can't get no satisfaction* . . . And then they do what with this tobacco, Walt? They roll it up and set light to it? . . . *Gonna take you up where you belong, higher than the . . .*' Above the Cook Islands, you are bringing up what looks like

Pacific coral: vivid yellow and black knots. Long-haul jets are a Hilton for germs, all breath and bilge on a kind of loop through the structure.

You bundle your five books, two of them half-read, into a bag. The very last in-flight movie before the Antipodes is about an American dog which inherits a fortune. By the Tasman Sea, you could do Little Nell's death scene without rehearsal. 'Try not to fly with a cold or respiratory infection,' says the airline magazine in its advice on how to enjoy your long-haul flight. 'Discomfort can result during take-off and landing as cabin pressure changes.' But what if you caught the bug in transit? Anyway, the descent into Christchurch reminds you of the scene in an Edward Bond play in which a character is deafened with a knitting needle.

'Good flight?' asked Jessica, at Christchurch Airport. I melodramatically bowed a depressurization-deaf ear towards her and allowed a theatrical release of phlegm into a handkerchief before answering that it had been a little gruelling.

'Oh, poor you. It's best not to fly with a cold . . .'

'Yes, well, I didn't have it when I . . .'

'You are a bit pale. But you'll still be able to get breakfast at the hotel . . .'

'I think I just had dinner . . .'

What Jessica actually said was *git brikfist it the hitil*. The Kiwi accent is a vowel-vice voice, in which the *e* is squeezed to an *i*, the *a* elongated to an *ee*. A New Zealander, for example, writes with a *pin*, and signals agreement with the word *yis*. Jessica's close friend Sarah was *See-rah*. Phonetically, the accent was very close to white South African but, in spirit, the voices were quite different. Perhaps it was merely a matter of projection of national image, but South African sounded cold and cruel to me – an ugly voice for what had been in recent decades grotesque ideas – while there was a warmth, and even music, to the clenched vowels of New Zealand. If this was not merely international prejudice, then the distinction was, presumably, one of pitch. The South African sentence landed with a thump; New Zealand ones finished in the interrogative lilt which was also an Australian habit.

On the road into Christchurch, we kept stopping at traffic lights, but it was purely from legal convention. There was almost never another car or person crossing. With the shrinking and bloating of the clock in the air, I had lost track, but, surely, it had been Thursday in Los Angeles.

'It's not Sunday, is it . . .?'

'Why? Oh, no. This is Friday morning rush hour. If you think this is bad, wait till you get to Timaru . . . Oh, I've booked you a hotel there. I got you three nights. The receptionist said: "Are you *sure*?" . . .'

Jessica laughed. I realized that this was my equivalent of the moment in more traditional travel books when the chief tribal scout tells the visitor seeking passage: 'No one take you to Alligator Bay, *sahib*. Fish lives there, you in heaven in ten seconds . . .'

Jessica had a friend who worked for the Park Royal, Christchurch's plushest hotel, a pyramidal prong in glass, fitted out in the American way of marble atriums and see-through lifts. My connection had secured me a suite for the price of a room. I was told that previous occupants had included Jackie Collins and Wilbur Smith, on promotional tours, and Sir Peter Ustinov. I wondered if he had written about it for an in-flight magazine.

One wall of the top-floor room was all window, providing a panorama of Christchurch, a pleasant and correct city, curled around a river, park, and cathedral, reminiscent of Canterbury, England, on which the place is partly architecturally based. The room had black furniture, offset by cream carpets and walls, illuminated, if you wished, from ceiling spotlights. The fridge was a miniature off-licence, with a vast genealogy of glasses laid out beside it. The bathroom had a sunken tub and a whirl-bath and three wash-basins, presumably for when the suite was occupied by rock stars entertaining more than one friend for the night. The towel rack looked like lambs asleep. There was also a gold-wrapped chocolate on each pillow, it being a peculiar assumption of expensive hotels that the kind of people who can afford to pay a labourer's weekly wage for one night's accommodation will suddenly go ape-shit with gratitude for a free piece of confectionery.

I blacked out from jet lag, and woke – in what was New Zealand's afternoon, my God knows what – to watch CNN, our age's new universal cultural glue. Because this American cable news service was now such a standard global fixture, a quick way of assessing the state of the economy of any nation was to check what appeared between the programmes on CNN. Poor markets used filler factual material where the advertisements should ideally have been. In Christchurch that afternoon, the gaps were being packed with a scroll of 'Important Dates'. When these reached 'December 24th – Chistmas Eve – Important family time in many countries', you knew that the New Zealand budget was seriously stretched. The rest was public information about condoms, and weather bulletins which ended with an estimate of that day's ultraviolet burning time. (One of the holes recently found in the ozone layer was directly above New Zealand.) Everywhere you went in the quiet world at that time, you saw the same warning initials on the posters: UV and HIV. Sex was death and sun was death. And the money was running out.

Jessica had arranged invitations to a series of dinners and cocktail parties around Christchurch, to help with my background research before I risked Timaru. 'I'm a bit worried that you're prejudiced in advance,' she said. There was a certain truth in this. Apart from the knowledge enforced by the psychological oddity of my wife's devotion to this distant nowhere – and the television advertisements for New Zealand Lamb, which had always been a central part of British culture – my previous perception of the place amounted to three pieces of factual bric-à-brac. The first – from, I supposed, some squib on a newspaper foreign page – was that British and Australian airline pilots landing at Auckland and Christchurch had been cautioned by the local authorities for making the chortling cabin announcement: 'Ladies and gentlemen, we have just landed in New Zealand. Please put back your watches fifty years.'

My second stored story was that the British police and army frequently sent informers, grasses, canaries – in need of a new identity when their cover was blown – to New Zealand, where they were given a different surname, a nose-job, and a flock of sheep. According to legend, there were often odd social incidents, in which a New Zealander would suddenly fail to respond when their name was shouted, or turn round when another one was called. It seemed to me that there was an interesting anthropological thesis to be written assessing the effect on the relative temper and interest of these two nations of the fact that Australia was a culture built on British convicts, while New Zealand was a culture built on British coppers' narks. I was also interested in whether it was made clear to the informers before they agreed to turn Queen's evidence that New Zealand was where they were headed if it all went wrong.

The third Kiwi detail I retained was that New Zealand was the world pioneer of research into, and treatment of, the debilitating viral illness ME (myalgic encephalomyelitis), vulgarly known as yuppie flu. What intrigued me was how – given that the symptoms were listlessness, tiredness, and a lack of will to do anything – they had been able to tell that the first victims had ME and were not merely New Zealanders.

But these were the prejudices of an outsider. My first impression on arrival had been – perhaps inevitably for a native of a country of fifty million who had frequently travelled and worked in a country of two hundred and fifty million – of geographical spaciousness and social intimacy. With three million residents, New Zealand had a city's population in a nation's space. At Christchurch, I had been fifth off the plane, and the previous four were all personally greeted by the ground staff ('OK, Bob?', 'Good to see you there, Rachel!'). The explanation was either a frequent flyer programme or an anthropological discovery of some moment: the last remaining industrial democracy in which all of the inhabitants were on first-name terms.

On the social round in Christchurch, I was surprised most of all by the solid Anglophilia and monarchism of the white New Zealanders. A liberal embarrassed by the baggage of Empire, I tended when in the Commonwealth to urge the inhabitants to overthrow the Governor-General and write their own constitution. This was in tune with the mood of the younger Kiwis ('We're going to git your Queen off our stimps and binknotes,' a girl warned me at a dinner party. 'Hiv Katherine Mansfield, Richard Hadlee, pipple lik thit.')

But the oldies were fierce Elizabethans, surrogate Londoners. Over dinner or drinks, they would suddenly ask me: 'How is the

Queen Mother's leg?' or 'Is the Duchess of York's new book as good as her first?' I had noticed in the newspapers that the big television offerings in the Christmas 1991 schedules were *HRH The Prince Andrew – Helicopter Pilot* and *Fergie – Portrait of a Princess*, Mountbatten-Windsor brown-nosers imported from Britain. Each was at least a year old, but the broadcasting authorities had presumably concluded that the monarchy was a sufficiently constant institution for this not to matter. I decided not to test these colonials' loyalty to the Crown with the London gossip that the couple might soon have separate residences as well as separate documentaries.

Jessica's father, a sheep farmer near Christchurch, had never visited Britain in his sixty or so years, but had learned the layout of the capital from maps and atlases. When his daughters had gone overseas on my wife's refugee programme, he had been able to direct them to Harrods and the British Museum, telling them where to change lines on the London Underground. It was an almost eerie act of mental fealty to the 'mother country', as his generation called it without irony, from which his parents had sailed in hope during a previous British recession.

The bungalows in which these prosperous farmers and bankers resided outside Christchurch were replicas of those you would have found in the Home Counties twenty thousand miles away, filled with genteel antiques, Turner prints, wooden Harrods boxes of loose-leaf tea. The manners of the New Zealand middle class were English manners but more staunchly taught and practised. For example, Jessica had somehow grown up believing that it was an insult to a supper guest to serve fewer than two vegetables (excluding potatoes) and that real friendliness meant three.

In the mother country, the approach to these things was generally a bit of steamed green or orange for visual contrast with the dull spuds. Hence, at dinner tables in England, Jessica would regularly flinch as the lids were raised from the porcelain pots, in what was perhaps the only known case of a carrot being a stick. That manners mattered so much in New Zealand was, clearly, partly a colonial inheritance taken to extremes (like the Indian civil service), but also perhaps, in this case, a characteristic developed as a defensive distinctiveness from the Australians next door.

However, as was suggested by Prime Minister Bolger's record low showing in the polls, politeness towards the government was lacking among all generations. Although cultural movements tended to reach New Zealand several years after their impact on Britain and America, the country had, oddly, been something of an ideological pioneer. The first Western democracy to allow women the vote, New Zealand had also hosted the world's first and most cosseting welfare apparatus. Such was the national pride in this structure that a New Zealander working in London as a cab driver had once told me that, when he informed his mother by letter that he needed a small operation, she telegraphed back that he was to fly home for treatment, rather than risk it in Britain.

The first among what would be many Conservative critics of this costly state embrace was Anthony Trollope who, in 1872, objected that 'the colony is over-governed, over-legislated for, over-provided with officials, and over-burdened with national debt'. But, three decades later, Asquith, the British Prime Minister, solemnly described New Zealand as a 'laboratory for the instruction of younger countries'. This patronizing compliment ignored the fact that it was countries of greater or similar age – Britain, Canada, Australia – which most diligently copied the welfare model. It certainly worked for New Zealand. According to legend, as recently as 1950 the number of unemployed was twelve..

But now there were twelve in some families. Since the middle of the 1980s, New Zealand had been at the front of the pack in another political experiment: the complete dismantling of a welfare system. Once again, it had become a laboratory watched closely by Britain, Canada, and Australia, though this time by the parties of the Right rather than the Left. In 1984, the Labour government of David Lange had inherited the problem of the islands' economic decline (partly a result of its old trading buddy, Britain, turning towards the European Community markets) and expanding welfare-related debts. The government's response had been severe deregulation.

The Kiwi dollar was devalued by 20 per cent, Air New Zealand and the Bank of New Zealand privatized (the latter sold, with cruel cultural irony, to the Bank of Australia), the top rate of income tax halved, and state pay-outs strictly limited. Family allowance was abolished and other benefits reduced in value by a quarter. Pensions were income-tested and the qualification age raised by five years. Free medical treatment was scheduled to be removed. This was Reaganism and Thatcherism stretched beyond the dreams of their creators. As a sort of symbolic demonstration of the demolition of the old provisions, New Zealand Rail withdrew the lifetime free passes of the nation's only two surviving holders of the Victoria Cross from World War I. The government called this 'a true enterprise culture'.

In economics as in medicine, experimental treatments are acceptable only if symptoms subside. New Zealand's did not. Unemployment doubled to 12 per cent during Labour's administration, and a quarter of manufacturing jobs were lost. The result was that a fabledly stable political system – the Anglophile egomaniac, Sir Robert Muldoon, had been PM for nearly ten years – gave way to an almost Italian jitteriness. In 1990 New Zealand had four prime ministers. Lange, a smart lawyer, left office after abandoning his wife for his speechwriter. His successor, Geoffrey Palmer, thought a safe replacement because of his low sex drive, was then feared too drab to be risked in the ballot and was replaced by Mike Moore, a stocky, demotic, charismatic cancer survivor. But Moore was not enough and, in the 1990 election, had lost to Jim Bolger of the National Party. It was Bolger, a starchy ex-farmer, who, fourteen months on, was scoring the single-figure charisma statistic.

This was partly because National had enthusiastically extended the policies of the party it had thrown out of office. Bolger's economic lieutenant, Finance Minister Ruth Richardson, monthly snipped away more of the fiscal umbilical cords connecting society's frailest to the state. The government's seventy thousand publicly owned houses for the poor had been handed over to the control of a corporation which charged the commercial going-rate. By the time of my visit, there were reports of schools introducing 'breakfast clubs' (a polite phrase for soup kitchens) for children going hungry at home. Not because of middle-class sentimentality towards the downtrodden, but because unemployment and business failures were now affecting the well-heeled too, Richardson had become a national bogeywoman, herself dubbed 'Ruthless', her policies called 'Ruthenasia'.

At my Christchurch soirées, I kept being told the latest Ruth joke, a rather strenuous clump of puns, but which I record here from anthropological interest as an example of New Zealand political humour: 'So Ruth decides, being virtually a min already, that she's going to have a six change. And the doctor says, what kind of cock do you want? We have all sorts. And Ruth says, well I don't want a Bulger [Bolger], and I don't want a Palmer [hand-gesture of masturbation], I think I'll settle for a longy [Lange].' A cultural analyst could have hours of fun unpicking the strands of contempt for male politicians (all pricks), and fear of female ones (pretend-fellas), wrapped up in that gag.

Most of the political comment you heard was the aimless anger of a betrayed electorate, stronger on complaint than alternative policies, but a friend of Jessica's father – another sixtyish sheep farmer, called Jim – was more reflective. Ixports, he thought, were the key.

'I think,' he said, 'that we are victims of history . . .'

'What do you mean?'

'Well, not just Britain and the Common Market – do you still call it that? – although that didn't help. But look at our ixports. First, lamb and butter. I'd never even heard the word cholesterol until two years ago, I'm feeling a bit sluggish, and my doctor gives me a blood test and starts reading the riot act about egg-and-bacon breakfasts every day. And when one of the girls said she was becoming a vegan, we thought it was like, you know, the Mormons. But now I have this rabbit-food stuff for breakfast, and this chemical spread on my bread, and we try to eat red meat only twice a week, although we are, if you like, biting the hand that feeds us . . .'

You could see that the advance of cardiac awareness and vegetarianism might be bad news for a nation living on its sales of lamb and butter. But Jim's other hypothesis was more novel: that a far distant nation of minimal military expenditure and significance had lost out from the end of the Cold War.

'The Eastern Bloc was a big buyer of wool,' he said. 'Every soldier in the Warsaw Pact had a thick greatcoat and some pairs of woolly socks. Come the thaw . . .'

It was hard to imagine a better illustration of the world economic order, which could not be denied, no matter how far away you were from the core.

'And take the Kiwi fruit . . .' said Jim. In the previous decade, this lime-coloured furry-skinned fruit – named after the flightless bird which was one national symbol and looking like the rugby ball which was another – had become a restaurant and kitchen hit. It was used, particulary in *nouvelle cuisine*, as the contrast ingredient for everything from meat to fish to cheese. As food became an art form, its colour had been another blessing.

'New Zealand's great new export,' Jim explained. 'Looks like we're going to be living off the little buggers for ever. But, see, the thing's really called a Chinese gooseberry, and we never got round to trademarking the name Kiwi fruit. So anyone can have a go and use it. Europe, for a start, starts farming them more cheaply. Now our boys are rushing round, trying to cross it with an orange, mate it with a strawberry, marry it with something, to produce a super Kiwi fruit . . .'

So New Zealand had lost out to fashion in its traditional exports and to competition in its new ones. It was – like so much of the quiet world at that time – a country in flux. Earnest businessmen at parties kept asking me, as if I were a visiting politician or diplomat: 'What do you think New Zealand should do? Look towards the trading bloc of Britain and Europe or turn to the markets of Australia, Japan, and Asia?'

It was not a subject on which I really had a view, but I tried to formulate one for them. In the past, I said, links between nations had been geographically illogical, because of the long-distance avarice of empire, such as the odd bond between the hemispherical extremities of Britain and New Zealand. In the future, however, nations would be united by proximity. Britain would look to its European neighbours. New Zealand – half turning, half thrown from the tit of the mother country – should look to Australia, America, and Japan.

They nodded, but the problem, which they could not acknowledge, was that they feared the Americans, as any minor country must, and had become estranged from them because of Lange's locally popular decision to ban nuclear ships and submarines from the islands' ports. The sensible amities were also restricted by the extent to which they disliked the Australians and Japanese. The former they regarded as philistine alcoholics, the latter as sinister workaholics. But then one of New Zealand's colonial inheritances from Britain was racism. In the colonist, this was directed at the later arrivals. In the colony, as in Australia, it was aimed at the early ones. When unemployment was discussed, I mentioned a statistic I had read that – while the overall jobless figure of 12 per cent was grim enough – *25 per cent* unemployment had been reached among the Maori and immigrant Polynesian populations.

'Ah, yis,' came the reply, 'but yer Maori doesn't want to work. We've tried to help yer Maori. Integrate, people say. But yer Maori doesn't want to integrate . . .'

The wide circulation of such views surprised me, as Jessica and her family were liberals. But I came to see that New Zealand, so often accused of resembling the Britain of forty years before, matched it particularly in the unthinking white triumphalism of daily conversation. Indians – discussed, in this country, mainly in a cricket context – were cheerfully described as 'curry-munchers'. When I mentioned an impressive speech I had heard from the National MP Winston Peters, whom I called the 'Maori MP', it was pointed out to me that he was merely 'part-Maori', as if to account for his talents, while 'part-Maori', used (incorrectly, as it happened) of the fallen David Lange, was apparently supposed to explain his animal lapse. On certain subjects, the New Zealand and South African accents really were blood tongues.

The significant difference was that New Zealand governments had behaved reasonably towards the Maoris. A tribunal had recently decided to return $400 million of fisheries to the control of the first settlers. But the whites resented this. The statistic far more interesting to white New Zealanders than that 25 per cent of Maoris were currently unemployed was the prediction that, by 2020, a quarter of all New Zealanders would be Polynesian (Maoris or Pacific islanders). The whites had what you might call the Cape shakes about this, as they blamed the other races for what seemed to be the increasing lawlessness of their nation. Auckland, on the North Island, a city with the world's largest Polynesian population, was striven by gang warfare.

'If you go to Auckland,' someone said, 'be viry careful after dark . . .'

'I should be OK in Timaru,' I said.

'Oh, yis? You theenk so? Things are pretty nasty down in Timaru. Oh, yis . . .'

I asked Jessica about this. 'Oh, yis,' she said. 'There was something in the paper. Maybe it won't be so boring after all . . .'


When I checked out of the Park Royal in Christchurch, the receptionist said: 'Where you trivilling now?'

'I'm going to Timaru . . .'

'Rilly? Well, don't stay long . . .'

'Why not . . .?'

'Well, it's the kind of place that doesn't really do anything . . . There's no industry. Nothing for tourists. And they're funny little pipple out there . . .'

'Oh, why . . .?'

'Hard to say. We had a nuclear accidint in Ni Zilland in '64, and pipple reckon something got into the water over there . . .'

'In what way are they odd . . .?'

'Oh, I don't think I could put my finger on . . .' He caught the eye of the other receptionist and laughed. 'Well, let's just call it incidents with sheep . . .'

'Oh, I see. You think they do it with sheep . . .?'

'You'd heard that somewhere else, had you . . .?'

'No. Well, not about Timaru. Just it's what the English say about the Welsh . . .'

'Oh, yis . . .?'

I mentioned in the introduction the phenomenon of territorial sensitivity – and the extraordinary extent of this in New Zealand will become apparent later in this book – so I should perhaps make it clear that it is not the opinion of the present writer, or of his publishers, that either Timaruvians or the Welsh do it with ewes. The above exchange is featured as an example of the kind of geographical smears – usually begun by urban dwellers about ruralists – which seem to be a global occurrence.

Even within countries which were not involved in wars or civil wars, there was this endless regional tension. It was what you might call Bully–Runt syndrome. Internationally, you had 240-pounder nations like the USA and Australia (the former with military and economic weight, the latter big through force of personality and lifestyle) looking menacingly across the play-yard at the bespectacled weaklings of Canada and New Zealand, who unconvincingly squeaked that they were not scared and that, anyway, there was no particular merit in being a vulgar thug. Nationally, the bully metropolitan cities had the same relationship with the runt country towns. The larger nations and towns would, I suppose, present the conflict quite differently, as penis envy from the other side.

The first thing you noticed on the road to Timaru was the silence. Almost any drive in New Zealand outside of the major conurbations resembled the scene in a nuclear holocaust movie in which the survivors venture out on to the burned, unpeopled, eerie Earth. The other peculiarity was the illusion of snow on the lowlands ahead, although it was Antipodean spring.

As you got closer, it was clear that this was the effect not of ice but of animals. Packed in, shoulder of lamb to shoulder of lamb, the country's ovine residents outnumbered its human ones now by a ratio of merely about 18:1, down from a high of 20:1. This was a result of the cholesterol and vegetarianism factors, and of the failure by the national meat marketers to establish the lamburger as a fast-food rival to the hamburger. Even so, this was probably the only country in the world in which people flocked to see *The Silence of the Lambs* believing it to be a public information film about oesophageal blockage in new-born sheep.

It cannot be denied that the sheep get great scenery. New Zealand is indubitably beautiful, but, for the British visitor, its pleasures – of remorseless gorse, invigorating air and vibrant birdlife – are the recognizable ones of Scotland. A hotter Scotland, it is true, but one without an Edinburgh or Glasgow. I could never lose the sense of being cheated. After twenty-five hours in the aluminium tube you turned out to have made the only twenty-thousand mile trans-continental journey which had the net effect of a round-trip. Embarkation point and destination uncannily matched.

Only up around Mount Cook did the picture offer novelty. The mountain streams and lakes were turquoise, an effect produced by the dilution of the high-altitude glaciers, and so, looking up, the water stood out in the mountains as a sparkling skein, like da Vinci's sketches of the arterial system. High above was the shimmering line where snow-cap and snowy cloud collided, confusing the eye. There was no doubt that New Zealand took a good postcard. The problem was what you would write on it.

In Timaru, I checked in at the Hydro Grand Hotel, which Jessica had booked. It took several jabs on the bell to drag a sad-eyed woman to reception.

'You're sure you want three nights?' she asked.

'Yes.'

'Will, see how you go and let me know . . .'

The Hydro Grand had once been an impressive building, its pink cupola and commanding view of beach and harbour remaining as proof of this status. Now, however, its paint was peeled, its facings shabby. This was nearly the end of December and I was only the fifth guest of the month. All the others – including an Alaskan couple and a Japanese pair – had stayed for one night each. The room had a white candlewick bedspread, bare pocked linoleum, and lavatory paper you could have used to slash your wrists. In that connection, there was a neat little postbox slot in the bathroom marked *Used razor blades*, presumably in case too many visitors to Timaru committed suicide using the same ones.

A message had been left at the Hydro Grand for me to ring someone whom I will call, for reasons of her own protection, Cousin Claire, a relative of Jessica's. Raised in Timaru, Claire was now a powerful attorney in Christchurch. She was back in town to spend the Christmas break with her parents.

'Oh, hi,' she said, when I called. 'I was sort of worried you were gitting the wrong impression of Timaru. I hiv a kind of loyalty to it. Jess said you're writing about the most boring places in the world . . .'

'Quiet,' I said. 'Differently interesting. Activity-challenged . . .'

'Oh, yis? Just there's fun to be had in Timaru if you know where to look. I'll pick you up at your hitil timirrow afternoon, show you around . . .'

'OK. Jessica said there's been some kind of trouble down here. People kept mentioning it in Christchurch . . .'

'Rilly? Oh, will, all small towns hiv their incidents, these days. I don't know what she'd be referring to spicificily . . .'

I knew from her manner this was not the truth, that she was doing PR for Timaru. So I went to the public library on Bank Street, and took out the back-number files of the *Timaru Herald*. After only a few flicks, I discovered what I thought Cousin Claire had been hiding. The previous week, Leif Wulff, a fifteen-year-old boy, had been stabbed to death in the town, walking back from buying a blank videocassette on which to record a Michael Jackson concert from TV. Another adolescent, charged with the murder, had, according to the court reporter, stood nonchalantly with his arms folded and a half-smile on his face while the indictment was read.

I was about to put the volume away when I saw another headline: MINISTER CALLS FOR NEW ASSEMBLY LAWS. The federal minister of police had urged in a speech that consideration should be given to the re-establishment of the old anti-association laws, under which public gatherings of more than three or four could be forcibly dispersed. Local officials had reacted enthusiastically to the proposal which, it was thought, might 'have an effect on gang violence such as that afflicting Timaru.'

So there were two Timaru taboos, at which Jessica had been hinting, and which Cousin Claire had been trying to conceal. I read on. Two road gangs – the Devil's Henchmen and the Road Knights – had established headquarters, and support, at opposite ends of the town. To date, there had been one stabbing, one shooting (both non-fatal), two incidents in which bullets were fired at the homes of rival gangsters, and several episodes of arson, including the torching of four trucks at a haulage company which had recently made a Road Knight redundant. The local MP was attempting to negotiate between the gangs, but so far with little success. The Mayor had called for a Christmas truce.

Surprise at such news from Timaru – the smiling adolescent murderer, the gang violence – depended on the assumption of a fall from historical tranquillity. But, in many cases, the safety of the past turned out to be a myth. The library was attached to a museum, which included a facsimile of the Timaru coroner's registers from the previous century, so I checked out 1891 and 1892, a hundred years before. In the first of the years, there had been six fatal accidents, none of them obviously suspicious. A reasonable score, you might suppose, in a community becoming industrialized.

However, 1892 had been juicier. A young girl, Jane McCrae, had drowned on New Year's Day. An adult male, Mr Henry John Bowles, had gone under the waves eighteen days later, and, on February 22nd, a Mr W. G. Oliver had thrown himself under a train at Temuka and been declared a suicide. In June, one Carl Hansen was reported 'crushed at Pleasant Point'. In July, there was what the *Timaru Herald* called the 'shocking suicide of William Ziesler', followed, the next month, by the 'supposed suicide on board the *Elginshire*' of George H. L. Durham, who had hanged himself at sea as, before the year was out, did James Tegg, on land. Flicking through the years ahead, you found the deaths reflecting the greater economic and industrial complexity of society: suicides of ruined businessmen, crushings of farmhands under miracle equipment. In Timaru, as elsewhere, then, the past was not always a better place.

The museum was a small and quiet spot, but then such a building can only work with the history given to it. Short on local events to reflect, Timaru's was reduced, at one point, to a caption reading: 'The last hundred and fifty years have seen major changes in the design of women's underclothing . . .' The most intriguing display was that devoted to Richard Pearse (1877–1953). Known locally as Mad Pearse, this Timaruvian is now widely accepted – from contemporary accounts and surviving prototypes – to have built the first workable aeroplane, constructed from filched farm equipment and bamboo, ahead of the Wright brothers. Unfortunately, because he lived in New Zealand, nobody noticed, and he died in obscurity as a bitter old man. His neglect may be seen as emblematic of the nation's wider problem.

Standing in front of a model of the 1902 Pearse machine which had been dismissed by the locals as a joke or a sin, I was struck by the enormity of the fact that, only ninety years later, I had flown from London to Pearse's birthplace in the space of a day. Communism, Freudianism, and aviation were the three great movements of our century, and only the third could claim to have survived intact to the brink of the next. As for Pearse, the invisible pioneer, it may partly appease his shade that when flight became so standard that Timaru built an airport it was named after him.

Leaving the Museum, I walked out on to Stafford Street, the main drag, which ran westwards from the harbour and docks to the single office-block and hospital at the other end of town. It was a strangely oppressive street, as every shop possessed, presumably because of the heat, a painted hardboard canopy, like the hat-brims of aunts crowding round a baby at a baptism. Apart from this concession to climate, Timaru was like a small British town of the early sixties. On hoardings, long-dead commercial tease terms like 'smorgasbord' and 'à la carte' and 'luncheon' tried to seduce the passers-by with whatever intact letters they had left. The clothes shops had creakily swinging names like the Distinctive Man and the Miss Timaru. A place called Skinworld turned out – perhaps disappointingly for some browsers – to sell sheepskin and leather coats and handbags.

The local Baptist church had set up a stall, on which a large sign read: 'December 25th is Jesus's birthday. Have a piece of his birthday cake'. Shirt-sleeved believers were handing out slices of fruit cake, with marzipan and white icing, in some kind of Mrs Beeton parody of the Eucharist. This was odd enough, but stranger still was that, on what was the last shopping Saturday before Jesus's birthday, in what counted in New Zealand as a reasonably sized town (population twenty-eight thousand), you could still have taken large strides down the High Street with your arms stretched out on either side. I wondered what it must be like to grow up in a town but without the crowd as your basic unit of social interaction. Half the people on the street were waving to someone else in a car: that giveaway small-town gesture.

But it was not just the paucity of shoppers which made the date seem surreal. Christmas in New Zealand was the seasonal equivalent of a phantom pregnancy: the symptoms unarguably present, but pointlessly, disturbingly, so. Carol singers squinted into the sun, dreaming of a white Christmas which could never meteorologically be. Fairy lights scarcely registered against the summer afternoon glare. Seasonal traditions rooted in an English winter of dark cold nights – mulled wine, twinkling lights, Yule logs – were transferred intact to 10 p.m.-dusk summer heat.

Down on the docks, an information board said: 'Arrivals: Nil. Departures: Nil.' This maritime scoreless draw was doubtless seasonal, but seemed more generally fitting. Back at the Hydro Grand, I took a bath – the enamel bore those caramel swirls which come to a hotel tub when it has seen too many bottoms – and looked with renewed interest at the slot for used razor blades. Just then, I heard police sirens and waddled dripping to the window. A phalanx of loudly chanting youths was rounding the corner from Stafford Street. A quartet of police cars, lights and sirens at top notch, was in pursuit. Interest and astonishment mingled in me. So the gods were mocking my project. I would have to ship out of the very first destination, Timaru, because of the outbreak of revolution.

I dressed and ran down to the street. The demands of the marchers – now that I could understand their slogans – were perplexing. 'Don't Drive Home!' they screamed. And: 'Watch Those Children!' The latter, at least, held some suggestion of protest movements – a gentler version, perhaps, of 'Hey, hey, L. B. J., how many kids did you kill today?' inspired in this case by the stabbing of the fifteen-year-old boy – but the first creed was seriously weird, suggesting a Luddite revolt against automation. Then one of the marchers handed me a leaflet. 'Timaru police and the young people of the town have joined together in this demonstration, which is intended to draw attention to the dangers of drinking and driving over the holiday period.'

Their voices drifted down towards the harbour. 'Don't Drive Home!'. . .'Watch Those Children!' I had stumbled upon the only known demonstration in Western political history in which the police and the students were on the same side. Then I began to wonder about the responsibility of the message being pressed. 'Don't Drive Home!' A sensible sentiment in the old Timaru, maybe, but these days pedestrians were being stabbed. Then a second procession of cars – civilian family saloons – joined on, behind the police vehicles. From the wound-down window of one of them, came another leaflet. 'Timaru's mini-cab drivers add their support to this campaign.' I bet they did.

\*

That night, I had a fish supper at a restaurant on Stafford Street, which would have been excellent except for the insistence on playing Slade's 'So here it is, Merry Christmas!' very loudly on the speakers in a doomed attempt to create a Yuletide mood. Reading a history of New Zealand, I was disturbed to find one of the few things I had marked down on the nation's credit side being reassigned.

The country's precocious granting of the vote to women – the centenary of which would be expensively celebrated in 1993 under the stern gaze of the current Governor-General, Dame Cath Tizzard – had apparently been an accident. The Liberal Prime Minister, Richard Seddon, was granite-facedly against the suffragette movement and had bullied, cajoled, and whipped parliament to throw out a female emancipation bill. However, his arm-twisting and procedural tricks so appalled two of his supporters that they changed sides, guaranteeing the measure's acceptance. So what the women of New Zealand would be commemorating in 1993 was not the dawning of ideological light, but the incompetence of male power games. It was a small example of the interpretative quicksand that national history could be.

Afterwards, I watched television alone in the communal viewing lounge of the Hydro Grand. Restricted to an abstemiously British three channels – with CNN and Rupert Murdoch's Sky on offer in the big cities – New Zealand television was, culturally, more seduced than producing.

The comedy was mainly two-year-old sit-coms from Britain, with Rowan Atkinson the latest sensation for his *Blackadder* and *Mr Bean* series. The news and current affairs were normally British, Australian, or American imports (both ABC and NBC news from New York were screened daily). Sometimes, the Kiwis adapted a foreign format for their own ends. Britain's nark-your-neighbour police series *Crimewatch UK* inspired a local spin-off, in which the laborious reconstructions of inconsequential offences – the theft of a handbag, the disappearance of a cat – became the object of mockery in Clive James's British series *On Television*, an anthology of appalling small-screen material from around the world. The New Zealand broadcasters then purchased James's show, as they did all British hits, with the result that viewers were outraged by this Aussie-Brit's mockery of them: a little morality tale about the dangers of the second-hand nature of their dealings in the medium. The limit of the original programming seemed to be *Holmes*, a chat show presented by a thin man in spectacles who was required to embody in one flesh New Zealand's answers to Terry Wogan, Michael Aspel, David Frost, Johnny Carson, Arsenio Hall, and Jay Leno.

Next morning, I nervously explained to the sad-eyed receptionist at the Hydro Grand that I would not be staying for three nights after all, but would be leaving that morning. Her look said: *I told you so.* I relocated to the Grosvenor Hotel, which was decent mock-American, and arranged for Cousin Claire to collect me from there.

She asked me about the Royal family: the Queen Mum's leg, the Duchess of York's daughters and books.

'By the way, people say that the Duke of Edinburgh has a love-child in Timaru. The Royal Yacht docked here once. But I don't suppose you can put that in your book . . .'

I had found that, almost wherever you went in the Commonwealth, you would be told of some bastard offspring of the Queen's consort. Given the physical and logistical impossibility of all the rumours being true, I assumed that it was an urban legend, one of those unprovable chain anecdotes which spread through communities. But an urban legend generally represented some submerged social fear or hope. In this case, I suspected that it was based on the perception – common even to ardent Royalists – that Prince Philip was the bad bod of the British Royals. But the stories spoke also of New Zealand's desperation to have Royal progeny of its own. When, for example, it was alleged that Captain Mark Phillips, the estranged husband of Princess Anne, had impregnated an Auckland girl, Jessica had referred excitedly in a letter to 'New Zealand's own Princess'. I had to disillusion her. Even if paternity were proved, Captain Phillips's sperms were commoners.

Cousin Claire was a bouncy woman, with a loud voice, known in her family as a Dionysiac and optimist. Even so, her attempt to be upbeat about Timaru deserved a medal.

'Unfortunately, the meat freezing plant is closed for the

holiday. They usually do tours. I thought I'd just drive around, show you some places you might not have picked up on as a first-timer. Jess and her friends are probably a bit, well, towny, about it,' she said.

'Tell me about the murder,' I said.

'Murder? I don't git you . . .'

'It's OK. I know . . .'

'Oh, will. I was worried you'd take it out of contixt. It's shaken pipple bidly round here. But what do you ixpict? There's a trind. You can't deny it. I know it's always timpting to rominticize, but it's actually not thit long since you lift your front door open as a mitter of course. The Prime Minister hid his home number in the phone book. There wiz this progrimme called *Crimewatch*, bit the joke was they niver had enough crimes to put on it. Not now . . .'

In a recent month, there had been twenty-four armed robberies in New Zealand. In modern memory, one would have been thought catastrophic. The previous year, the country had suffered its first mass slaying. In the coastal pocket of Aramoana, a youth called David Gray had wiped out thirteen people, a third of the population, before turning the shotgun on himself.

'Why do people think it has happened . . . ?'

'Will, the government says it's too much violince on TV and in the films. Some say it's racial, but that doesn't really stand up . . . The Church says it's the Divil. Everybidy ilse blames the government. The economy . . . Of course, a lot of pipple say bring bick hinging. But the kid here was killed by another kid and you can't hing kids . . .'

So the borders of the quiet world were pervious. By now, Cousin Claire had driven up into the hills above the centre of the town.

'Now, if you look on the lift, you'll see some of the nicest houses in Timaru . . .'

She waved at some unusually plush bungalows – in New Zealand, if your house had two storeys, you were either in prison or you slept in the office – with fussy gardens.

'Tell me about the gangs, Claire,' I said.

'The gings? Oh, listin, what kind of book is this going to

41

be . . .? Now, I was going to take you to my old school. There's an exhibition of local sculpture, in the grounds, sid to be viry good . . .'

'The gangs . . .'

'Oh, will, I'll drive past the hidquarters for you, because it's obviously what you want. But, you know, I hear these ging boys aren't all bad. One old girl I know, frind of my parints, she has one as a next-door neighbour and swears by him . . .'

'Oh, yes? Swears at him, you mean . . .'

'No, I mean it. He does her shopping, gits her washing for her . . .'

Given that Timaru had already shown me a protest march organized in co-operation with the constabulary, I would not completely have bet against the town harbouring well-mannered gangsters, but it seemed more likely that Cousin Claire represented a bad case of residential generosity.

Down on the Washdyke – the industrial region of Timaru – we found a wasteland compound, on which stood a square of high wooden fences, topped all round by coils of barbed wire. Through the open gates, we saw a corrugated-iron shed. Splayed in front of it were motorbikes, beached in different stages of dismantlement. As we watched, a bike roared out of the gates, and deafeningly revved towards the centre of the town. Its rider wore a black helmet, with tinted visor, and a studded leather jacket, on the back of which was spelled out in bolts: Henchmen.

Now I understood. Perhaps the previous week's murder, and the armed robberies, were evidence that the modern world was catching up with New Zealand. This, though, was an example of a far more common process in these parts: New Zealand catching up with the modern world. Timaru had just got the sixties, thirty years late. Before I left, there was further confirmation. Someone told me that poppies were being stolen from local gardens and flower shops by pot-heads. There it is, man.

To see in 1992, I went to Nelson – a South Island beach resort where New Zealanders traditionally celebrate New Year – with Jessica, her sister Gemma, and a party of their friends. You really might have believed, again, that the whole of the country knew each other. Everywhere Jessica and Gemma went, they met a friend. Phone calls would come in to the hotel with invitations to Hogmanay thrashes being held at Nelson. There was a welcome flow of the wines which, in my opinion, constitute New Zealand's one indisputable reason-to-be.

The men I met at the celebrations were calculatedly macho. A prominent national sportsman, who was rumoured to be a homosexual, was ridiculed as the Kiwi Fruit. They also kept encouraging me to try bungee-jumping. This sport – in which you throw yourself from a bridge into a ravine with a long piece of knicker elastic tied between your belt and the bridge – had originated in New Zealand. Only in a culture of unusual monotony could such a practice have become established. It resulted, presumably, from the desperate need for a buzz. Bungee-jumping would never have begun in New York, where you could get much the same adrenalin rush just by going out to buy a loaf of bread.

The rougher among the men said things like: 'We want to git your Queen and her Governor-Gineril out.' It was supposed to provoke, and they were disappointed when I said I hoped they soon succeeded. The more serious males said: 'What should New Zealand do? Continue to look towards the trading bloc of Britain and Europe, or turn to the markets of Australia, Japan, and America?' I gave them my answer. They grimaced, and said the Japanese were weird and Australians bozos.

In fact, whatever their protestations, the influence of the vast magnetic island to the north was everywhere apparent in their manner. Where the older New Zealanders were Brits with thinned vowels, the younger islanders were Australians off the bottle, or mainly off the bottle. A friend of Jessica's, who had played rugby nearly to All Black level, took me aside and whispered: 'Next time you come out, we'll show you what you might call a man's New Zealand . . . What you've seen so far is, no disrespect' – he nodded at my hostesses – 'a girls' New Zealand . . .' I scarcely dared imagine the agenda he was suggesting. Bungee-jumping? Rugby? Beer drinking? Sheep shearing? Kick-a-Maori contest?

You thought, from far away, of New Zealand as a soft and fluffy country, innocuous. I kept finding something harder there: an extreme sensitivity about their own nation coupled with an intolerance towards others. One day, in a crowded café in Nelson where I was lunching, a holidaying sheepbreeder and his wife, placed on my table, struck up a conversation. After the general stuff about residences, destinations, professions, prime ministers, the man said: 'You must have a lot of Jews in England . . .'

I was still fretting about the premiss of the question, when he continued: 'One thing about NZ, you don't get a lot of Jews . . . I think it would be true in Britain, wouldn't it, certainly in America, that Jews occupy more positions of power – relative to population – than anyone else . . .'

'Well, it depends how you put it. Certainly, Jews in the West tend to be successful, industrious. It's almost all middle class, without an underclass. That is one of the interesting things about them as a people . . .'

'Interesting? But that's because of the Great Jewish Conspiracy. They all help each other up. A Jew appoints a Jew and so on. Look at history, everybody always hates the Jews. Myself, I've never had any difficulty understanding that. Because of the way they are . . .'

I am aware of the dangers of extrapolating a nation's nature from what might very possibly have been an isolated bigot. Even so, hearing this towards the end of my stay, I didn't think, What a very odd thing for a New Zealander to say, but rather the opposite. Maybe it was all those coppers' narks starting new lives down there.


For most of our stay at what were theoretically Nelson's Golden Sands, it rained torrentially. The nation which the Maoris called *Aotearoa*, the land of the long white cloud, was, for us, the place of the stubby grey one. In mitigation, the hotel announced an innovative daily competition. Anyone collecting twenty spots of rain on the page of a broadsheet newspaper during any daylight sixty seconds would be given a free bottle of the local Chablis or Riesling.

'Sixty . . . fifty-nine . . . fifty-eight . . . fifty-seven . . .' counted Jessica or Gemma each morning, looking at a watch.

'One . . . two . . . three . . . four . . .' I counted, watching the raindrops blotch the sports pages. I wondered if this would become the new national craze, replacing bungee-jumping, another hedge against empty hours.

We won so many bottles that we soon scarcely knew whether it was raining or not. Denied the beach, I spent a lot of time watching television and reading newspapers. Both, in different ways, attested to the charming low-key nature of New Zealand. The December 31st edition of the local newspaper offered a front-page report on Christchurch's New Year celebrations, under the banner headline: NO FUSS EXPECTED. Another splash, about the British New Year's Honours List, was: CBE FOR SHEEPBREEDER.

But my favourite – of that day and, indeed, of my whole stay – was: BEACH TOILET STILL SHUT. The paper reported: 'A new $25,000 toilet at Diamond Beach Habour remains shut over what would normally be its busiest period, because of an electrical problem . . .' It was a news culture in which an unused loo was a scoop.

And, on television, the main channel's 1991 round-up included, in its section on 'New Zealanders in the News', John Tanner, an emigrant Kiwi, whose route to celebrity had been the murder of his student girlfriend, Rachel Maclean, in Oxford. You assumed that they must be desperate for the homegrown known.

As a gift of its position, New Zealand gets each New Year first: a small excitement which even cynical visitors could share. We welcomed the future in a Nelson restaurant with what the wine guides called, with increasingly inappropriate disdain, New World champagne. Next day, with rain forecast only for the early afternoon, we were lying in the sand dunes with a bottle of New Zealand Marlborough Chardonnay. At 1 p.m., we raised our plastic glasses to the British New Year, which was just striking twenty thousand miles away. I closed my eyes, crossed my fingers, and wished for a safe passage through the quiet world in the year ahead.

# CHAPTER TWO

# THE DOWAGER EMPRESS'S REVENGE

## Melbourne and Canberra

Just before I arrived in Australia, the Prime Minister, Bob Hawke was putsched by his own party, although it is doubtful that he used that word himself. An iron-haired bruiser, an old Union hand who could have played without direction a boxer's corner man in a remake of *The Fighter*, Hawke was a glorious example of one of the ways in which committed Australians differentiated themselves from Britain, their old colonial overlord: refusal of the mind-your-language rules. In my Melbourne hotel room, I watched Hawke's first television appearance since his fall. The presenter began by explaining that Mrs Hawke had been billed in the newspapers to appear, but had been forced to cancel. 'That's right, Mike,' the only just ex-Prime Minister said. 'Frankly, after all that's happened, Mrs Hawke's a bit *buggered* . . .'

If a senior British politician had used that word on television, the switchboard would have been singed with calls, most of them demanding his resignation. But speech was one of Australia's statements of liberation. The Hawke interview example had depended merely on social relaxation, but many others held more invention. One of the international arrogances of the British was the claim to be exceptionally adept at what they pointedly called the Language of Shakespeare or the Queen's English. In fact, English was fine for the rotund quote on a public occasion, but Australian and American (from which the British regularly stole bravura neurological insults like 'the lights are on, but there's no one at home . . .' or 'his elevator doesn't go all the way to the top . . .') really cleaned up on the colloquial. Although, in the case of Australian, it was usually a matter of dirtying up.

Aussies had a spray of euphemisms for urination – 'shaking hands with the wife's best friend', 'pointing Percy at the porcelain' – while cooking up for the penis itself culinary off-cuts like 'pork sword' and 'tummy banana' and, for the place at which Percy was pointed, 'dunny'. In the form of extended metaphors, the language offered images as vivid as 'sore as a dingo's donger in the breeding season'. Some had been popularized by the Australian entertainer Barry Humphries, others invented by him for his cartoon character Barry McKenzie and his theatrical creation Sir Les Patterson, supposedly the Australian cultural attaché in London. Satire and real-life proving seamless, some of Humphries' nonce Oz had now fed back into spoken Australian.

Snobs and the British, sometimes interchangeable sets, might object that little of the linguistic invention reached above the belt. But, in my view, such exuberant euphemism was a sign of the cultural vibrancy which typified Australia. Its filth showed a poet's ear. A braver critic than me might have mentioned the attractively assonantal play of *g* and *o* sounds in 'dingo's donger'. (And consider, as contrast, the nominal poverty of British invention in the same area: mainly borrowed boys' names, like dick and willy.) Where the New Zealand accent made relatively tactful departures from the inherited English vowels, the Aussie one gave them a screw and a twist like an arm-lock.

Alert readers – and, in particular, aggrieved New Zealanders – may have noticed a new enthusiasm in the tone of the text. I should make clear that it is a tribute to the democracy of this enterprise that Australia is included at all. It is among my favourite countries in the world, Sydney my most loved city. Australia had struck me, on my first visit a few years before, as a sensible America. It was a nation with the same wild range of landscape, from beach to desert to throbbing metropolis, but discreetly peopled – 5 per cent of the US population in a nearly equal acreage – and these including considerably fewer psychopaths and neurotics. Australia was an America in which the populace was not possessed of the belief that it was specially blessed and directed by God, with a particular vocation to bully smaller nations. An America in which they played cricket instead of baseball.

However, during the research for this book, when I was trawling the memories of travellers for the most activity-challenged, the most differently interesting places they knew, there were so many votes for Melbourne and Canberra, Australia, that I felt obliged to consider them. After detailed examination, the selectors agreed to their inclusion, but with one proviso. It will become apparent as the book goes on that sections of this investigation differ significantly in scale. Some chapters tackle entire nations labelled (libelled, their residents would say, whether or not their accents were Australian) as places of calm: for example, New Zealand and, later, Canada. Others are restricted to a single city: Brussels, Belgium, or Milton Keynes, England. Even there, a distinction may be made between activity-challenged places which are microcosmic representations of the national condition and those which are interesting aberrations from it. It is under the last flag that Victoria and Canberra have been admitted.

Because of this distinction – and because readers of an often critical book may sometimes ask themselves, 'Well, what *does* he like?' – there now follows a presentation of the wider case for Australia: what you might call a swoon interlude.


Australia offers perhaps the only recent example from the quiet world of outgoing cultural influence. It was mentioned in the previous chapter that New Zealand television is an anthology of British and Australian offerings. But British culture of the eighties and early nineties would have suggested, to an outsider, a different post-empirical hegemony.

Among the most popular four television programmes in Britain were *Neighbours*, a soap opera set in a Melbourne suburb, and *Home and Away*, a Sydney-based serial. In music, the highest-grossing performers, at least for the hormonally challenged young, included Jason Donovan and Kylie Minogue – who had started singing after acting gave them up in *Neighbours* – and the band INXS. I had once lived in a block of London flats in which the young Australian actor playing a character called Martin Dibble in *Home and Away* was staying while pursuing a recording contract. In the mornings and evenings, packs of schoolchildren would gather on the pavement outside, chanting, 'Dibble! Dibble! Dibble!' until the shocked Aussie, who was regarded as no one much at all back home, emerged to sign autographs. It seemed one of God's better jokes against the British Empire.

In the gaps between the programmes, too, commercials for Australian beers like Foster's and Castlemaine XXXX began to challenge Budweiser as the macho glamour-import beer. In London theatre, two of the most lucrative shows of recent seasons had starred Jason Donovan and Barry Humphries, the latter in his role of Dame Edna Everage, the drag (and dragon) social queen from Moonie Ponds, a Melbourne suburb. Australian journalists – like Clive James, Robert Hughes, and Germaine Greer – dominated British print and television. Sydney novelists, Peter Carey and Thomas Kenneally, won (and, on other occasions nearly won) the Booker McConnell Prize for British and Commonwealth Fiction.

For decades, articles had been written about the Americanization of Western culture: *Dallas* and Coca-Cola and 'Have a nice day!' Now, in Britain at least, it seemed there was a new story: Aussification. It was true that the same retaliatory dominance had not been achieved in the world's central cultural market – the USA – but, even so, there had been improbable Hollywood success for *Crocodile Dundee*, a movie about an outback character, starring Paul Hogan. Former Australian art-house directors like Bruce Beresford, Peter Weir, and Philip Noyce had achieved significant careers in California. And, in what might be seen as the ultimate nod of acknowledgement from the industry, Meryl Streep had learned an Australian accent to play the mother in a film about the famous outback case in which a couple claimed their baby had been kidnapped by a dingo.

Non-film business had shown a similar trend, with Rupert Murdoch, Alan Bond, Kerry Packer, Robert Holmes à Court, and numerous other Bruce-tycoons monopolizing the stock markets and media industries of the globe.

Aussification ranked as one of the quiet world's most unpredictable export booms, as surprising as the way in which Scandinavia, against expectation, suddenly began to produce major playwrights in the nineteenth century, and great tennis players in the twentieth. As an occasional cultural commentator, I had been required to explain the new Oz influence on Britain. It was tough. The soap opera boom, for example, clearly broke historical precedent. The genre had always been regarded as escapist. The success in Britain of the country-village radio drama *The Archers*, for example, was generally attributed to the urban-dwellers' secret dream of rural retreat. *Dallas* and *Dynasty* were watched, critics felt, because they permitted the reticent British vicarious immersion in ten-gallon glamour. It was what you might call the hope-on-a-soap theory of television viewing.

The popularity of *Neighbours* wrecked this thesis. Although, in its later ratings pomp, it would have a death, divorce, and suicide rate to rival any of the American dramas, it first came to notice as an unusually low-incident soap. In *Dallas*, gunshots chimed the hour instead of clocks. But, in *Neighbours*, a cliffhanger was when a kettle fused and the man of the house had forgotten where he put his tool-box. When I had first started watching, the characters were excitedly talking about what I took to be a 'poisoned moose'. I envisaged a queasy behemoth, perhaps gorged on toxic berries, charging towards this corner of Melbourne. In fact, the threat turned out to be from a pudding made with spoiled eggs: a 'poisoned mousse'. This was typical of the serial's concentration on small domestic mishaps.

The hope-on-a-soap theory, therefore, could not hold. Was it really plausible that the secret desire of Europeans, who led busy and interesting lives, was to do bugger all in Melbourne? Emigration and vacation figures suggested that it was, or that at least they dreamed of doing so in some part of Australia. The nation had managed the profitable trick of making its lifestyle enviable and magnetic to others. This was partly to do with volume of sun, proximity of beach, and the sartorial common denominator of thongs, which were the main visual images of the artworks of Aussification: the sense that all days in this nation were holidays. Certainly, people routinely drank as if they didn't have to get up for work. An outsider could easily see this relaxation as optimism. It was a nation to which people were drawn in the hope of being reborn, not religiously but domestically or professionally or sexually. Divorcées and redundants fled there. Students loaded around its coasts.

Close up, it was true, some of the languorous national attitude was exposed as cynical, slobbish, philistine, and bigoted. The relationship between New Zealand's whites and its Maoris or

Polynesians looked like power-sharing in comparison with the attitude of Australians towards Aborigines. New Zealanders might have slandered the Jews in café conversation with strangers. But, in Australia, coach drivers – a central profession, given the spaces between the places – would do lengthy routines on the speakers for what they assumed to be the amusement of the tourists. 'Know what an Abo calls his woman? A *gin*. So, if you hear an Abo saying he's going off to have a gin on the rocks, don't think he's ordering a drink!' There was another one, a topical gag for the last few years because of the large number of Aborigine youths committing suicide in police cells. They usually hanged themselves from the ceiling. Hence, 'What do you call five Abos in a police cell? [*Pause. Guffaw.*] A mobile.'

It might be pointed out that the men who joked about Aborigines calling their females *gins* referred to their own women as 'towel-warmers'. This was a reference to the traditional hier-archy.of youthful Australian relationships: the guy bronzed and upright in the surf, the girl ready to rub him down when he was done. Whole layers of Australian men still thought Feminism was a brand of sanitary towels. Most breathtakingly, white Australians complained that the Aborigines were pissed all the time. 'You know, your Abo believes that there are hidden lines drawn beneath the surface of the earth. Only an Abo can see them. Know what they're for? Help him find his way home from the bar.' It was true that the first settlers had come to believe too enthusiastically in the white tribal myth that the god of happiness lives in a bottle. But, given the main leisure activity of majority Australians, this was, to adapt the vernacular, like the dunny saying the arsehole stank.

Australia, though, was devotedly politically incorrect. In Perth once, I had seen a drive-in off-licence, a bloody-minded denial of the general Western movement to separate the car and the bar. In fact, the odd thing about the process of cultural Aussification was that the nation had been brave, or cynical, enough to cash in on this negative image. When the back of their Land-Rover hung perilously over a cliff, the Aussie sports in beer commercials expected their wife to jump off the back to raise the odds of saving their consignment of beer. Murdoch's *Sun* was a satirist's parody of what a stereotypical Australian might do to a

British newspaper. Compare this with the way in which American movies and commercials romanticized the nation's past and present.

But a country and its inhabitants were not inseparable: a deal which most people did with themselves when visiting France. I was not often sorry not to be an Australian. I was frequently sad, though, not to be in Australia. I had first gone on a press trip. I warmed to the wine and the cricket and the way the politicians swore. But my true conversion came in Sydney. Because of television and cinema, mine was the first generation of travellers for whom a visit to a new location could be ruined by a feeling of familiarity. It was just possible that, in earlier times, a voyager would say, at the Taj Mahal, 'Oh, it's smaller than it looks on the woodcut.' Or, in Florence, 'Well, once you've read Forster, it's not a surprise.' But the phenomenon of accidental wonder-loss was almost certainly a modern one.

Such was the casual travel accomplished by the average television viewer or magazine flicker that the voyager of today could have been once too often to a place before they got there. You went to New York and the sensation was not, as travel once was, of a curtain pulled back, but of stepping through the glass of a television set. That which you had already seen was rendered three-dimensional. There was not necessarily a loss of excitement or enjoyment. It was wonder which had gone: the first gasp of astonishment was replaced by a grin of confirmation.

But, then, one afternoon in Sydney Harbour, I discovered what it was to be shocked by a sight: what it may have been like when travel was a search for incredible pictures rather than a response to them. Perhaps it was simply that, despite Aussification, the place had still been less relentlessly previewed on celluloid and videotape than America. Or maybe it was that the Antipodes still transmitted, to the English visitor, a sense of distance, of total remoteness, which merely transatlantic locations no longer could.

In North America, I always retained a subconscious connection with my homeland, aware of being only a few hours behind the English day. The celebrated, but now tangible, topsy-turviness of Australia – the fact that, as you breakfasted, dinner was being eaten in Britain – removed that safety rail. In a world shrunk by jet engines, you could still, making this trip, feel a touch of Columbus.

The country even seemed to have a distinctive light, so that your irises felt always slightly widened, as if from a painless migraine. Perhaps this helped the country's sights to seem like a brilliant mirage. The light was at its brightest, and most singular, in the middle of that Sydney afternoon. I toured the harbour on a two-hour cruise. The boat went slowly, for the eyes and cameras of the travellers, but it was not a crawl. The length of time needed for the trip gives some sense of the scale of what is the largest natural harbour in the world. Beginning to chug around the uneven circumference, you looked up at the heights of Hunter's Hill, the cliff-edge residences of many of Australia's millionaires. The rich folks' view – across the azure waves, through the cage of the great bridge, to the Opera House crouched on the opposite shore – was the world's classiest executive toy.

Then the boat ducked and bobbed under the Harbour Bridge. The world's big bridges divide between those worth looking from and those worth looking at. Sydney's was emphatically in the latter category. Its skeletal dark steel, arched across the harbour like a vast raised eyebrow, could not be called beautiful but was magnificent for its arrogance, a cathedral of engineering.

Half-way through the journey, we rocked across the mouth of the harbour, where the rhythms of the sea made the sheltered bay waters froth and boil. In the nineteenth century, a boat of early immigrants had been smithereened there, minutes from port after months at sea. Sailing around the other side – the boat now a bobbing dot for any millionaires looking across from their steep and steeply priced retreats – we reached the Opera House. The architect had wanted to suggest white sails, but, witnessed, the images were more chimerical. From the side, they looked like a clutch of nuns, with their cowled heads bowed in prayer. From the front, the hoods looked like the open beaks of birds. Even well prepared by representations, I gasped. And envied those travellers of the past for whom such shocks were commonplace.

End swoon interlude. Spool reality. In January 1992 – when I flew in to Australia, from New Zealand, for this project – the light was as bright as before, but the national optimism was dampened. Nearly 10 per cent of the workforce could now, without impunity, drink as if they didn't need to get up in the morning, although the question was whether they could afford to. The Bruce-tycoons of the late eighties had been largely ruined by the recession, discovering that to live on a Sydney cliff-edge had been to tempt a metaphor. The best views in the world were now up for sale, flirting with reluctant purchasers by lowering their prices ever further. Alan Bond was on the brink of imprisonment for financial irregularity.

It was the state of the economy which had putsched Bob Hawke and left his wife feeling a bit *buggered*. The party had replaced him with Paul Keating, a Treasury minister known as the Undertaker, because of his mordant manner, and a politician so volcanically demotic that even Australians commented on his swearing.

A high percentage of those comments came from Melbourne. It was my hunch – on which I would wait for total confirmation until Victoria, British Columbia – that places named after the Dowager Empress, her relatives, or friends were almost guaranteed to be a bore. (Melbourne was a nineteenth-century British prime minister, who had crawled at the young Victoria's court. Two Australian guidebooks described him as her son, but this was presumably a Republican smear.) At one point, the list of nominations for my itinerary had resembled a biography of the British Saxe-Coburg-Gothas: Victoria, Alberta, Victoria, Melbourne.

Adding detail to my thesis, the city of Melbourne in the state of Victoria was a bossy and conformist place. A friend of mine had once been stopped there by a traffic cop for, as a pedestrian, crossing the road at a diagonal. He had been not merely cautioned but sent back to repeat the walk on the straight and narrow. It was said to be the only city in Australia where a question about where you went to school was seeking not information but status. And, though the nation as a whole was notably unsoppy about God, Billy Graham, who had done a number of successful gigs there, had called Melbourne 'the most moral city in the world'.

Late the previous year, I had interviewed Barry Humphries in London, and he had regretted that a crucial aspect of his act was missed by audiences in England and America. That was, he thought, its Australian social precision. For him, Dame Edna could only have come from Melbourne because her stratospheric pretension and vaulting snobbery were merely an extreme version of its diurnal values. Despite its confusing longitude, it was 'the Home Counties in the South Seas'. Sir Les Patterson, on the other hand, a dribbling dipsomaniac who thought *Tosca* was Italian for wanker, could only, Humphries suggested, have come from Sydney. While I was in Australia, that statement of Humphries's was quoted in the *Melbourne Age*, though only the part about Sydney.

The relationship between Sydney and Melbourne was like that between Liverpool and Cheltenham, or Chicago and Connecticut. The first named found the second named dull and priggish, while the latters thought the formers rough and ruined. When Melbourne had won an award for 'best laid-out city', the riposte had come from Sydney: 'Laid out means embalmed, doesn't it?' Melbourne was fond of explaining that it had been settled by free pioneers, while Sydney was a more or less reformed gaol.

The capital of Victoria was secure, or pushy, enough on this point to have turned the old prison into a museum, where tourists were invited to gawp at a waxwork of Ned Kelly swinging in his cell. Another Australian city might have been embarrassed about the inevitable European travellers' gags, but, for Melbourne, the restoration of the building was a monument to civic rectitude. It was a declaration that, elsewhere in the nation, they might tell you that Ned Kelly was a hero, but Victorians had known what to do with him.

My soul was already sold to Sydney, but I found nothing in Melbourne to lead me to remortgage it. Most alarmingly, it shared a feature with Timaru. The less smart shops had oblong plywood sun-visors hanging from their fronts. Turning a corner, I saw a sign saying Canberra Tourist Board, and was intrigued, because that city was my next destination. But the shop was an empty shell with whitewashed windows. *The Canberra Tourist Board office has closed down*, a sign revealed. The phrase sounded mocking and ominous.

One of the poshest Melbourne shops was dedicated to the

work of Ken Done. He had become Australia's household artist, designing ranges of T-shirts and placemats and coasters which – using a fruit-bowl palette of reds, oranges, greens, blues, and yellows – made patterns from national symbols like the Opera House and the kangaroo. Looking at them, I reflected on the extent to which Australia was what you might call a primary-colour culture. Its banknotes flashed like parrot feathers, eschewing the green of the oldest Anglophone banks. The Rugby shirts were old gold. Kerry Packer – who had changed the game of cricket by buying up the best players for a private tour – had pointedly taken the players out of whites and put them in rainbow shades. It was as if Australian eyes needed brightness, like children with mobiles, or they were compensating for the borrowed colours of what was still the national flag. The Aborigines could also tell you something about the Australian preference for primary colours.

Melbourne, though, was the most muted of Australian cities, perhaps because there was less embarrassment than elsewhere about its surviving ties. The streets and awnings beneath them spoke of imperial pride: Elizabeth Street, Queen Street, King Street, Dickens Café, Hardy Bros – Appt. to HMQ, Savoy Hotel. You could not call it Little England Complex, for it was imitation on a greater scale: Big England Complex. The only other place I had ever seen which was so devotedly olde English was New England.

Bob Hawke, although bristlingly non-submissive in demeanour, had never raised the question of the relationship with the Crown during eight years in office. There was, though, a gathering Republican movement, brewing from Sydney. Melbourne, I guessed, would be loyalist in any civil war. The Royal Botanical Gardens was British in both name and nature – a vast flowered park with snooty tea shops – with only those of the exhibits whch depended on climate betraying its location.

I walked up to the Shrine of Remembrance, the Melbourne war memorial, centrally positioned on a hill. The guidebook promised 'extraordinary views of Melbourne'. But a vantage point is only as good as what it gives you prospect of. You could go a mile above Melbourne, and put on kaleidoscopic spectacles, and the sights would still be banal. However, the memorial itself was moving, as cenotaphs in the old Empire always were. The names of the dead from the 1914–18 war were proudly chipped into marble on all the walls of the memorial, or curlicued into a book of remembrance, of which a different page was displayed each day.

But these Australians had died for Empire. In the Republic which the nation must surely one day become, they would be devalued as fodder for an idea which had gone, and would be forgotten. Perhaps Melbourne was just a naturally depressing place, but I was sunk into gloom and vestigial guilt by the thought. To die young in battle was bad enough, but to do so for a tenuous association, perhaps later to be revoked, seemed the soldier's cruellest fate. I somehow doubted that, even if forced to accept a republic, stuffy Melbourne would turn the memorial into a tribute to the victims of the British. The names on the memorial would simply become an historical anachronism.

The shrine had been carefully designed and positioned so that – on the eleventh hour of the eleventh day of the eleventh month, the time of the climax of the First World War – the light through the roof would illuminate the word 'love' in the phrase about greater love having no man, which was carved into the floor. But the trick of the light had not come off and had to be annually faked with spotlamps. There seemed to be a moral there about the treachery of national remembrance.


Back at the hotel, I rang Sally, a friend from London who had arrived in Melbourne that day for a family wedding. Her brother was marrying an Australian. The families were meeting at dinner that night.

'Do you want to have lunch tomorrow?' I said.

'I'm going to Sydney tomorrow . . .'

'But you only got to Melbourne last night . . .'

'Yes, I know. And it's awful. I was in tears of boredom by this afternoon. There's nothing, just nothing. I'm going to Sydney until the wedding. Lunch on Thursday . . .?'

'I'm going to Canberra . . .'

'Canberra? But people say it's worse than Melbourne . . .'

Oh, God. I checked the theatre pages, but the big show in

town was Lloyd-Webber's *Phantom of the Opera*, the artistic Esperanto of that time. I saw that *Neighbours* was billed in the papers as receiving its 'season première', one of the Australian language's borrowings from American, the other being the tendency of receptionists to say 'Have a nice day!' (For all the success of Aussification, there was also traditional Western cultural slippage of this kind. But then men like Murdoch, Packer, and Bond were displaced Americans, Murdoch having even become one for business reasons.)

The 'season première' confirmed that *Neighbours*, having begun as the soap in which nothing took place – which I now saw to have been a documentary portrait of Melbourne – had succumbed to the event dementia of the trans-continental super-soap it was. The first of the 1992 shows actually ended with that Methuselah scene in a hospital ward, with the last line before the titles being the doctor's 'Glenn, I'm afraid it's unlikely that you'll ever walk again . . .'

There had been a drowning and a shooting in the previous few weeks, and a fugitive criminal on the loose in the close. Several other characters had hurriedly 'gone to Brisbane', which was the traditional plot opt-out, except for one actor who had really annoyed the producers and been exiled to New Zealand. Aunt Helen, a series matriarch, suddenly an Electra of the Melbourne suburbs, was given the line which is always the subliminal admission of soap opera scriptwriters that they have gone too far: 'We're having a bad run of it in Ramsey Street . . .' The production values remained thrillingly minimal: the legs of the newly paraplegic Glen moved visibly under his blankets, the sea in which a swimmer nearly drowned was clearly a tank, with pictures of sand back-projected.

I ate in a seafood restaurant. The constant proximity of fresh fish was one of the benefits of the arrangement of Australia, an almost ideal civic plan in which all the cities were ranged around the coast with a virtually deserted (because desert) middle: what the tourist board called the Red Centre and Australians called the GAFA, or the Great Australian Fuck All.

At the next table were – I learned from overhearing – a young Melbourne businessman and an old college friend, who was passing through the city for work. Businessman A had recently married. Businessman B remained a bachelor, on what seemed to be a traditional Australian model.

> BUSINESSMAN B: 'Who was I with when I last saw you, mate? Julie? No, I'm not with Julie. See, I was porking this English girl I met at a party. Julie finds out. She goes back to Adelaide. The English girl goes back to England. No worries. I'm up to my neck in them. And I *mean* my neck, mate. They expect you to do that stuff down there now, some of these sheilas. It's not natural . . . You must miss all that, mate, now ya married . . .'
>
> BUSINESSMAN A: [Unconvincingly] 'Nah. Well out of it, mate . . .'
>
> BUSINESSMAN B: 'She sounds nice on the answerphone, your wife, in as much as . . .'
>
> BUSINESSMAN A: 'Oh, she's good value . . .'
>
> BUSINESSMAN B: 'Have you found it hard to adjust, being married . . .?'
>
> BUSINESSMAN A: 'Well, I guess there are pros and cons, in as much as you can't be out with your mates every night but, as I told you, she's good value . . .'
>
> BUSINESSMAN B: 'Like, where does she think you are tonight?'
>
> BUSINESSMAN A: 'She *knows* where I am tonight. I'm with you . . .'
>
> BUSINESSMAN B: 'But does she think you're somewhere else . . .?'
>
> BUSINESSMAN A: 'It doesn't go like that. I said, "Look, mate. I'm going for a drink, maybe a meal, with my mate." She says, "OK, mate . . ."'

I had once worked with an Australian who also called his girlfriend 'mate'. Perhaps it was an echo of primitive societies: a rare case of literally Neanderthal Australian male behaviour. I fantasized about an Australian Valentine's Day card, with the endearment: 'You're good value, mate'.

There was little matey about my hotel, which followed the American fashion, as seen in New Zealand, for a fake marble atrium overlooked by vine-clad balconies, from which transparent elevators rocketed from floor to floor. It was typical top-end accommodation in the quiet world. Many of the guidebooks used little drawings to indicate a hotel's facilities: sketches of a swimming pool, a fax machine, a tennis racket, a butler, a Nautilus machine. This hotel in Melbourne had so many little pictures that its guidebook entry resembled a Japanese novella. Beyond my comfortable means, it had become reachable through a recession special deal. For those still in work, the world was a buyer's market that year.

I was lucky to be there. It was comforting to discover, however, that there were a number of small drawbacks to residence in ritzy hotels which – if I had been a rich man paying the full whack – might have taken the gilt off the existence.

First, there was Credit Card Terror, the sweaty moment when the receptionist swiped the electronic stripe of your plastic sugar daddy through the slot, to decide whether you were rich enough to check in. I saw someone fail the test, and their instinctive but shifty yell of: 'I'm well below my limit on that card.' The second potential danger was Chocolate Ear. Because of the inexplicable keenness, already mentioned, of the best hotels to leave candy on the pillow, it was possible, if retiring to bed jet lagged or well quenched, to miss it. One morning in Melbourne, I woke to find melted chocolate, marzipan, and crinkly paper crushed against my head.

Thirdly, the use, for security reasons, of numberless credit-card-like computerized keys, could also be a problem for the over-stressed traveller, who might easily forget the number. Asking at reception the question 'Excuse me, which room am I in?' and having to prove who you were before they told you, seemed to me the adult equivalent of telling the infant teacher you had had a little accident. Fourthly, there was 3 a.m. Scratch, the disturbing noise resulting from the efficient insistence of the night staff on pushing under the door, as they arrive, international faxes or copies of the bill to facilitate Express Check Out. I was woken three or four times in this way. It seemed bizarre. You ladled out money for comfort and it was like sleeping in a house with a mouse in it.

On my last day in Melbourne, I went to the cricket; if you liked the sport it could never be a wholly unrewarding town. It was also the only time you saw the dowager empress's buttoned-up town with her skirts hitched up. Australia was playing a one-day game in the species known as day-night – disliked by the game's purists, admired by its financiers – in which they started after lunch, the red ball was swapped for a white one at dusk, and the game was played out, in the spangly outfits, under floodlights. The appalled old guard called it pyjama cricket. It was an adoption by the penurious mainstream game of one of Kerry Packer's breakaway inventions.

The crowd was as large and boisterous as a football one. When the home country hit a four, young men with skin like bullion, wearing nothing but luminous Bermuda shorts imprinted with pictures of citrus fruits, jumped to their feet and sang a verse of 'Skippy the Bush Kangaroo', marking the line-breaks with a swig from a tinnie of Foster's. For twenty years I had wanted to attend a cricket match in Australia: the rough equivalent, for any non-fans who have wandered in, of seeing *The Ring* in Bayreuth. So the day was Christmas for me, except that I made one terrible discovery.

For some reason, it seemed that every spectator at an Australian match arranged to be accompanied by someone who either (a) knew nothing at all about the game, (b) was deaf, or (c) on whom the first person had some serious personal dirt, for blackmail purposes. For whatever reason, the companion sat meekly while the first spectator explained to them each detail of the game. So every other seat held a commentator, statistician, and team biographer rolled into one Australian with a loud voice.

'Oh, that's going to go for one down to fine leg . . . Two, if Hughes fumbles, but he hasn't . . . you may think, mate, it's better to be hitting fours and that's what pleases the crowd, but, in this form of the game, ya quick singles can win ya the match, no worries. That makes the run rate 2.93. Not great. But on this pitch it will take some getting. See the keeper, there? Practises every morning in the car park of the hotel they're in, throwing a golf ball against a wall, reckons if his eyes get keyed in to a golf ball, the cherry's going to look like a cannon ball, time he gets into the middle . . . See the new leggie in the Test last week? Action kind of reminds me of old Pongo, played seven Tests and eleven one-day internationals, sorry, mate, *ten* I think it was, a while back. Just been charged with larceny, shot up a post office.

Know how many former Australian Test players have faced criminal charges . . .?'

And so on, for the eight hours a game took. Or three in this case, because the rain came and the match was abandoned. My relationship with Melbourne was becoming like Job's with God.

Back at the hotel, a fax had arrived from Jessica in New Zealand. It read: 'Hi! Place in uproar! Mayor of Timaru has denounced you in national media . . .' I had sent home to my newspaper a short taster of my experiences in Timaru, which had just been published. Included in Jessica's fax was a copy of an article in a Kiwi magazine. Headlined 'WHADDYA MEAN DULL?' the piece began:

'It seems yet another English journalist has found good sport in poking fun at the quaintness and under-population of one of his country's former colonial outposts. Clive James, himself of antipodean stock, once did it to our do-them-in TV programme *Crimewatch*. And now Mark Lawson, a scribe for the *Independent* newspaper in London, has stuck it up Timaru . . .'

I had been warned that New Zealanders were a few skins short when it came to criticism and this was underlined by the meticulous book-keeping of piques: the old James gibe objected to again in connection with mine. The reporter, a native Timaru-vian in exile in Christchurch, had been sent back to do a refutation. He kept saying I was wrong, but the only excitement he reported which I felt guilty about missing was that the karaoke craze had reached the town. He even tried the old drab-place backlash tactic of listing all the significant people born in Timaru. These, for the record, were: 'Champion boxer Bob Fitzsimmons, Olympic runner Jack Lovelock, concert pianist Michael Houston . . .' It was not made clear whether any of them had remained there.

I turned back to Jessica's fax: '[Cousin Claire's real name] has been absolutely great about it. But Tony, my other cousin in Timaru, is spitting. He thinks I am the friend who made the "party in Timaru" remark and that the party was one of his . . .' I faxed back to Jessica, under her real name, that sources would be protected. I would use pseudonyms for all my contacts in New Zealand.

I switched on the television news. President George Bush – visiting Japan on a tour cancelled twice because of Bush's vulnerability to suggestions that only foreign policy interested him – had fallen off his chair at a banquet in Tokyo and thrown up over the Prime Minister's trousers. Food poisoning was the White House line. But, having fallen over while running the previous year, this remarkable trump – falling over while sitting – was seen by some as an ominous beginning to his re-election year.

Next morning on the plane from Melbourne to Canberra, the national capital, the view seemed more sanguine. A wide meaty man, who looked as if he might have been an Australian politician, cackled at his neighbour: 'Papers say it may affect Bush's re-election. *What*? Falling over, chundering your lunch? Bob Hawke did that all his career and he was elected three times . . .'

From the airport I took a taxi downtown. One of the guidebooks I was using was Fodor's. It was a feature of this series that its write-ups always sought out a bright side: a neutrality presumably based on the calculation that such works were to help someone who had decided to go somewhere, not to help them choose whether to visit. Even so, I had discovered from use that Fodor's operated a hidden code. The formula 'Some people question ——'s charms, but those who live there say: to know ——is to love it' was as close as the books came to saying: residents-only parking. In the taxi, I checked Fodor's on Canberra: 'It's detractors use many pejorative metaphors to describe it: "Monumentsville", "A city without a soul" . . . those who live there will give you the unanswerable proclamation that "to know Canberra is to love it". . .'

Oh, God. And the code turned out to be right. Canberra was the great Australian civic cock-up. What might you think should be the qualities of a national capital? Well, chiefly, that it should be steeped in the country's culture and history or somehow representative of the national narrative. In young countries, a place associated with a battle of liberation or the signature of a revolutionary document was generally the best choice. But Australia had manufactured a capital on unpopulated sheep land, a shabby compromise between the rival claims of Sydney and Melbourne, the scrub chosen being roughly equidistant between them. The bulk of the population have always lived in the bottom right-hand corner of Australia, as if it were a bag that had been shaken.

The confederation of states had been joined in 1901, necessitating a federal town. An architects' competition to design one had been won in 1913 by a Chicagoan, Walter Burley Griffin, a disciple of Lloyd Wright, who dreamed up a place ranged round a central lake. Wars and squabbles delayed completion until the 1950s, when the architect got his small reward in the naming of his central concept Lake Burley Griffin, a name which somehow led you to expect fat mythical animals to flock there.

What you, in fact, got around it were fat political animals. Two thirds of Canberra's workforce were in government and, most of them were, sensibly, mainly resident in Sydney. So, from Friday lunchtime (or maybe Thursday) to Monday lunchtime, and through all recesses, Canberra was empty. It was a city in which no one lived from choice.

The heart of the town was a circle and triangle. The sphere was the bulbous grass mound which the parliament building topped. From the road around its circumference, two main drags, Commonwealth and Kings, radiated out, making a compass shape, with the legislative buildings resting between these arms.

Given that the only history the city had was its own construction, the nearest to a local museum was the National Capital Planning Exhibition. This building beside the lake proudly promised a 'talking model'. This seemed a few notches down in astonishment from the 'talking dog' which ancient hucksters used to promise, but I gave it a try. There was a wooden representation of Canberra, on which individual buildings lit up and explained in a modulated Australian voice what they did. The final voice spoke what was presumably the consensus view of all the bricks and windows: 'Canberra is now a true reflection of the national identity.'

But that was just what it was not. It was tough enough to build up any town from nothing – I shivered as I thought of

Milton Keynes, a later stop on the project – but a *capital* from scratch was madness. Canberra was political tofu, history substitute. Even its tilts at history seemed bizarre. In the middle of the lake was something called the Captain Cook Memorial Jet, a water spout which could shoot four hundred and fifty feet in the air. But what did it have to do with Cook? Had the captain won the long-distance pissing competitions over his ship's edge?

What Canberra had successfully done was to accumulate culture. There were five million books in the National Library of Australia, a cool and columned Parthenon wannabe. The National Gallery of Australia, a bright white box with wide white stripes of windows, had assiduously acquisitioned pictures national and international. (Warhol and Pollock particularly, perhaps another symptom of the Australian eye for brightness.) Yet these collections were kept in a confected city, readily accessible only to politicians and students.

The new parliament building, however, was undeniably impressive. There was a defensive cultural jumble-sale style to much of Canberra – the library bowing to Greece, the war memorial copying a Byzantine church – which was another element in the sense of ersatz history, of a country unsure of itself. The construction of a parliament might easily have borrowed a form from the mother country, and the original granite rectangle had. If you were determinedly cynical, you might see the new house, only four years old, as Le Corbusier with corks. But, for me, it had the original Aussie brio of the Sydney Opera House. The torso of the building was a white square, with regular wide, high windows reaching from the ground nearly to the roof, so that the effect was of interlocking T-shapes or, more appropriately, of cricket stumps. From the flat roof rose a central glass dome, around which craned four steel pincers, joining in an aluminium ring which enclosed a two-hundred-and-fifty-foot flagpole flying the Australian flag.

It was bold and fresh and paid homage to nothing except Australia's self-confidence. Inside, I walked the gallery of the portraits of the wide and meaty men who had been Australia's prime ministers, including Harold Holt, who had the distinction of being the only Western leader literally to sink without trace, gone off a beach, presumed drowned, in 1967. (A subsequent book suggested that he had been kidnapped by the Chinese in a midget submarine, but this entertaining thesis was now discredited.) Hawke's leaving date and Keating's painting had yet to be displayed.

The gallery also housed a display of constitutional documents. I read the opening clause of the British parliamentary act of 1900: 'Whereas the people of New South Wales, Victoria, South Australia, Queensland, and Tasmania, humbly relying on the blessing of Almighty God, have agreed to unite in one indissoluble Federal Commonwealth under the Crown of the United Kingdom of Great Britain and Ireland . . .' And I wished Australia free of this antique humiliation.

As I walked back down the slope outside, an English visitor was taking a picture of the parliament.

'Oh, *God*, it's just like sodding Blackpool Tower,' she moaned.

I stopped and looked back up at it. Like *Blackpool Tower*? This really was, I thought, taking pommy grudgingness about Australia too far.

Then she said: 'That was too high to get in one sodding picture as well.'

In the National Library at Canberra, I had read nineteen-day-old English newspapers, the most recently available. I spent an hour devouring them. On a hot day in a foreign country, this was even worse than it sounds. The papers were those I had read on the plane the day I left England. I couldn't even claim to be catching the news from home. I was reaching for it on the rebound now. It was obviously time to go and feed my national habit at the prime supplier.

Some time during the twenty-five hours westward at thirty-three thousand feet – between the complimentary Australian Riesling, Chardonnay, and Shiraz, the ever-popular Mozart in his short and tortured life and the movie about the millionaire inheriting a dog or the dog inheriting a million – I thought about my experiences of Australia. It was a tale of three cities. Sydney: vivid, original, assured, beautiful. Melbourne: derivative, prim, chilly. Canberra: a committee city, a programmed capital, yet housing a spirit which deserved its own political system. What Australia as a nation had achieved – which New Zealand conspicuously had not – was to blueprint a character and culture of its own.

And then I was home, to a Britain in recession and on the brink of an election, and to prepare for the next stage of my investigation of the quiet world: a young place, like Australia and New Zealand, but one in which the questions of imperialism and cultural influence were seen from a different perspective.

# PART TWO

# NORTH AMERICA

# CHAPTER THREE

# THESE MEAN STREETS

## Peoria and Normal

Like a runner doing stretches to tip the muscles off about what was coming, I liked to read the American popular press on the flight across the Atlantic. That way, you arrived with the mind half-acclimatized, beginning to shed European attitudes to taste, sentimentality, and irony.

In *USA Today* – the breezy colour graph-and-laugh broadsheet which had become America's first seriously national newspaper – I learned that the first chain of fast-food restaurants for dogs was scheduled to open in the States. The walk-in joint would offer quarter-pounders for hounds, pizzas for pooches.

I was English and I laughed and thought: I wonder if hot dogs are on the menu? I also speculated about whether this marketing initiative was the result of some politically correct legislation intended to provide the four-legged with equal opportunities of junk food. But the man in the seat beside me – a beefy Chicagoan wearing a baseball hat indoors, who had exchanged names as soon as we sat down – leaned across and said: 'Summen funny in the paper, Mark?'

'Oh, no, just . . . it says there are going to be fast-food restaurants for dogs . . .'

'No kidding? Where they gonna be stationed?' said Bob, as I knew him to be.

'Oh, er, it's starting in California . . . Wouldn't it just?'

'Hope it spreads out our way. Listen, I've often thought of giving our boy a bite of burger, but he has kinda delicate bowels. But this thing, the burgers would be special for the dogs, right?'

'Well, it looks that way . . .'

That he referred to a dog as his boy was no surprise, given his preferred noun for the jet on which we were headed for Chicago.

'Know what this puppy is?' he had asked as we waited on the runway.

'Sorry?'

'I don't recognize this puppy. It's kinda like a stretched DC-10.'

I am quite good on the species of aeroplanes, not from any childish glee at the machinery – which I suspected was Bob's involvement – but from neurotic scrutiny of safety rates for various designs.

'I think it's an MD-11,' I said. 'It's the upgrade of the DC-10.'

'You mean the rear doors don't fall off this one!' roared Bob, referring to a few unfortunate events in the seventies which were what frequent flyers tried not to think about before they started trying not to think about Lockerbie. A number of people in the cabin turned round and gave him the grimace usually prompted by public flatulence.

'Business or pleasure you're going to Chicago?' asked Bob.

'Oh, er, holiday. Vacation. I'm only passing through Chicago, then around Middle America, then Alaska . . .'

'Alaska? Let me give you a tip about Alaska. Minimize your city time. From Alaska you go home?'

'No. Canada. Then home.'

'Canada? You got a loved one dying there?'

'No. I . . .'

'You mean you're going to Canada and you don't *have* to?'

He gave that low whistle of disbelief, accompanied by an exaggeratedly slow headshake like someone testing the progress of their recovery from whiplash. It was the gesture successive generations of American men had learned from the male leads in television sit-coms. It was what you always got when you mentioned Canada to an American. The relationship between the two countries was, like that between Australia and New Zealand, another case of bully–runt syndrome.

The pilot crackle-crooned that we had reached our cruising altitude. For the flyer prone to fright, this is a moment of elation. He knows – particularly if he read too many alarming articles with graphs in *Time* and *Newsweek* after Lockerbie – that most plane bombs are primed to activate when maximum height is reached.

Bob put on his complimentary headset and watched the film, in which Steve Martin played a middle American guy unsettled by his beloved young daughter's marriage into a grand Yankee family.

I returned to my acclimatization programme with the native papers. I read that a Witches' Defence Group was trying to have *Hansel and Gretel* banned from public libraries on the grounds that it contained negative role models of necromancy. Luckily, Bob was too busy guffawing at Steve Martin falling into a swimming pool to ask why I was smiling. But it was clear that I needed much more time in the de-Europeanization chamber before reaching Middle America.


My relationship with the United States might be summarized as a case of coming to mock but staying to pay. Appalled assignments had eventually, if a little grudgingly, given way to awed vacations.

In English newspapers, there is a vast market for stories about American barbarism or wackiness. This commercial opportunity exists because of the confused yuk-yummy attitude which most Britons have instinctively held towards America, since the resented necessity of her intervention in the Second World War and subsequent loud sharing of the credit. And, as most British students educated since the 1960s and Vietnam are virtually guaranteed to possess at least a vestigial anti-Americanism, it is an opening which is enjoyably exploited, each new ideological or cultural solecism from across the pond topping up both supply and demand for such articles.

In a way which its proud and puppily trusting citizens scarcely begin to appreciate, the US is a freak-show for those in Western Europe. The place is seen as a warehouse for scariness, a laboratory for obsessions, a national equivalent of a smoking beagle. America was a country where the bullshit threshold was at least ten times above approved European Community levels.

In my eight years to date as a journalist – mainly spent

reviewing television and writing magazine articles about politics or what British newspapers call the Arts and American publications call Culture – there was one phrase I had employed more than any other. It was that popular European curse: Even in America.

But, even for America, the year 1992 was shaping up as a strange one. Perhaps this was partly because the Millennium was due, if you thought about it in the diary measure Americans most regularly used, the presidential election after next. The big-number years have always made people go funny. Around AD 1000, there were gatherings on hills of sects who believed that God preferred to work in round figures and that He would pull the plug as the three zeroes came up. As 2000 loomed, you gloomily knew you would be getting the descendants of these people looking doleful at your door in a couple of summers' time.

But far more eerie than the millennial phenomenon was the creeping feeling in America that the nation itself would be lucky to reach its two-hundred-and-fiftieth birthday. Only two hundred and sixteen years old, a young country by old-world standards, America was showing the geo-political equivalents of neck wattles, leg wobbles, liver spots, and incontinence. The remarkable aspect of this was that, only a year before, with the Gulf War seemingly won, the country and its president had seemed to be in their smug and strutting prime.

George Bush, due to seek a second term, had looked like an untouchable incumbent and the '92 election a waltz for the Republicans and a dance of death for the Democrats. In the middle of '91, George Bush's approval rating had been, neatly, ninety-one. A year later, it was heading for the thirties, as indeed, in a numerical parallel less appetizing to Republicans than the one above, America seemed to be. The story of this reversal will stand – along with the sudden dispatch of Margaret Thatcher in 1990 – as an awful warning to politicians of the speed with which the glories of their world can pass.

Bush had been undone by the recession. During the first presidential primary of '92, I had talked to the owner of the Paugus Diner ('Booth Service') in Laconia, an industrial suburb in the formerly lush, plush Republican state of New Hampshire. The proprietor was an Italian-American with a grain-sack belly, slicked hair, and a face like a shank of ham. 'I've got a guy in there – working minimum wage – supporting a family of five,' he said. A while back, he growled, he had advertised for someone to wait tables. He'd been unable to call his suppliers all day. The phone had been jammed. There had been two hundred and fifty calls minimum. He had voted Reagan twice and Bush once but never, no way, Bush a second time.

Bush's other burden was a growing doubt about exactly what had been won in the Gulf. The smart car sticker of the time asked: 'Saddam Hussein still has his job. Do you?' This was perhaps a reminder to the President that voters are usually more interested in their own pockets than global pockets of influence. The government had also belatedly accepted that, for two decades, all the goodies and sweeteners they had bought for the people – those expensive insurrections against governments with different views from the US, the maintenance of gas prices at around a symbolical but illogical dollar – had been bought on the executive American Express card. Do you take plastic? That'll do nicely. Now, at the top of the monthly statement, it read: Payment due – $400 billion – Payment received – Nil. Please return your cards and call this number urgently.

The President's involuntary refusal of the sushi at the Tokyo banquet was now widely seen as symbolic. Even without that, the removal of his thyroid after his collapse while jogging the previous year had left him with an indentation in his neck and a tendency to pallor and thinness. A clotted public orator even when confident, he was now, in confusion at his yo-yo in the polls, coming up with stuff like cut-up poetry. 'Remember Lincoln, going to his knees in time of trial and all that stuff. You can't be. And we are blessed. So don't feel sorry for – don't cry for me, Argentina,' he told a campaign crowd in New Hampshire.

Much of the unpopularity was Bush's fault. When his primary campaign seemed doomed in 1988, he had saved himself with the catchy promise: 'Read my lips – no new taxes.' He reneged a year later. Unimplemented pledges are the plasma of politics, but it was doubtful that another exponent had been foolish enough to be caught in possession of such a straightforward, day-glo, undoctorable whopper. The career of George Herbert Walker Bush had come to embody the expedient mutability of which all voters subconsciously suspect politicians. He had become an exquisite representation of slipperiness, his tax reversal and his finessing from support of planned parenthood to abhorrence of abortion merely the most visible signs. Read his flips.

But Bush was also the victim of something in the water. In a way which he would surely resent until the end of his life, Bush's huge approval ratings after the Gulf were now revealed to have been merely evidence of the volatility of a public desperate to find a definition of itself. There was a looming sense of doom in America, a perception that established politics had failed. Many pundits had said that – after being motivated and defined for thirty years by the Communist threat – Americans seriously needed to find a new enemy. What few people had predicted was that they would choose George Bush.

People were rooting around for an extreme solution. All bets and psephology had proved treacherous. On the Democratic ballot, the New Hampshire primary had been won by Paul Tsongas, a small dour Greek, despite the fact that – after the thrashing four years earlier of Michael Dukakis, a near-clone in nationality, stature, and manner – the Tsongas candidacy had seemed as miscalculated as a Republican running for president after Watergate on a platform of recording his own phone calls and bugging his opponents' offices. Eventually, Tsongas had been seen off by Bill Clinton, the bright but allegedly priapic governor of Arkansas. Again wrecking the conventional wisdom, Clinton had proved that there could be life after tabloid death: a singer who claimed to have been his mistress had splashed across the trash mags tapes in which he appeared to accept her compliments on his ability at cunnilingus, not previously a proven vote winner.

What had also set tongues wagging in New Hampshire was that Pat Buchanan – a demotic columnist and star of those political discussion programmes the Americans sweetly call shout shows – had nearly beaten Bush on the Republican ballot, despite being regarded as a joke candidate when he announced his campaign. But, at that stage, few in Washington appreciated the primaeval instability of the electorate. As part of the press pack following Buchanan's campaign, I had driven up through the wind-sculpted snow and frozen lakes to a big house in the woods above Laconia.

Here, rich Republicans – Reagan-ravers disgruntled by Bush – had organized a coffee afternoon for Buchanan.

On the wall hung a painting of Abe Lincoln. There was also an array of framed family snaps. The expected horses, children, and sepia ancestors were offset by photos of our host, holding a machine-gun and surrounded, in what looked to be a sunny country, by olive-skinned youths in battle fatigues.

'Where was that?' I asked.

'Nicaragua.'

'What were you doing there?'

'Providing humanitarian aid.'

I retreated to the rest room. There was a rack of reading matter. On offer was a set of brochures for a military book club. The titles for which members were invited to apply included *Forgotten Legions: Obscure Combat Formations of the Waffen-SS*. Other suggested texts were *How to Get Anything on Anybody – The Encyclopaedia of Personal Surveillance* and *Homemade Grenade Launchers: Constructing the Ultimate Hobby Weapon*.

Given that Buchanan's slogan was 'Take Back America', the last title in particular induced a certain unease. And the image which kept returning to me as I moved among these well-heeled desperadoes in their wooded retreat was of the white South Africans interviewed on television when President de Klerk proposed the ending of apartheid. These Americans, too, saw their birthright threatened and might literally fight to defend it. If a new theme was emerging from the Even in America pieces dispatched to England during 1992, it was this: Getting Even in America.

My other experience of the strange new rip-tides in American political life had come while leaving a campaign meeting in New Hampshire. In the wintry dusk, walking back to the hotel, a stumpy, powerful figure jumped out from a shadowy doorway.

'Hey, mister!' it hissed.

Taking it for a vagrant, a victim of George Bush's economic policies, I avoided its eye and speeded up. So did the figure, sliding along behind me on the icy sidewalk. The pursuer caught up, swung me round, flung out an arm towards my chest. A punch? A gun? A blade?

It was, in fact, a small white sticker. It said: KILLEEN '92.

'Hi,' said my assailant. 'I'm running for president.'

The speaker was revealed as a woman in her early sixties, with a cap of tightly cropped grey hair and lipstick which was traffic-light bright. Her clothing featured elaborate strata of nylon and wool, like an Arctic equivalent of a Russian doll. Her name was Caroline Killeen. She was running for president on the Democratic ballot.

All electoral systems attract no-hope hopefuls. But Campaign '92 in America had drawn a record number. It was also the case that their motivation was not wry or ironic – as British joke candidates, at least, have tended to be – but apocalyptic. Among the also-rans running were a lot of old men with hellish visions of America's destiny, a pack of people with bad dreams, a whole band of candidates with Jesus as their running mate.

My accoster, Candidate Killeen, had as her campaign head-quarters a shelter for the homeless. This was decidedly innovative, given that the modern American presidential candidate tends towards two or three houses and a frequent-stayer card at Marriott Hotels. With similar thrift, the official Killeen battle bus was a rickety bicycle. Her budget for campaign literature was minimal. Voters interested in studying her ideas in private needed to accompany her to the local photocopying shop, where they could pay for a reproduction of her leaflets.

'Why did you decide to run?' I asked.

'I looked around me. Things are bad in America. I think it's time we have a woman president. After two hundred years of these guys, I think it's time we had a cyclist in the White House too. Me, I'm a life-long cyclist, who trusts in a higher power . . .' Here, she fished a wooden crucifix from one of her layered jackets and caressed it. 'Twice, in fact, I studied to be a nun . . .'

'Really? Why did you leave the convent . . .?'

'Hey, this I'm saving for my memoirs . . .'

Soon, it seemed that everyone in America was running for president. Paul Fisher, the seventy-eight-year-old president of the Fisher pen company, was masterminding his campaign from a suite in the Howard Johnson Inn. The room was busy with word processors, laser printers, and an alp of paperpacks of a book called *The Plan*, written by Fisher and published by himself with a dust-jacket encomium describing it as 'the most important book for 1,000 years'. Perhaps an ancestor of Fisher had written the previous hot volume during the last bout of millennial trembles.

'Take this,' he said. 'It's a space pen. The capsule is sealed and pressurized. It writes at any angle, also at fifty degrees below zero and four hundred degrees above. This is the exact model used on the Space Shuttle. It's also used on Russian space flights. I also own the most valuable patents on erasable ball-pens . . .'

'Why are you running for president?'

'Pardon?'

'He's a little deaf,' a burly aide intervened. 'You'll have to shout . . .'

The aide turned and bellowed at the candidate: 'Are you having trouble with your device?' Fisher was clearly bidding for the Ronald Reagan constituency. The device was primed by the aide.

'Why are you running for president?'

'I first ran in 1960. Ran against John F. Kennedy. I got over ten thousand votes. In a normal year, I'd have won, but Kennedy got a record vote . . .'

'Have you run since . . .?'

'No. I'm running this time because things are so bad. I'm very concerned about the environment, pollution, the economic situation. No American government has balanced the budget since 1930. This year's federal deficit was the largest in history . . .'

An old man with bad dreams. After that, they were everywhere. In the middle of the night, I was woken by a scratching at the door of my hotel room. I switched on the light to see an A4 sheet edging across the carpet like an SAS rescuer. It turned out to be the electoral platform of what appeared to be the nocturnal campaigning candidate. His leaflet argued: 'The answer may be some form of divine intervention.'

Then, on a flight to New York, I was transcribing from my notebooks on the laptop table when my neighbour leaned across.

'Excuse me, are you press?'

'Oh–um–er–yes.'

'That's great. I'm running for president.'

'Oh. Which one are you?'

'I'm the New Age candidate, running for the Human Ecology Party. My name is Da Vid . . .'

'David?'

'No. Da space Vid. It's a name I took a few months ago. I've had a series of psychic identities . . .'

Scraggily bearded but seriously tanned, Da Vid was dressed entirely in purple: baggy pants and a smock top, with a knitted mauve winter hat resting in his lap. As far as could be ascertained from his laid-back campaign literature, a Da Vid administration would establish Alcatraz and Jerusalem as 'International Centres of Peace' and the world would be soothed and purified through the global dissemination via television of 'Artainment', a channel broadcasting gentle colours and sounds. We would also eat a great deal of blue-green algae.

Even in America. Well, yes, but this was mild compared to what was about to happen. Easy to see at the time as a joke, the people in the Laconia woods and the record numbers of presidential also-rans in New Hampshire soon proved to be an omen. A few weeks later, and with Buchanan slipping back, H. Ross Perot, a vertically challenged Texas billionaire, let slip on a CNN phone-in show that, if the American people chose to place his name on every presidential ballot, he might agree to run for the White House. Washington guffawed but the people stormed their state officials to add the tycoon's name. Perot – who spoke in twangy metaphors about the American government being like a car which needed a mechanic to 'get under the hood and fix it' – was soon regarded as the populist outsider who would go to Washington and throw the old guard out.

Even in America, it seemed bizarre that a billionaire – who had, in fact, made his money from computer-processing government business – could successfully pose as one of the folks, standing to take back the government for the little guy. As a jug-eared dwarf, Perot also provided a severe corrective to the prevalent view that modern politics was a beauty contest. But the Texas tycoon was a lightning conductor not a messiah. In retrospect, it was clear that the crisis of American democracy had been simmering since the early eighties. Reagan, for example, had been elected by talking about the government being the problem. The minds of the American electorate moving slowly but surely, someone finally said, in about 1987: 'Hang on a minute, he is the government!' The election, on Reagan's wave, of the routinely two-faced Bush had focused disillusion with the power élite. But perhaps this analysis was too flattering to voters' motives. What threatened Bush was what always finished politicians in the quiet world. People were shaking their pockets and were terrified by the silence.

I realized that America was a controversial election to this book's house of representatives of the quiet world. Of course, strictly, the USA belongs to the noisy world; may, indeed, epitomize its democratic manifestations. Confirming this perception, Los Angeles had erupted, in the May of the year of my journeys, when a white jury imaginatively found not guilty four white Los Angeles cops accused of assaulting a black motorist, Rodney King.

Fortuitously – for all except the Los Angeles Police Department and the American way of life – the original arrest, including what looked like a beating with batons, had been recorded by a passing amateur cameraman. The King cassette became the second most important home video in American history, after the Zapruder images of Kennedy's assassination. It also apparently denied the late President's dreams of harmonious racial integration. More than fifty people died, and millions of property dollars were lost, in the riots which followed the acquittal of the cops. Front pages of newspapers in countries equivocal about the USA carried pictures of state troopers armoured like Robocop, warily guarding the charred frontages of torched stores. Even in America.

But this was the American nightmare. It had never been the aim or the point of life in these latitudes. The dream had been of the quiet world: home, family, God, patch of grass, car. It was a hope still enclosed in the phrase Middle America. John Updike has said that the term Middle America was not widely used before the social disruptions of the Vietnam War which, if true, confirms the status of these towns as controls in the American experiment. And, thus qualifying for this project, Middle America had become code, both at the edges of the continent and beyond, for a way of life which was boring and small-minded or, shall we now say, activity-challenged, differently prioritized.

I had made my selection because of, respectively, a cultural association and a linguistic one. Peoria was shorthand for typicality, a litmus-test city. 'Will it play in Peoria?' asked those in the businesses of politics, marketing, and entertainment about some new policy or product. Impressively, the phrase had spread to the same industries in Britain and Australia, where practitioners asked not if it would play in Bognor or in Wagga-Wagga, but in Peoria. Accordingly, English writers were drawn there magnetically every time it seemed that America was on the edge. You fled from the mean (as in shitty) streets of New York or LA to the mean (as in average) streets of Peoria.

As for Normal, I had once met a man in Chicago, who had told me the name of the town in which he had grown up.

'Good God. And was it, like, well, normal?'

'Normal as fuck. When we were kids, we used to fantasize that there was this other town called Abnormal, that they let you go to when you were grown up . . .'

Both communities were strictly too big – and slightly too far to the right of the land-mass – to fit the classic symbolism of Middle America. I could have gone to one of those wackily named places – Scrotum, Nebraska, or Instep, Iowa – where there are barely enough residents for a baseball game and the oldest of them still spoke to English journalists and writers about the time when Truman came through on his campaign train.

But what the hell. I was drawn by the history of the words to Peoria and Normal, traditional tranquillities in Illinois.


As the MD-11 banked over Chicago's O'Hare Airport – named for one of the big-shouldered political hustlers who made the place famous – I stashed away the newspapers. They reported that Ross Perot had become the only independent presidential candidate in history to reach 40 per cent and to lead the polls. I had also discovered one more Even in America piece: at the University of Iowa, a degree course was now being offered in – stop those European irony muscles twitching – Elvis Presley. The course professor argued that the King was a musical equivalent to literary post-modernism. I envisioned theses like: *Hound Dog at*

*Heatbreak Hotel: Canine and Catering Imagery in the Works of Elvis Presley.*

The pilot began to let the plane down in steps. I tried not to remember the statistic that, unless there is a bomb in the hold, the only really dangerous parts of air travel are landings and take-offs, when the vast but flimsy tin cigar in which you sit is subject to maximum stress. But, on this occasion, we made it.

'This is some neat puppy,' said Bob, as the wheels eased on to the tarmac.

At O'Hare, all the immigration officers looked like heavy-weight boxers. It would be politically incorrect to make the joke about the men being quite formidable as well.

'Stayninshargo?' my interrogator asked.

'No. I'm going on to Peoria.'

'On poipose a visit, ya put plezza? Shudda be bizniz?'

Since the bad business in New Zealand, I always lied about why I was in these places.

'No, it's a holi . . . a vacation.'

'Rilly? Na much plezza in Poria . . .'

It was clear he was suspicious. I had visions of being seized as a narcotics baron: 'Judge, the authorities first became suspicious when the accused claimed to be taking a vacation in Peoria . . .' And the jurors would all gasp with laughter, and slap their sides and shout, 'Whaddayaknow!' and I would spent my adult life eating prison hamburger.

But he finally passed my papers, with a shrug. I had a drink and bought the *Chicago Tribune*: 'Correction: A page 1 story yesterday mis-stated the percentage increase in Chicago murders so far this year. The 355 murders through Monday represents an increase of 8 per cent, not 12 per cent.' I was pleased to be merely in transit. Then I walked for about four miles across fake airport marble and found the check-in desk for my connection to quiet America.

The flight from Chicago to Peoria is a short commuter trip, so you get a propeller plane. The odd thing about these aircraft is that even the technologically illiterate refer to them by the manufacturer's name. A passenger on a jumbo jet speaks of 'this plane', rather than 'this 747', but, on a propeller-driven flight, you quite regularly hear people saying 'When is this Fokker going to land?' or 'How old is this Fokker?'

This is probably because, limited to an altitude about a third of that attainable by jets, the commuter planes are unusually vulnerable to the effects of weather. Certainly, as my craft rocked towards Peoria like a drunk trying to walk the wrong way up an escalator, I wondered both how old the Fokker was and when it was going to land. 'We've, uh, caught a storm,' apologized the single stewardess. 'In a bigger plane, you can ride above it, but this one . . .' A sudden bump left her unable to finish her sentence, but this was an improvement on the passengers, who were too gibbering to begin one.

It was on this flight that I constructed an explanation for the notorious piety of modern Americans, an urgency of worship otherwise confined, these days, to the East. Because of the range of their terrain, Americans take planes like those in more clenched territories use trains or buses. Only in a ballet corps or a brothel do so many people have their feet off the ground at the same time. Therefore, if it is true that all human beings believe in God during turbulence at thirty thousand feet – and there is empirical evidence that even atheists wobble when the seat-belt sign comes on suddenly – then Americans, many of them flying twice a day, are almost automatically more likely to believe. Those flying in Fokkers have an extra prod to religiosity. (A few days after experiencing this insight, I saw a television commercial for one of the Bible-bashing, wallet-draining US faiths. 'We live in *turbulent* times,' it nudged the viewers. QED, I believe.)

If this theory is correct, then on the Fokker from Chicago to Peoria that day there must have been novenas and confessions trailing from the plane like the jet-stream it unfortunately lacked. When the storm began, I had just taken possession of the complimentary orange juice. For the next few minutes, I kept inadvertently toasting the man in the adjoining seat, the jolts forcing my forearm upwards in a wedding-guest reflex. This was irritating, until I realized that it was worse in front – where a man kept accidentally baptizing his colleague with bourbon – and behind, where a young college lecturer (as he had revealed himself to be on the inevitable instant introduction) gruntingly bequeathed his lunch to a waxed bag.

I was sitting half-way down the plane, in my traditional perch by an emergency exit, and trying to lose my flying fear in a book. This was proving annoyingly difficult, as it was a post-modern thriller which gave away the ending on page one. As a result, I kept looking up. I soon became aware of a pattern of sights and sounds. From behind, my ear kept being drawn to a recurrent squelch or splash, like a rubber boot coming down in melting snow. I looked round, and wished I hadn't. It was another passenger saying an agonized goodbye to lunch.

Looking upfront, I noticed that the stewardess kept teetering down the aisle, leap-frogging one hand from seat-back to seat-back for support, and clutching in the other a slopping, squashy bag, an opaque version of the clear ones in which children bring home goldfish won at fairs. I realized, and wished I hadn't, what was going on. More or less happy to slop out food to passengers, all stewardesses dread becoming involved in the reverse journey.

So it was a relief when we began to lose altitude deliberately, as opposed to the involuntary drops which had punctuated the trip. The arable patterns of Middle America came into view: dry brown fields with deep green trees clumped around them. I thought that it looked like beef and broccoli on a plate, then wished I hadn't, as the climate threw in another movement which the pilot had not programmed. Then the ground hit the plane like a parent slapping a naughty child.

As we slowed to a halt, the college lecturer, now the colour of the trees we had just seen, said: 'Was that the flight from hell or what?' Up front a young woman in a business suit wise-cracked with a dry mouth: 'First time I ever barfed on a plane. It's sort of good to know the bags hold it without leaking.'

In most parts of the world, the passengers could have reassuringly reflected: Well, I won't be flying again for a while now. But some of these people would be going back up into the same weather pattern later that night. If I had been an investing type, I would have bought heavily in TV evangelists.

★

My Peoria hotel ran a courtesy van from the airport. From the small commercial terminal, it doubled round to the airfield where the private jets arrived. There we picked up three thirtysomething men in Brooks Brothers shirts with button-down collars, which looked as if they had confined a tie until lunchtime.

'No bags?' queried the driver.

'We've just flown in for dinner,' said the senior Brooks Brother. 'We're going back tonight.'

I was made apprehensive by the subtext of this: that Peoria was not even a stopover prospect. I was booked in for several days. On the road downtown, the Brothers – who were rich from being in Money in some unspecified way – bitched about the office. They bubbled with the bad luck of others: 'He bets the farm on the stock, thinking it's win-win . . . Now he's fifty down on paper!'

Fifty thousand? Fifty *million*? Whatever the sum, they all chuckled at this. It was clear that anecdotes of the financial losses of colleagues fulfilled the function given to dirty jokes in other male cultures.

Listening in, I felt only marginally intrusive, for it was equally apparent that most of the point of such conversation was that it might be overheard by the poorer or the less cool. The senior of the trio turned to a chortling autopsy on his boss (the men seemed to work for rival concerns). He told a harsh yarn about how the man's temper, which seemed to be legendary, had led to his near-banning from a country club. A second Brother had just joined in with the legend of his furious denunciation of some office junior, when the third – whose small round tortoiseshell spectacles branded him the conscience of the team – suddenly said: 'Their kid drowned in the swimming pool . . .'

It was clear that he was playing unfair by intruding reality, but the others momentarily dropped their hey-wow office-gossip voices, as you might lower a flag.

'Yeah. That was tragic . . .'

'Awful . . .'

'Apparently, with their kids now,' said the original reaper of this grim news, 'she sits there, right by the pool, just staring. Even if she's spoken to, she won't look away . . .'

I wondered why the third man had turned the conversation so

deliberately from money to mortality. Had he felt edgy because his friends, with their talk of win–win and fifty down on paper, were sounding like eighties voices in a nineties when the money luck was so clearly running out? I also thought about the anonymous woman, crouched by the swimming pool as her surviving children splashed, afraid to move her eyes at all.

You could glimpse a whole existence – mournful, guilty, twitchy, protective – in the one sentence spoken about her. Although we didn't like to think about it, we all had this shadow life, as anecdotes – cruel, amusing, sometimes, if we were lucky, loving – for other people. That woman's tragedy and marriage were free entertainment, time-wasting, for people whose only connection with her was that her husband exercised professional power over one of them.

But the Brothers kept the flag lowered for less than one minute. After what he clearly regarded as sufficient respect for the dead kid and his broken mother, the one of the three who worked for the drowned child's father said, his voice hey-wow again: 'Tom's flying in, last weekend of August. He's keen to get the boys together. Might be a fun weekend . . .'

'Shit. I gotta wedding,' said the middle Brother. 'Family. I wonder . . .'

Then we reached the Père Marquette Hotel in Peoria – one of those calculatedly antiquated places with dark wood, chandeliers, and a light-up sign above the elevator which said *This Car Up* and *This Car Down*, from before literacy gave way to arrows – where the Brothers had booked a room each, merely to shower and dress in before their dinner.

Peoria is pronounced Pee-ooria, which makes it sound even more distressingly like an infection of the urinary tract ('I'm sorry, sir, it's peoria, but if you take these, it will soon clear up.') But, as it turned out, it was an interesting weekend to be there. I had thought as I squeezed through the lobby that the guests looked generously proportioned even by American standards and, as I checked in, I saw a banner slung from the roof. It read: WELCOME ATHLETES AND COACHES – US OLYMPIC WEIGHTLIFTING TRIALS.

This made the atmosphere of the place accidentally surreal, so that you felt like an extra in a David Lynch film. Elevators the makers claimed were safe for eight people were, that weekend, stalling with four. Also, I had at first thought that the Père Marquette was a sordid hotel. Walking down the corridor to my room in the late afternoon, I saw trays outside several doors, with smeared plates and jugs containing dried residues of syrup and gravy. After twenty-four hours, I realized that, leaving and returning to your room throughout the day, you would see that the trays were there and then gone, cleared and then re-appeared, and I understood that these were the weightlifters, being fed every couple of hours, like new-born babies.

At breakfast on the first morning, a competitor and coach team was wedged into the next table. The weightlifter's order combined meals and cuisines in a way which made it sound like a Dadaist poem constructed from a restaurant menu: spicy chicken wings, salad Niçoise, hamburger with egg and fries, blueberry muffins. As the first wave of plates arrived, another coach was passing the table. The eater's trainer acknowledged his peer: 'I'm just making sure he don't go on a diet or something!'

Because of these special guests, the café was seating two to most booths, instead of the intended four, so I was asked if I would mind a stranger joining me. He was called John and worked for Centel Cellular, the local telephone company. The name of Ross Perot came up, as it always did at that time. I asked if he had a chance.

'Well, a lot of people have this feeling now that *something's gotta happen.* Like in really hot, muggy weather, when you think: This is gonna break. Now, if you believe that, then Los Angeles was the first thunder. And people don't see politicians sorting this out. Like people keep saying now, the gangsters used to be in Chicago, now they're in Washington. So people figure, well, Perot, he couldn't do any worse . . .'

Perot was playing well in Peoria. The city's residents were people who had believed Ronald Reagan when he said it was morning in America again, and had now woken up to discover that he had shown them a doctored clock and it was approaching midnight. The pathos of the Perot phenomenon – and, more generally, of the retreat from Bush – was that it was as if the

American people were seeking their own Havel or Walesa, a people's hero to save them from the tyranny of government.

And yet from what was this figure to provide liberation? Not Communism, but the very system of government for three decades gloatingly (and in a number of small countries forcibly) promoted as its transcendent nemesis. In all but the significant matter of personal liberty, triumphant American capitalism now resembled defeated Soviet Communism in the gulf between ideological promise and administrative reality.

After breakfast, I went walking round Peoria. My guidebooks had been vague on what to do. One warmly recommended the Christmas lights, which was something of a dampener for this mid-June tourist. So I just opened my free hotel map of the downtown and made orderly progress around what, it soon became clear, was an orderly city.

There was a sense of propriety and discretion everywhere: even the town's two skyscraper office blocks were bashfully low and drab by the standards of the genre. The buildings essentially divided between financial services (banks, insurance, investment) and churches, Mammon's buildings huddled together in the centre of the town around Main Street, God's distributed among the outlying blocks, where the schools and houses began. That was the lifestyle being proselytized: pray, earn, pray, earn, an existence of knit-purl regularity. The only approved deviation was shopping, now, as elsewhere in America, increasingly confined in quarantine camps called malls, on the outskirts of the town.

The variety of buildings enshrined to religion was astonishing. You could worship a different god on every block, hear a different creed on every street. One of the Presbyterian churches – a monstrosity in pink rock – had been converted into three restaurants, but the rest were still under the old management.

The Franciscans ran their operation from a clean limestone construction in the middle of Peoria. The wider Roman tendency seemed to own most of downtown. A white plaster Messiah and Virgin stood, like security guards, at the ends of a lucrative slab of property, which included the huge neo-Gothic St Mary's cathedral and a variety of administrative buildings.

Peoria is a key station of the cross in American Catholic

history, having spawned Bishop Fulton Sheen, one of the first priests to realize that, if Christ were alive today, he would be making a fortune from the broadcasting circuit. Sheen presided over radio's *The Catholic Hour* and TV's *Life Is Worth Living*. The current Bishop of Peoria – John Myers – was himself gathering fame with his right-wing brimstone attacks on liberalism in the Church. His first pastoral letter had suggested that Catholics pro-choice on abortion should cease to receive the sacraments. Like Perot, this stuff was playing well in Peoria, although a disgruntled member of the clergy said that Myers was 'running for Pope'.

Shifting from my left foot, I walked to the First United church, which had a fussy-turreted bell tower and a plaque which promised: 'And the truth shall make you free.' There was a Scottish Rite cathedral and a Christian Assembly church. Going for a stroll in almost any direction was like attending an Ideal Church Exhibition, a sort of Expope '92. One of the publications I consulted claimed there were three hundred and thirty-nine places of worship in the Peoria area, servicing a population of three hundred and fifty thousand.

Even though I had facetiously theorized during the storm that American devotion was due to air miles flown, the amount of prime US real estate given to Jesus needs serious consideration. Liberals and secular outsiders often made the mistake of forgetting the extent to which the United States is a Christian country, in a sense far more significant than that in which Italy, for example, is a Catholic one. Religion was not yet mere repetition. The regular public recitation of the line 'one nation, indivisible under God' is a far more reliable clue to the national psyche than, say, the tendency of the English to sing 'God save the Queen'. The latter was habit; the former was imploration.

An objective reading of the televised addresses to the nation of most modern American presidents – the Baptists Nixon and Carter, the Fundamentalist Christian Reagan and the Episcopalian Bush – would suggest a relationship between politician, country, and God similar to that believed in by French kings. The more distressing manifestations of the American century – McCarthyism and the tendency to invade smaller nations follow-ing different ideological creeds – were best understood as politics blackened by the intolerance and evangelism to which religions tend: you are either for me or against me.

The weird afterlife of American celebrities – the fanatical adulation, the books, badges, and posters, collected by people who would even tell you that Elvis or President Kennedy was not really dead, that their tombs were empty – was more easily comprehended if you accepted that it sprang from a culture in which icons, statues, and resurrections were routine points of reference. This was a nation encouraged by its leaders and teachers through two centuries to believe that it was especially blessed. And at least some of its presidents – one of them, Reagan, at a time when apocalypse was within man's scientific scope – had believed themselves to have a personal relationship with God. So some of the convulsions gripping America at that time were due to the dawning fear of cosmic abandonment.

The dedication of the nation to the deity also dictated the shape of American values. As most of the religions prevalent in America – apart from Mormonism – preached monogamy, the morality followed from the godliness. As a private ideal, this was admirable enough. The pity was that the obsession had now polluted the nation's politics. All candidates for high office were routinely asked the A-question ('Have you ever committed adultery?') and the D-question ('Have you ever abused drugs?').

For reasons not entirely clear to the foreigner, an acceptable answer to the D-question was: 'I experimented once or twice with drugs, while young, but did not enjoy it.' However, to the A-question, the only approved response was 'no' and, if they did not believe you, they would hide behind your garbage bins until they caught you out. It seemed to me that the situation clearly called for a canny candidate to adapt the acceptable D-answer to the treacherous A-question and reply: 'Yes. I experimented once or twice with adultery, but did not enjoy it.'

The real point was that this random sexual standard would have disqualified most of those modern presidents America now regarded as considerable (Kennedy, Eisenhower, Reagan, Franklin Roosevelt). It was beginning to seem that St Paul could never run for office in America because the *National Enquirer* and *New York*

*Post* would print reproachful anecdotes from the period before he fell off his horse. Bill Clinton remained more Saul than Paul, but if he were able to reach the White House despite being pursued by rumours of woman-chasing and draft-dodging it would be a vital breakthrough in American maturity. I thought of lighting a candle for him in one of Peoria's three hundred and thirty-nine places of worship.

Exhausted by my morning's ecclesiastical orgy, I trudged back downtown for lunch. The streets were so empty that I might have been in Scrotum, Nebraska, or Instep, Iowa. After peering at a few threatening menus and forbidding frontages, I chose a place on Main Street, which had blood-red carpets and walls, varnished wood tables and similar surrounds, with silver, shippy handrails. It was called Encore!, but there was no evidence that previous customers had taken up the invitation. The restaurant was completely empty half-way through the lunch hour.

Either to reduce expenditure or to increase atmosphere, the lighting was subdued. But, after I coughed operatically for a while, a middle-aged woman appeared in a lighter patch of blackness which was probably a door.

'Oh, er, are you open for lunch?'

'Sure,' she said, in a tone which judged the question foolish. Then she turned and yelled, 'Jolene! A customer!' in a tone which seemed to judge the fact surprising.

By one of those bits of restaurant lore which will never be revealed to the mere eater, the first four tables in the deserted room at which I tried to sit down were forbidden. Finally placed where Jolene wanted me, I examined her through the gloom. She was wearing a schoolgirl costume. She was joined by two colleagues matchingly dressed. I was the only customer in a Lolita theme restaurant.

As I ate my cheeseburger, two pieces of jailbait, one of them clearly on her first day, leaned against the wall and languorously chatted.

'Always this quiet?'

'Often. I think they oughta get some entertainment in . . .'

Mind boggling, I lost myself in the *Peoria Journal Star*. The headlines included: CASE INVOLVING POLICEMAN'S INVERTED WATER

METERS UNRESOLVED and PUBLIC HEARING SET FOR IMPROVEMENTS TO ROUTE. I scanned the features teasers on the front page: 'The interest in dwarf trees is growing and it's easy to see why – Lawn & Garden, B1'.

On the Letters page, there was support for Perot but it was clear that the latest humourless morality crusade of the Republicans was also playing well. At that time, Vice-President Dan Quayle – the only known example of a four-word Even in America article – was attempting to deflect the extra attention forced on him by Bush's physical frailty with an appeal to the stony groins of his party's core supporters.

Quayle had imaginatively suggested that the Los Angeles riots had been caused by an episode of the sit-com *Murphy Brown* in which the title character, played by Candice Bergen, had given birth to an illegitimate child. Although Quayle believed in a constitutional amendment banning terminations – and, therefore, in any approximation to the real world, must logically have supported illegitimate children – he had indicated that, before being enraged by the Rodney King verdict, the residents of Los Angeles had been depraved by the sit-com incident.

'Ha ha ha ha ha ha ha ha ha ha *ha*,' said the liberals and the non–Americans. But not in Peoria. 'What a gladiatorial spectacle we are witnessing, as the national press and their "enlightened élite" cohorts sharpen their scalpels in preparation for yet another Dan Quayle bloodletting,' wrote Bob Hoerr to the *Journal Star*. 'It may jolt these pompous keepers of the moral flame to learn that millions of us are not lining up at the trough to partake of their moral swill . . . Anyone with a modicum of sense knows that Mr Quayle is correct – maybe not politically correct, but correct none the less . . .'

'I for one agree most heartily with Mr Quayle,' added D. L. Bainbridge. 'Our society is dead because of the everyday illegitimate births by Hollywood stars . . . This filth is being piped into the minds of our children through the movies and TV . . .' Rita Rheinhart echoed: 'Hooray for Dan Quayle for speaking out . . .'

You began to see why a schoolgirl theme restaurant might be deserted. After lunch, I visited the Peoria Historical Society. I learned a lot there. In particular, I discovered how travel writers achieve those laconic laid-back narratives of the history of a place in which they have just arrived.

The story of what, three hundred years later, would become the only conurbation to win the All-American City Award three times begins in 1673. A Jesuit priest, Père Marquette (later a hotel), accompanied by a secular traveller called Louis Jolliet (subsequently a restaurant), were sent on an expedition by the comte de Frontenac, Governor of Canada. It was believed that, if they followed the river now called the Mississippi – which the Jesuit rapidly named the Concepçion in a piece of Mariolatric insurance for his journey – they would eventually reach China. They travelled in two canoes with five crew.

Soon realizing that the Concepçion did not reach the Orient, they arrived at what we now know as Memphis but were turned back by the friendly Illini Indians, a part of the nation called Algonquin (later also a hotel), who warned that they risked meeting the Spanish. The Indians advised that the party returned to Canada along the Illinois. This was, they said, a less torturous waterway. During the return leg, Marquette and Jolliet met the Peoria ('People of Fire') Indians, who fed and rested them. Finding time for a business transaction, the Jesuit baptized a dying Indian child. More than four hundred years later, the location of this salvation is commemorated by a plaque on what is now Grand-view Drive.

In 1680, the French explorer Robert Cavalier Sieur de la Salle – drawn to the region by the availability of fur for the fashion-hat trade back home – established a fort near Lake Peoria, intended to prevent the English and Spanish from exploiting the common market in animal skins. In 1691, the French defences were joined by Fort Louis II and, as spiritual back-up, a Jesuit Mission. In 1763, Britain was ceded the territory in the French and Indian war, but failed immediately to occupy it and the French remained.

In 1812, during internal machinations among the Algonquin (involving, one assumes, their deadly rivals the Marriott, the Hyatt, and the Holidayin), French Peoria was burned by Americans who believed that there was Gallic support for Indian insurrections. This was mistaken prejudice and the French settlers were later compensated by what was described in the histories as an act of Congress. It must be assumed that this means government money rather than sexual favours.

It was in 1819 that the first seven American settlers – including Joshua Fulton (later a road) and Abner Eads (subsequently a street) – arrived. Within a decade, the potential of the town's river and fields had been seen. John Hamlin built a flour mill in 1830, the first business in Peoria. In 1837, Andrew Eitle established a brewery and, in 1843, Almiron S. Cole set up a distillery. Subsequently, Peoria levied the greatest amount of internal revenue tax on alcoholic beverages of any district. But, even then, the residents were more likely to organize a piss-up than to participate in one. The place had a reputation for propriety and piety.

If a Peoria man said, 'Did the earth move for you?' he could be assumed to be talking redistribution of soil. Bordered by farm land, the town pioneered the steel plough and earth-shifting equipment in general. Later, in 1925, the Caterpillar truck company was established there. Cleverly painting its vehicles buttercup yellow like children's toys, Caterpillar was dented by the depression of the thirties but rose to priapic liquidity through the building of the Interstate highway system. In 1992, it was still Peoria's biggest employer with twenty-one thousand jobs surviving the recession.

Peoria was incorporated as a city in 1845, by which time it had around five hundred inhabitants. Peoria's American political reputation dates from 1854 when Abraham Lincoln delivered a three-hour speech – how the modern reader thanks God for the soundbite – as part of a debate on slavery and thus launched his public career. 'The people's will is the ultimate law for all,' Lincoln said. This sentiment is now chiselled into the concrete outside the New Courthouse.

In the 1890s, Peoria, which boasts the fourth oldest theatre in America, became established as a significant vaudeville venue, a big-time booking. Those who like to suggest that the question 'Will it play in Peoria?' was admiring rather than pejorative in origin date the phrase from that time.

In the forties and fifties, when the census returns began to suggest the microcosmic qualities of the spot, Peoria became established as the test-marketing capital of the States. Its inhabitants, although they seldom realized it, were privileged to purchase trial merchandising lines which stores elsewhere did not, and might never, stock. It was a land of banana-flavoured milk and low-fat honey. From this distinction comes the other possible application of the phrase 'Will it play in Peoria?'

The city's reputation as a political bell-wether, established by the Lincoln speech of 1854, was consolidated by its status as a commercial rehearsal room. As electronic campaigning methods shrank the distinction between a world leader and a peanut bar, the people of Peoria were thought equally useful for deciding whether Americans would bite on either. Cementing the perception, in 1980, Ronald Reagan delivered the final speech of his campaign there, achieving the bonus of a piece of symbolic Lincoln cross-dressing to which he was never averse. It also helped that one of the most respected of second-tier American politicians – House Minority Leader Bob Michel – was the representative of Peoria.

In the recession of the 1980s, the brewery and the distillery – Peoria's heirloom industries – went bust. Caterpillar was rocked by oriental competition. However, workers had diversified into insurance, direct marketing, and telecommunications. The Greater Peoria Economic Development Council claimed that the area was therefore spared the biggest fiscal frights of the early nineties – the local growth industry of making seals and perforations for packaging is particularly cited – but, in the middle of 1992, unemployment had reached 7.8 per cent, just above the national average of 7.1.

On the way back to the Père Marquette, exhausted by my telescopic rendition of the three hundred years of history since the original appeared in his canoe, I decided to stop for a frozen yoghurt. In the Twin Towers – a small downtown arcade, or baby mall – I had a choice of two delis. One was completely empty, so I went for the store with two people sitting at a table outside. As the electronic doors split for me, the couple stood up and followed me in. They were the staff.

As I chipped with a plastic spoon at the icy mound, I looked

around the shops. You would have thought there had been a
bomb scare. But, refreshed, I decided to prolong my city tour.
The local tourist board noted in its brochures that Peoria is
'precisely the size of Paris'. But, if so, Peoria proved that size did
not matter. It was what you did with it. The tourist board also
claimed that the city was known as the Little Apple, because of
its image, culturally, as a sort of smaller New York.

When I read this I thought: When people talk about the
duplicitous professions, they always cite journalists, politicians,
and estate agents. Why did they never say tourist boards? And yet
these people were clearly inveterate pup-sellers, professional
Pinocchios.

For example, I kept seeing leaflets for a construction called
Peoria Heights. It boasted linen shops, sweet shops, dress shops.
Or, more precisely, shoppes. One sure sign that you have entered
tourist hell is that the spelling gets terrible – shoppe for shop or
even, in extreme cases, ßhoppe; olde for old. There is one
exception to this rule: the graffiti on the walls of inner cities are
often grammatically imperfect as well. Perhaps the rule should
be: bad spelling on brick = danger, bad spelling on varnished
wood = safe.

In fact, the Little Apple claim by the tourist board could only
have been true if you were seriously into church choirs. Beyond
that, there was a restored paddle-steamer on which you could
have dinner and gamble at small-stake tables. And, at the Play-
house, there was a Sondheim, but it was one which had already
flopped in New York. Perhaps the litmus-test city was now being
seen more patronizingly, and those forced off Broadway
shrugged: 'Well, let's see how it plays in Peoria.' At the Civic
Centre, the main cultural event seemed to be the Olympic
Weightlifting Trials.

I asked the lady selling tickets, who looked fiftysomething,
what she thought of Peoria. She said, 'I lived here all my life. It's
fine. I just wish there was more to do . . .'

It was easy to think, if you were youngish and had some
money and some luck, that sensible types lived where they wanted
to. But for most people still it was never an option. You kept the
geographical hand you were dealt. You had to remember this
every time you sneered: Why would people live here? Residence

was two thirds inertia. And the US census showed that Illinois was one of the states with the highest proportion of sticker citizens, people who still lived where they were born.

But if tradition was one spur, history was another. Recent American history. They lived in Peoria, many of these Americans, not because of what was there, but because of what was not there. There was no mayhem yet. Research showed that, as the brand-name cities broke down, people were moving out, not to the traditional innocence of Scrotum or Instep, but to transitional suburbs or, in the architectural buzz phrases, 'second-tier cities' or 'edge communities'. They looked like a city and felt like a city but, as yet, they didn't smell like a city. The strong possibility of being bored to death was probably better than the extinction opportunities on offer on America's other streets.

Back at the Père Marquette, I watched the television news. Representative Bob Michel of Peoria had made a nervous speech urging Americans not to throw out the political system – polls were showing that voters believed that all incumbent politicians should be kicked out – in a fit of recession-induced fury. For years, everyone had prophesied that anarchy in America would come from black anger. Perhaps Los Angeles proved that it would. But a new possibility was brewing: that the anarchists might be the middle-class whites. Which was stronger? The anger of never having had or the anger of losing what had been?

Next morning, I caught the Greyline bus to Normal. Three of us were leaving Peoria that day. There was a young guy in fake (I guess) zebra-skin knee-length trousers and a leather waistcoat over a bare, hairy chest. Hair also lay in rope-thick black ringlets down his back. There were three tattoos on each shoulder, like winning lines on a fruit machine. For discretion, he wore shades.

He was staring ahead in what looked like a chemical reverie, but, after half an hour, he turned and said: 'Is this *train* going to Chicago?' I froze. Was 'train' hippy for bus? Or was his head telling him at this moment that he was travelling Amtrak? Or – a third possibility – was it a quote from something? It was a line you could imagine bluesily crooned – 'Eeeeze this train gooooooing to Chi-car-go-oo-oh?' – in the manner of 'Hey, buddy, can you spare me a dime?'

In the end all I said was: 'Normal.'

'Shit,' he said.

The other passenger was a blonde girl in faded denim shorts and white T-shirt. She kept giggling to herself, a delighted eyes-alight peal every few minutes. She was either remembering what had recently been happening to her or anticipating what soon would be. Either explanation was intriguing, as it was objective evidence that fun was possible in Peoria or Normal.

The non-human cargo was equally bizarre. As we had waited to board, I had seen, being stashed between the wheels, boxes marked RUSH HUMAN BLOOD and ATLANTIC SALMON, both packed in ice. And so we cruised through Illinois, past endlessly repeating breezeless fields, the hippy, the giggler, the plasma, the salmon, and me.

When we arrived at the bus dépot, I took a cab, leaving behind the hippy, who was drooling at a stunned bus company employee: 'Where do I get the train for Chicago?'

The cab driver asked if I was on business. I lied.

'I have to say, sir, Bloomington-Normal wouldn't be my choice of a hot vacation spot . . .'

'*Bloomington*-Normal?'

He explained that Normal had a neighbouring community called Bloomington. The local politicians had decided to double-barrel them like a married couple and call the result the Twin Cities, with a hopeful but doomed nod at Minneapolis-St Paul.

'Have you thought what you're gonna do?' the driver asked.

'I thought I'd just hang around . . .'

'Well, you can try. There's not a whole lot to do. It's a conservative place. Malls, taverns, banks, churches. Helluvalot of churches . . .'

There were fifty-two thousand people in the Twin Cities, he said, and twenty thousand of those were students. The Illinois State University was situated between the communities. Apart from that, he said, you had mainly working and retired insurance salesmen, who were cautious people, well, they were bound to be. The biggest employer had been the State Farm Insurance

Company, which insured property and cars across Illinois and beyond. About a decade ago, Mitsubishi had moved into town, doubled its size. That was where the work was. So it was a strange place now. Old sleepy folks who had lived there all their life, car workers, students. It was a dead place, artificial.

'So why do you live here?'

'Because, one, I was born here and, two, I never got away . . .'

Residence was two thirds inertia. I reflected on how cab drivers had made a disproportionate impact on travel literature and journalism. They were quoted in newspapers and books only slightly less often than senior politicians. There had been one in a *New York Times* page one-piece that morning, about political opinions in the Midwest: 'said a construction engineer, *now working temporarily as a cab driver.*' They were articulate, opinionated, a good, quick dyspeptic fix on somewhere. I wondered if tourist boards realized how much brochure hyperbole they punctured.

'What are the girls like in London?' he asked.

Political correctness – and, to be honest, sheer poverty of data – caused me to pause, but I also felt the quite unexpected pull of national loyalty. Suddenly, I was a spokesman for English femininity.

'They're, er, nice. A bit more . . . reserved than American ones, possibly . . .'

'That right? Here, you'll find it's middle-aged ladies or college girls. The college girls you'll have no problem. They'll come through just on that accent of yours. I'd fake it if I could. I was married once and . . .'

Around the English-speaking world, it was a vital rule that you never let a cab driver, assuming you got an English-speaking one, loose on the subject of crime or sex. Luckily, we reached my hotel. It was called Jumer's Château, a re-creation, on abandoned farm land, of a German castle. It had Disney-Gothic towers, the menu was heavy with bratwurst and Black Forest gâteau, and, for some reason, there was so little light in the lobby that you had to listen for the tinkle of the elevator to know where it was. Perhaps the intention was a thematic representation of divine twilight from Wagner productions.

After stashing my bags, I felt my way back to the entrance, losing a chunk of knuckle on a raised whorl of the fake-ancient wall plaster, and caught a taxi to a mall. We passed the First Church of Christ Scientist, the church of Jesus Christ Mormon, the Mennonite church, the church Triumphant.

In the mall, a lot of the fashion shops had girls' names – Julie Cool, Tricia Teen, Bobbi Beau, that kind of thing – but Marie Celeste would have been more appropriate. Your footsteps echoed on the marble as if you were the first tourist of the day in an Italian church. There was even a similar sweet sickly smell, though not of incense, but of cookies, candy, ice-cream. Some stalls claimed thirty-three or forty-five flavours but they remained in refrigerated rainbow limbo, with no takers.

A novelty shop on my left was selling – or so the sign said – Talking Plantpots. I assumed it was an attempted exploitation of the theory that conversation motivated flora. The pots vibrated as they spoke and, as I passed, one toppled off the shelf and rolled across the floor and round my feet. 'Hello, hello, hello,' the plantpot said. Even in America.

At last, another shopper crossed my path. He was an old man in a shirt so loud it almost strobed in the strip-lighting. He had a limp so severe that you thought of a bad school actor in *Treasure Island*. He nodded greetings and shouted in the unknowing holler of those going deaf: 'And they say the economy's getting better . . .'

Well, yes. In the bookshop, I remarked to an assistant how quiet it was and she said: 'Well, it's Friday!' But, next day, when I made the same observation in another shop, the employee beamed: 'Well, it's Saturday!' The Republican defence of the economy had come to this: people didn't shop at weekends!

In the bookshop, all the non-fiction volumes had titles like *What Went Wrong?* and *Who Will Tell The People?* and *The Losing of America*. It might be added, for anyone interested in this national psychology through bestseller lists, that the other non-fiction hit of the period was a handbook on euthanasia. For a European, visiting America just then was like hearing that a rival you had always disliked had been diagnosed with cancer and thinking: I never wanted them to *die*.

I groped my way back through the lobby to my hotel room.

If the model was Teutonic, the taste was all-American. There was a ring of bulbs around the bathroom mirror so that brushing your teeth was like being in *Sunset Boulevard*. I read the *Bloomington-Normal Pantagraph*. The front page featured a photograph of thick lines of people winding round the local travel agent's. In a desperate attempt to encourage travel during the recession, several airlines had halved or even two-thirded their fares. The reaction had been as hysterical as everything else was in that country at that time.

Hardening the market, two of the flyers had filed for Chapter 11, an exotic American law which meant that, although you were effectively bankrupt, you could carry on as if you were not, your creditors unable to touch you. The regular acceptance of this pretence might be taken as a comment on the unreality of late twentieth-century American economics. In the same connection, on the Letters page, a local wrote: 'Uncle Sam is broke. Mother Hubbard's cupboard is empty. Our cities, states, government have huge deficits. Let's give Ross Perot a chance. He can't do worse . . .'

I flicked through the tourist board publication *Bloomington-Normal Points of Interest*. Unfortunately, I was too late for *An Evening with John Denver* but *Cats* was on. It usually was. The cultural Esperanto of the world was McDonald's, Coca-Cola, CNN and Andrew Lloyd-Webber. Somehow, I failed to feel any national pride at the inclusion of one English element in an otherwise American quartet. But I was discovering on this project that, no matter how far you flew or drove or walked in the quiet world, you could pretty well always get a Big Mac, cable news, a plastic cup of cold aerated caffeine, and watch a tenor pussy, baritone diesel engine, or Paris romantic with a really serious skin problem, courtesy of England's would-be Puccini.

I switched on the TV and saw an item about a support group established for US parents whose children demanded expensive computer games: the group used the slogan 'Just Say No', a non-ironic borrowing from the anti-drugs campaign. But why couldn't they just say no? Even in America.

It seemed to me that this vast advice market was one of the defining characteristics of the USA. You were always amazed by the sheer number of organizations, the lists of initials, advertised in the phone directory and in public places. There were lessons on everything in America; support groups for all known conditions and difficulties. The politically right-wing in Britain and its antipodean former colonies used the phrase 'nanny state' to condemn welfare systems and government hand-outs but it was possible to argue that America, which made a public religion of individual achievement, had become a different kind of nanny state, one based not on hand-outs but on handbooks, on an entire network of support groups and counsellors telling people what to do next.

The media teemed with pressure groups, their profligacy forcing ever more cumbersome titles. To protest against a planned Spike Lee movie about Malcolm X, there sprang up something called the United Front to Preserve the Legacy of Malcolm X and the Cultural Revolution, whose supposedly snappy acronym UFPLMXCR resembled an oculist's chart or the line of a keyboard.

But the only support group for someone in my condition was the Bloomington-Normal Tourist Board and they would only treat you if you were prepared first to stand up and admit: 'My name's Mark and I'm an Andrew Lloyd-Webber fan.' On the table in my room was a leaflet promoting the 'Summer's Coming Dance – with Billy Valentine and his Band'.

I had been reading *Outerbridge Reach*, the latest novel by Robert Stone, the great chronicler of American imperial decline. Stone's book had been inspired by the story of Donald Crowhurst, who, in a round the world yacht race, had faked his apparently victorious process by sending back fictional co-ordinates. Reading the book, I reassured myself that – if any of the places I visited proved to be just *too* differently interesting – I might fake it, like Stone's hero. This reminded me that I had not yet booked the flight from Normal to Chicago which would connect me with my plane to Alaska.

I dialled American Airlines but was connected to one of those robot monologues on what to do next with your telephone: 'To expedite your call, press 2 on a touch-tone phone. If you have a rotary phone . . .' Touching 2 got you another humanoid: 'For non-continental flights, including the Caribbean, press 1. For internal continental flights, press 2 . . .' Systems like this were much on my mind at the time. Ross Perot had suggested, to great public enthusiasm, that America might be governed by phone-in: what his people called Electronic Town Meetings. At times of international crisis, the voter would apparently dial a special number and sift the possibilities: 'If you favour nuclear attack, press 1. If you prefer stepped-up economic sanctions, press 2. Those wanting air cover for humanitarian relief supplies, stay on the line for an operator.' Even in America.

But you had to wonder if the technology was up to it. I was simply trying to provide air cover for myself and I couldn't get through. For two hours, every time I pressed 2 on my touch-tone hotel phone, there was the angry hammering of the busy signal. Belatedly, I realized that it was because of the cheap offers from the troubled airlines. Everyone was flying somewhere. It was the Great Middle American Refugee Crisis. Hard on my previous fantasy about not actually going to some of the duller places, I was faced with the possibility of not actually leaving one.

I eyed the lengthy list of numbers for use by the differently abled and otherwise-birthplaced. I pressed the number for speech and hearing-impaired but that was consistently jammed, so either a Deaf-Mute Convention was being organized in some faraway state or there were a lot of people as dishonest as I was. I rang the number for Spanish-language bookings, but they answered in a language I didn't understand and, when I spoke in English, put the phone down. Eventually, the trans-atlantic number had mercy on me.

At Bloomington-Normal Airport next morning, the terminal had two cardboard signs, reading Ticketing and Check-In. With my usual lunatic caution, I was hours before the first flight of the day but the place was teeming with people. It was the busiest building I had seen in Peoria or Normal. At first, I assumed it was the Middle American Refugee Crisis, but then I noticed that almost none of those in the airport carried luggage or reported to the check-in desks. They headed straight for the restaurant or for the viewing gallery upstairs.

When I went to the restaurant, I realized that the airport was a hot social venue. Families came here on outings to eat and see the planes. On the menu, all the food had names from aviation. A big burger was a 747, a smaller one a Single Prop. I wondered if the DC-10 made you shit yourself and fantasized about a burger called an Air India, which would arrive forty-eight hours after you ordered it. I also thought of the poor children in Bloomington and Normal.

'Bobby-Lou, we're going to the airport!' Pop would say.

'Great! You mean we're leaving here?' the child would reply.

'Hush your mouth, child. We're going to see the airplanes.'

'Aw. Is that *all*?'

Then my flight was called and I took the Fokker to Chicago – turbulence again making the plane a cross between a vomitorium and a chapel – and then a more stable 737 to Seattle. There was no doubt about which side the pilot was on in the bully–runt relationship between America's famous places and its open spaces. His voice on the intercom was big-city laconic, with an urban-phallic attitude to the wastes over which he flew us.

'Folks, any stuff you see down there for the next hour, that's Montana . . .' he drawled. And: 'Not much to see down there, folks. Only difference is, those of you on the left have got South Dakota, those of you on the right have got North Dakota . . .'

It was at Seattle that I felt insanity advancing. There was a two-and-a-half-hour wait late at night before the Anchorage connection. I trawled the airport for an English paper but all that was available was an Everest-sized pile of the late Robert Maxwell's *The European*. I was prepared to update my mantra of cultural Esperanto. McDonald's, Coca-Cola, CNN, Andrew Lloyd-Webber, and unsold copies of *The European*.

I flicked through the newspaper. Then I tried to lose myself in the ingredient information on an apple-juice bottle I had bought. 'Contains apple juice concentrate from New Zealand,' the label revealed. I felt pleased for the beleaguered country where my journey had begun. Reading *The European*, while drinking the residue of New Zealand apples on the western edge of North America, I felt the epitome of the modern global citizen: all barriers of trade, information, and travel collapsed by jet engines and telephone lines.

But that feeling only occupied me for a minute and soon I was flicking back through *The European*. I saw a box headed:

'European Competition'. The first question was: 'What is derogation?' Well, it was something to do with the way power would be shared between individual countries and a united Europe, wasn't it? The second question was: 'In no more than fifteen words, what should be the first task of a Prime Minister of Europe?' I brooded. *To irritate the British Conservative Party and rub Baroness Thatcher's face in it as well*, I concluded. Exactly fifteen words. I looked to see what the prize was. 'Win the exciting *Eurocracy* board-game devised by Jacob Hoeksma of Amsterdam!' the paper urged. Brussels – The Board-game. It was a chilling reminder of the perils which lay ahead before this journey could be brought to its conclusion.

I was staring grimly ahead when a figure crossed my line of vision. A young, pale, bearded man was standing by my table. He held out one hand, shook it, and then pointed the other at his open mouth. I wondered if this was another 'Even in America' story. Some Seattle by-law which allowed rentboys to solicit for fellatio and masturbation by gesture but not speech. He held out his hand, shook it, pointed the other at his open mouth. I pretended to be reading *The European*.

He slapped a small card down on the table. It said: 'HELLO. I AM A DEAF–MUTE. I AM SELLING THIS CARD TO MAKE A LIVING. PLEASE WILL YOU BUY ONE?' I hadn't actually been planning to buy a new piece of small white cardboard that year, what with the recession, but I dropped a dollar on the table. He placed another card down on the table. I turned it over. It said: 'I LOVE YOU'. I wondered if I had been complexly propositioned: a case of the love that *can* not speak its name.

It was an unsettling episode. Even in America. And I had not yet reached its true extremes.

# CHAPTER FOUR

# CONTINUING SERVICE TO DEAD HORSE

## *Alaska*

America, largely through the luck of an Indian heritage it has until recently disowned, is blessed with poetic place-names. For example, I have always had an ambition to visit Nebraska, seduced by the sound of it alone, although Americans always tell me that my faith would not be repaid if I were to see it in the flesh and earth. On the east coast, they reckon that the derivation is not from tribal myth but from the same root as 'nebulous'.

In Alaska, the words on the road signs are more prosaic. There are the namings of patronage, like Fairbanks, a once-politic sop to Taft's now irrelevant vice-president. Then there are the labellings of laconicism, such as the top-edge settlement called Dead Horse, a self-deprecating homage to the American joke about the one-horse town where the horse ain't feeling too good. But, above all, there are the baptisms of pragmatism. The starkest example is Anchorage. At the other end of the century, it was where the ships stopped.

At this end of the century, its main name-recognition in the West was as another kind of port. The thirsty 747s anchor there briefly on their way through to Japan and Indonesia. The most attention the average European paid to Anchorage as a destination was as a name in the second, lesser row of rotating dominoes on airport departure boards, the one marked *Via*. Millions of crumpled travellers – slow-stepping like astronauts or infants from the twin effects of tedium-relieving alcohol and airline seating – have wandered among the Eskimo dolls and freeze-dried packs of Atlantic salmon in the terminal where a gormless polar bear stands guard, a fearsome Arctic predator now made by taxidermy a cuteness for the tourists.

Most, after an hour at Anchorage, shuffled back to their refreshed jumbos. One of the few travelling to, not through, I took a taxi into town. It was nearly midnight, but as luminous as summer noon in Europe, glare muddling the view. The road was lined with firs, big Christmas trees. Beyond them were the large Christmas puddings of the surrounding mountains, the white sauce of snow running down them.

I checked into the Anchorage Hotel on E Street, a neat and unshowy accommodation with antique furniture, marred only by an overdose in paint and wallpaper of a colour which I would have called pink but which was perhaps intended as salmon. Certainly, most of the food on the local menus proved to be of the same hue.

At the end of the arrival formalities, the receptionist said: 'Oh, and don't go out walking after dark.'

I nodded sombrely, the old safe-traveller neuroses locking on. So even here, I thought, on the antiseptic edge of America, the streets were to be feared. It was only an hour later, when I was stuffing towels and newspaper into the incandescent cracks around the heavy blackout curtains in the room, that I realized I had fallen for the ancient Alaskan hotel clerk summer joke. There was no dark to go out after.


The next morning, just after the artificial distinction of dawn, I breakfasted in the hotel lobby. I was surprised to find that Anchorage supported two daily newspapers: the *Times* and the *Daily News*. A regular word in both that morning was 'Perot'. Alaska had been one of the first states to place the people's billionaire on the presidential ballot.

The main headlines were a local angle on a global story. The governor of Alaska was attending the international ecological summit in Rio de Janeiro. The state had a stake in the subject because of the 1989 Exxon Valdez incident, in which a floundering oil tanker black-washed the top shore of Alaska and gave its wildlife a cruel shampoo. The papers reported that the sea otter mortality rate had tripled since the spill.

The other main fret in the press was a parochial blow-up over an exhibit at the town museum. A piece of sarcastic modern art which involved the laying of the stars and stripes on the floor was regularly being rolled up and removed by splenetic veterans. Even in America.

I strolled downtown. Sleep had been restless or, perhaps more precisely, light. In all long-distance travel, the mind becomes a con-man to the body. Every frequent flyer perfects the strategies for winding up the interior clock: the eye-mask, the darkened room, the brandy night-cap, the caffeine pick-me-up. But the Arctic summer entails a double deception. Even when the body acceded to the new regime of day and night, it was reminded daily of the old arrangements by the surprising visual stimuli where dark should be.

In the slice of light called day, there were other shocks to the body. For the first few minutes, I felt slightly legless and chesty and wondered if something was going wrong with my lungs. In fact, I realized as the feeling eased, there was something going right with them. They were stunned by the oxygen content of what they were processing. Cut off from their usual European supplier with his dirty fix, they were experiencing carbon monoxide cold turkey. In the days when consumptive patients were advised to take the air, this was the substance indicated.

The purity of the air – though presumably gradually being undermined by the place's status as a gin-joint for jets – is helped by the plausible reliance, impractical in larger America, on foot over car. Already manageably compact, Anchorage had the extra pedestrian-friendliness of an idiot-grid system installed by the army engineers who laid it out. If you could count to fifteen and spell to P, you could get around its wide streets and deep, clean sidewalks. At 4th and E, I found a shopping mall and, within, a large department store. Even on the edge, this was recognizably America. There was only one thing missing. Shoppers. I was the single customer in the store.

From a culture where commerce meant crowds, I was fazed by the isolation. The assistants were giving the covert scrutiny which in Britain meant you were suspected of being a shoplifter. Here, it was becaue you were suspected of being a shopper. Though no economist, I began to wonder how capitalism in

Anchorage actually worked, if this was a representative example of the relationship between supply and demand. Trying to find something to buy – for the first time ever in a shop, I was feeling the moral pressure usually induced only by charity tins – I idly constructed a conspiracy theory. Was it possible that the federal government secretly subsidized these stores – that every department, not just the one with the untouched perfume, was a cosmetic one – to allow the US citizens of these circumference zones vicariously to share in American commerce?

Such a deception would be a rational extension of the national strategy. Despite being a country of five time zones, variegated terrains, and jumbled cultures, the USA made a brave attempt at homogeneity. Every town had a production of *The Phantom of the Opera*. In Anchorage, I was able to buy *USA Today*, the same paper sold earlier on east coast streets, and carried it past McDonald's and Waldenbooks, branches of chains which I now knew to be properly national.

A connoisseur of the small-screen appalling, I had been anticipating in Alaska a kind of down-home moose-and-caribou TV, a hickish, amateur stab at the sophisticated medium seen elsewhere. But, in my Anchorage hotel room at 7 a.m., I had just watched NBC's breakfast show *Today*, apparently happening live but, in reality, a time-delay recording of what New York had seen four hours before at its own dawn. To an extent which I had not expected, Alaska – the penultimate American state in terms of admission to the union and the ultimate in terms of northern land mass – was encouraged to feel part of the team. The American day was the American day, whatever time and distance said.

This is not to suggest that all of America was equally enthralling. I was already beginning to wonder whether the whole day allocated to Anchorage on this project was a Calvinist diligence. On my walk of orientation, I was up to N and 12° by midmorning, and slowed pace to space out the sights. The first of these, commanding a knoll above the railway station, was the bronze statehood statue, celebrating Alaska's admission to the USA in March 1959.

The word 'statehood' cast a clearly deliberate shadow of that other break-out noun 'manhood'. We were encouraged to reflect that, on the celebrated date, America's Arctic afterthought cast off the virginity-stigma of territorial status and lost its cherry, got its rocks off, with California, Texas, New York, and the other US bruisers. Attempting to convey this, the monument intended to show a bust of Eisenhower, the president who made the statehood invitation, symbolically protected by the national emblem. Unfortunately, due to vulgarities of perspective and facial impression, the impression the monument actually gave was that Eisenhower's head had been torn off by a bald eagle.

I called in at the tourist centre where a notice predicted at most a couple of hours of relative gloom during the night. It was seeming increasingly likely that Alaska represented the ultimate time-activity ratio nightmare: nothing to do and twenty-two hours of daylight in which not to do it. I formulated a strategy for Anchorage. I would have lunch, then do the museums, galleries and graveyards, the latter a recommended sight in a guidebook, which, before arriving, I had found surprising but now didn't. Then, as a self-indulgence for my glum thoroughness, I would telephone home for the cricket score.

It was a blazing day, so I was surprised to find that the pavement cafés had a choice of empty tables on the sidewalk, while the customers huddled stuffily inside. This perversity was soon explained. It was a legislative pettiness in Anchorage that licensed premises could not serve alcohol on the street.

Not wholly consoled by fizzy water with the pink dish of the day, I walked to the town's Museum of Art and History at 6th and A. Among the paintings, the landscapes were the most rewarding, particularly if you were interested in the techniques of artists working within rigid limitations. The trouble for the Arctic artist was colour. Montherlant once observed that happiness writes white: for readers to have a good time, characters must ideally have a bad time. Alaska's canvas talents soon discovered a similar truth of their own. Snow paints white.

An oil like *The Sleigh Team*, by the neatly named George Albert Frost (1843–1907), came perilously close to that old art-class joke about a blank sheet depicting a white cat in a snow storm. You could sense the relief with which Eustace Paul Zeigler (1881–1969), in his studies of Alaskan fishermen, swooped on the contrasting blue of summer sea and sky. Working with their clamped palates – depicting ice, sea, and sky in bravura shadings of white, blue, and violet – the region's artists forcibly pioneered a painterly discipline equivalent to the writer's haiku. It was noticeable that, later, Ziegler turned to charcoal on white paper, merely leaving his virgin canvas to provide Alaskan background.

The section of the complex allocated to History had far more to work with. As elsewhere in America, attention was being given to the achievements of the native peoples. Eskimos – a term which the race continued to accept in preference to the goody-goody white-man phrase Native Alaskans – were subject to a particular variety of historical disrespect. It was not the racism of fear and perceived sexual inferiority (which whites displayed towards blacks), nor the racism of dismissive contempt (shown by Australians to Aborigines, New Zealanders to Maoris), but rather a sort of racism of anthropomorphism. Eskimos were seen as cuddly creatures with furry hoods and fishing rods, human dolls who did not possess gonads or votes.

Not content to settle for retrospective sympathy alone, the Inupiat peoples of Alaska had commendably secured significant interest in the government and business of the state. This was pleasing to liberals but, in their rehabilitation, Eskimos had proved a special dilemma to the colonially guilty. For a start, they wore so much real fur. Politically correct in terms of redressed territorial theft, they lacked some other modern pieties. When, in 1988, two late-migrating whales became trapped in the ice off the north coast, environmentally concerned reporters from America and overseas sent back to their green-leaning readers stories of a heroic rescue attempt supervised by Eskimos who were, though this detail was somewhat fudged, maintaining their strength by snacking on whale meat.

In the building of the Alaska which was robbed from the first settlers, there had been three phases of trade. In the eighteenth century, the Russians hunted otters and seals for the clothes trade in the fashion business's equivalent of the Cold War. The Inupiat hit back – to the extent of scalping some Soviets in a retaliatory hunting of their own – but were forced to begin their two-hundred-and-fifty-year wait for the dawn of political correctness. In the mid-nineteenth century, Russian colonial contraction after Crimea – and the shortage of furry sea creatures caused by the earlier orgy – put Alaska on the transfer market.

In that age when land was sold like football players, William Seward, the American secretary of state, secured it from Alexander II for $7,200,000. The columnists bitched, dubbing the frozen nub 'Seward's Icebox'. The discovery of gold brought a warmer interpretation of the purchase. When the gold, like the otters and seals, gave its eventually inevitable answer to human greed, the icebox was forgotten again. But Alaska was a prominent example of a luck economy, in which chance consistently renewed a place's usefulness or wealth. First sea and then geology had kicked up riches. Now political history did.

Modern Alaska was a product of American foreign policy, consolidated by American domestic policy. The Japanese threat to invade mainland America during World War II led to the spending of one billion dollars between 1941 and 1945 on securing the enticing cat-flap which was Alaska. Any chance of the big-spending military leaving – after the Japanese had accepted defeat and a pacifist constitution written by General MacArthur – was removed by the territory's convenient (at least for its stature and finances) proximity to Russia, with which the Cold War had now been joined. Vital to the American nightmare, Alaska subsequently became key to the American dream when the Atlantic Richfield Corporation hit oil, a lauded resource in the hungry industrial culture of which, in 1959, Alaska had become an official part.

Now, the Cold War was over and the oil beginning to show signs of going the way of the seals and the otters and the gold. Alaska needed some new luck. In the absence of a visitation, it was struggling to make some. Anchorage was bidding for the 1996 Winter Olympics. The town's Centre for the Performing Arts – a pink brick pavilion – already cheekily featured a motif of interlocking rings.

The State Governor had also just floated the idea of a water pipeline from his lake-packed state to desert California, the southern neighbour where the drought was so tough there was a flourishing business in spray-painting straw lawns green. But, at the moment, his pipeline remained in the pipeline. The more plausible option was the importable resource of tourism.

I was doing my bit. Leaving the art and history museum, I headed for the cemetery, as recommended in the guidebook. The

Inupiat graves had whalebone crosses but, otherwise, the place was the usual morbid walkabout among stones, wind-blown flowers, and bad, sad chiselled poetry. Whatever they did for tourism, the gravestones seemed unlikely to encourage immigration. The sums produced by subtracting the life dates were so small that I doubted my maths.

Subsequently, I was told I had been correct. Alaska was a place associated with premature deaths. Perhaps because of the absence of other distractions – another bloody day in purgatory – heavy smoking was routine and serious drinking not unusual. Youthful suicide was also reportedly prevalent. Certainly, in the newspaper death columns, numerous entries for the young reported death as having been 'at home', with no explicatory history. Another bloody day in purgatory.

Anchorage, it was becoming apparent to me, was a place in which any excitement – like empty pavement tables on a summer day – turned out to have a drably rational explanation. For example, I had noticed during the morning that the streets of the town featured an improbable number of beautiful women, far beyond the per capita incidence even in chic Western capitals. Then I worked it out. They were over-nighting air hostesses, an optical illusion of beauty, teasing a drab town.

It was a doleful note on which to end the day. However, I felt a certain elation, as I had now earned the reward of the day's cricket news from England. Receiving the information from a wife with no interest in the game is not always ideal ('Who got the wickets?' 'Oh, something like, oh God, I remember thinking it was the same name as a place . . .' 'Salisbury?' 'That's it.'), but, after my day's sight-seeing in Anchorage, even scrambled facts were a joyous prospect.

From the Anchorage Hotel, I dialled the fifteen digits which, in the modern world, found south-west London in fifteen seconds.

'What was the score?'

'It rained all day. They didn't play.'

Next morning, I caught the 08.30 train from Anchorage to Fairbanks. People in offices waved animatedly as we chugged out, which gave a sense of what constituted an event to the residents of the town. They had never met us, but you would have thought we had given them the best sex of their lives the night before.

The Anchorage–Fairbanks trip took twelve hours – through stations with names like 'Ship Creek' and 'Hurricane Gulch', evocative of childhood comics and the *Perils of Pauline* – but I was getting out after nine, at Denali Park, the wildlife reserve which was Alaska's main tourist trap. The train moved as slowly as a commuter service for those employed only on February 29th. But I was more used to this by now. The Alaskan pace of life had much in common with the work-deferring one which Europeans attribute to the Spanish. It was not only when inching down the track to Fairbanks that I thought of a line from 'The Whitsun Weddings', Philip Larkin's train poem: 'All sense of being in a hurry gone.' Larkin had meant Hull, his lifelong dislike of travel shielding him from more universal applications of his line.

For most of those on the train, though, the sense of being in a hurry had gone, long before. They were the superannuated, widowed or divorced, people free to go on long, rambling journeys, like students with money. There were also a few students without money, some anachronistic hippies. So the travellers you met in Alaska divided between the retired and the opted out. People either had a yard of hair or an inch.

In my carriage, there was a hippy couple in denim and leather who, as soon as they boarded, snapped back the moveable armrest dividing their double seat, improvised an embrace, and slept for nine hours, their dark lank tresses entwining like vines on the trellis of the seat-leather. They are in the corner of a snap I took and if anyone editing a picture-dictionary ever gets stuck on the idiomatic expression 'shagged out' they can have it.

The train was empty enough for us to have a double seat each and a buffer of empty leather front and back, but that wasn't going to stop Americans chatting to you. My nearest north-west neighbour soon strolled down to introduce himself. He had a fussily cut grey beard and a worried manner. This was the day's only train to Fairbanks on the state's only route there but, at every station, he took out the timetable and checked that he was where he should be. My closest south-east neighbour had wandered up to join us. English and unused to such casual intimacy, I missed their names in the preliminary blizzard of introductions, but I caught that he was from Texas and she from South Carolina, so in my head I called them Tex and Carol.

'My wife passed away last year,' explained Tex.

I looked away. Carol crossed herself and shrilled: 'I'm sorry!'

Carol, it transpired, was herself a widow. Tex confided further to two people he had known for twenty seconds: 'We always planned our trips three or four years ahead. We were kinda organized . . .' I had a vision of wall-charts and diaries, red lines and sticky paper dots. 'So when cancer took my wife, took her like that' – he snapped his fingers – 'there were arrangements in place . . .'

Carol asked me outright if I had 'lost someone too'. I spun the cover story: sabbatical, wife unable to get time off work. They asked where I was from. London, England, I said.

'I love your brogue!' exclaimed Carol, and I started looking at my shoe, before I realized. Middle-class middle-aged Americans spoke an antique English which was possibly the product of their religious tourist visits to Stratford-on-Avon. Later, Tex told me, in the connection of England, that he had 'visited a tavern in the borough of Newbury'. He pronounced it *burrow*, but otherwise he might have been out of Christopher Marlowe. When Carol said, 'I loved *Brideshead Revisited*' – which is what Americans say to the English when they get really desperate – I went to the restaurant car for lunch.

Here, because of the prices, there were more of the retired than the opted out. From native Yankee distrust of the different, intensified by geriatric medical necessity, they treated Alaskan menus with the watchfulness of despots fearing a coup through doctored food.

'An "Alaskan All-Day Breakfast Burger". What would that be, son?' one oldster in a baseball cap quizzed the steward.

'Sir, that's kinda like a sausage and egg McMuffin, but with reindeer meat?'

'*Reindeer* meat?'

The steward said, in a canny piece of target marketing, that reindeer meat was famously low in cholesterol. The baseball cap risked it. So did I, opting for the reindeer sausage. It was like very gamey veal, and tasty enough, as long as you could suppress the subliminal image of Father Christmas saying to Mother Christmas: 'Say, Rudolph's late home tonight. Do you think he's OK?'

At another table, a second grizzled couple were having their own menu seminar with the steward, though this time from special interest rather than suspicion. The man had worked in the spud business all his life and he wanted to know the provenance of his hash browns. The steward brought the sack for him to examine.

'Now that's a really interesting potato,' he told his dazed spouse, who was entering into a full understanding of the lines in the marriage service about for better or for worse.

Back in the carriage, putting down a novel in which nothing much happened in Nottingham and looking out of the window, I began to see why those travelling this route might become fascinated by potatoes. Alaskan scenery was at best relentless. You got thirty minutes of trees – lines of pines, the leaves so hirsute they hid the trunks – and then a flash of lake, before the leaves danced back on for an encore, like an endless chorus line of empty, self-supporting skirts.

On the early part of the journey, there was the occasional habitation, like Wasilla, a 'bedroom community', the American for what the English called a dormitory town. Wasilla had a McDonald's and a video shop. Homogeneity again. Then there were trees, trees, trees, lake, trees, trees, trees, until we reached Matanuska. This town was famous for its supernatural legumes. The twenty-two hours of summer sunlight, combined with uncorrupted soil, resulted in fifty-pound cabbages, vegetables like medicine balls.

Then it was back to the bushy green kaleidoscope until Talkeetna, where a local chef gave President Warren G. Harding botulism on a state visit in 1923, thus bringing Calvin Coolidge to the White House. Perhaps because of this, Alaska is now rarely on the campaign trail. Frankly, a candidate would have to be mad to trek up here, which meant that Alaska's modern political exposure had been restricted to a visit from Richard Nixon. Unfortunately, however, he failed to order Warren G. Harding stew.

After Talkeetna, we resumed the coniferous merry-go-round.

By mid-afternoon, a lake was like a Christmas present. In the circumstances, I became more diverted than I would have expected by watching the way in which lakes melted, Alaskan nature's reverse version of the celebrated entertainment to be found in the drying of paint. A winter lake becoming summer water broke up in patches, which took on a strange poached-egg effect: bright white irregular circles with a raised bubble of dirtier white in the centre.

Infrequently, there was the treat of a ravine, including the serious vertigo-moment of the aforementioned 'Hurricane Gulch', nine hundred feet across, two hundred and ninety-six down (although that word is banished from your vocabulary during the crossing) and spanned by a relative plank of a bridge. Tex told me that bungee-jumping had become big in Alaska, from which we may perhaps conclude – after New Zealand – that it is an inevitable cultural development in places of deep ravines and deeper tedium.

The trees came back on, by unpopular demand, for one hour more now only.

'This must be a bit dull after Texas,' I suggested to Tex.

But Americans of his kind dread giving offence and so he only said: 'Lot more trees, it's true.' Carol said that she planned to see the whole of America before she went to her grave. This was her thirty-eighth state. I told her that, with a car, you could pretty much see the whole of England before you went to your bed. But Americans of her kind dreaded even you giving offence to yourself and so she said: 'But England's beautiful.' Tex put in another good word for Newbury, where he had visited the tavern.

Tex and Carol and I, though, had homes to go to after this. Why did people make their homes in Alaska? The stewards on the train were mainly high-school graduates working summer break. Most of them were off to college soon and I assumed it would be off and out.

'Oh, no,' said a steward called Tony. 'I'll come back and settle here.'

Tony had been born in California but his dad, an attorney, had moved up to help the still baby state in a mood of missionary zeal. The more you talked to people, the more you saw that

Alaska had attracted idealists, clean-slaters, rat-race refugees. But these children of the refugees seemed to share the idealism.

'Why do you like Alaska so much, Tony?'

'Oh, it's clean. And I kinda like trees.'

It was not a response I'd ever contemplated and so I looked at him as if he'd just said he did it with sheep. Confused, I turned to Krystyn, a stewardess who looked like Chris Evert when she first hit Wimbledon.

'Do you plan to leave?'

'No way.'

'What's the attraction?'

'Oh, like I've been to lower forty-eight . . .' As if to make sense of its size, Alaskans rationalized the 95 per cent of America from which they were separated as 'lower forty-eight', the number of states in the contiguous land mass. 'And lower forty-eight is fine, but it's kind of *fast*. The people are nicer here. And, like Tony said, there are the trees. I really like trees.'

All you could say was that they were in the right place. I got off the train at Denali and checked into McKinley Village, a wooden hotel complex used mainly by package tours for geriatrics.

Old age as a second childhood is an endlessly repeated conceit but I had not – until my passage through Alaska – appreciated the extent to which package tours for the retired wealthy so exactly resembled school trips.

In every group of such tourists, there was the self-appointed clown, cheeking the tour leader, constructing dumb puns from place-names, and regularly reddening the females present with smutty jokes. Each party too contained the dull-eyed runts who, at every stop, were plucked back from the wrong coach just before it pulled out. And, on geriatric holidays, as on class outings, at least 50 per cent of the logistical energy consisted of insuring against urinary mishaps.

The only serious difference was that a tour leader's attitude to miscreants was not a teacher's. Because they were paying, the irritations of the second children were met not with screaming or detention but preternatural understanding: 'Yes, Madam, I can see that the B on that other coach looks like a C. I'll talk to Head Office about it tonight . . .'

Most of the tourists were duos (except where doubling with in-laws formed quartets) and many of the couples were, in two senses, uniform. The men wore baseball caps, looking suddenly twenty years older when they took them off. Their strawberry jump-suited wives yelled into their better ear, counting out pills for them every four hours. The more technologically adept prompted their medication with watch alarms. It was the geriatric equivalent of the infant feed: drug-suckling. In another regression, they called each other 'Mommy' and 'Daddy'.

The mommies were reading Rosamund Pilchers. The daddies carried around a copy of James Michener's novel *Alaska*. I found Michener a chore to read but admired his strategy beyond words. He had pioneered a kind of map fiction, which perfectly exploited the American obsession with territory. Every citizen bought the Michener about the region in which they lived (*Chesapeake*, *Texas*) and then, when vacationing in another, purchased his work set there (*Alaska*, *Hawaii*). For those brave enough to leave the States, there was his *Caribbean*. In my view, his only marketing mistake was to have written *Space*, which as yet lacked a travel tie-in, rather than *Stratford-on-Avon*.

Our brochures described the trip to inner Alaska as a 'wilderness experience', but, in truth, we were roughing it in strictly controlled conditions. I almost wrote laboratory conditions, but, even on the wilderness experience, our privations were more those of pet mice than research rats. The well-swept wooden cabins lacked television (my first long period in the quiet world without CNN) and telephones (ditto for cricket scores) but a shower was provided, although its natural constituency was slim midgets.

A central reception cabin contained a pay-phone and a café, but room service and laundry were outlawed. Accordingly, I swilled my mucky underwear and socks, piling up since Peoria, in the face-basin and draped them over the wooden rail of the reception cabin steps to dry. When I returned from a wildlife tour, the rail was empty. A receptionist explained that the clothes had been confiscated because a guest had found them offensive. I understood that Bible-belters might object to men displaying their underwear in public, but *if they weren't in them at the time*? Middle American moral standards clearly could not relax even on vacation.

As I carried my knickers away in the brown paper wrapper traditionally provided for socially explosive material, I checked out the noticeboard for the evening's Denali leisure options. The hottest sell seemed to be 'Alaska Cabin Nite' at the Wilderness Dinner Theater. The promotional notice promised 'an evening of rip-roaring entertainment and a family-style all-you-can-eat dinner'. This suggested courage in the organizers as, for American diners, the words all-you-can-eat have the effect which the dropping of a glove once had on duellists. Having myself fought a lifelong struggle with bulkiness, America was the only country in the world in which I regularly felt skinny.

When we had all-you-can-eaten, 'Fanny Quigley and her crew' would show us 'ol' Alaska in its gold-mining heyday – with tall tales, great songs, and foot-stomping music'. Ignoring my self-imprecations in Peoria against any public event deliberately misspelled, I booked a ticket for the Cabin Nite.

If I hadn't been composing a sarcastic account in my head, I doubt that I would have got through the nite. My worries set in on the courtesy bus, when a pink jump suit said: 'You guys going to the Cabin Nite? You're gonna have a great time! We went last night, only we didn't have our camcorder, only our flash camera. If we'd known what the entertainment was like, we'd have taken our camcorder. They said we could come back in tonight to film.' I thought: *That* bad, huh?

I only had with me my flash camera, but I didn't use it. Nor did I think of asking permission to return the following night with a camcorder. Mainly, in fact, I contemplated arranging to pay a second visit with a machine-gun. In a wooden hut, slung with mining helmets and fake-sepia gold-field maps, we were seated at long wooden tables. An inconvenient spare man, I was placed next to a big lady from Maine, who confided that she had once shot a moose. On my other side were two beaming Japanese. We soon discovered that we had not one word of shared language between us.

The performers – who were also the waiters and waitresses – wore gingham and frills. The head girl told us that her name was

Fanny. She instructed us that, every time she shouted 'D'y'all know what?' we were to scream back: 'What, Fanny?' We had a practice. I sullenly mouthed the words soundlessly, like boys whose voices were breaking had been told to do in the second-form end-of-term concert. But the sound which bounced around the hut showed no sign of missing my contribution: 'Wha-aaa-t, Fa-aaaa-nnn-eeee?' Even my Japanese neighbours made a brave phonetic stab at it. Some people were taking pictures of their spouses shouting.

Her being called Fanny was, I think, a small subversion inserted by the performers. Although the word is a more junior vulgarity in the States than in Britain, I suspect they had done it for the same reason that one of the performers at similar ancient, traditional, medieval tourist banquets in London usually has the Shakespearian soubriquet of Bottom. If you dreamed of playing Hedda Gabler or Willy Loman, and now you were stuck as performer-server at a traveller's snack-and-act, you too might find it cathartically amusing to have your super-annuated vacationers and Bible-belters yelling 'Bottom!' or 'Fanny!' every few minutes.

But off-off-off-*off* Broadway as she was, the actress could not be faulted for her gusto. 'Now, there are one or two rules at Fanny's tavern!' she yodelled. 'No cursing and no spitting! Now, on y'all's tables, y'all have a flagon of ale and a pitcher of good hot strong black coffee!'

'Do you have decaf?' asked one quavering voice, perhaps failing fully to enter into the authentic Gold Rush experience.

We began with ribs and beans. As they spooned out the food, the server-performers sang: 'Hello, hello, we know you're feeling beat / We know y'all craving food to eat / So welcome y'all to Fanny's tavern / We hope a good time y'all are havern.'

And, apart from me, it really seemed that w'all were. The Japanese were treating this no-play as if it were a Noh-play. I reflected on the extent to which tourism benefits from the deep desire of the tourists to justify the expense by enjoying them-selves. While we were eating, one of the chefs put on a pair of floppy ears and ran past the window of the tavern. 'Look, a wild hare!' said the wench-thespian nearest to my table. She put a hand on my shoulder and whispered: 'You, sir, look like the kind of man who can spot a wild hare. Why don't y'all stand up and shout, "Look, a wild hare!" right now.'

'Er, no thank you,' I said.

Server-performers were clearly trained to use only minimum force. She shrugged and yelled herself: 'Look, a wild hare!' One of her colleagues aimed a fake shotgun at the chef in floppy ears, who howled, and ran back to the kitchen to prepare the second course.

I skipped it, hearing a joke about 'hare today, gone tomorrow' in the distance, as I walked back to my wilderness hotel. I realized that another reason why she had been called Fanny was that the word Funny was not in their vocabulary.

But Fanny was just fun. Our real reason for coming to Denali was that we might see a mountain and we might see some animals, although, depending on the season, it was possible that we would not see either. This was as close as you got, in quiet-world tourism, to risk.

The mountain was McKinley. At twenty thousand feet, it was a third lower than Everest but, in the gazetteers of mountaineering, was highly prized because its rise from plain to peak – what climbers call the 'uplift', a technical description with a metaphor hiding behind it – is greater than that of the Nepalese skyscraper. Hundreds of teams of hopeful scalers left from Talkeetna every year. There had always been fallers. But, suddenly, in 1992, the climb had become as dangerous as ordering Warren G. Harding stew in Talkeetna. On – or off – McKinley, it was the worst year in history for slips, with eleven dead early in the season.

Safe travellers, though, had come to Denali only to peer at the peak from a distance. It was a rough rule of twentieth-century tourism that, in the towns, you were taken to the top of man-made heights in order to look down in awe while, in the countryside, you were taken to the bottom of nature-made heights in order to look up in awe. The two styles of sightseeing: ant and giraffe.

Denali's other potential animal viewpoint was eye to eye with a bear, caribou, or moose, the main advertised attractions on the half-hearted half-day safaris which were the place's other pull.

Ideally, between your eye and the animal's there would be the plate-glass of a coach and dozens of metres of tundra. The park staff, however, were careful to prepare you for greater optical proximity.

Although it is common for Britons visiting the USA for the first time to comment on the politeness and efficiency of leisure industry employees, the regular visitor soon appreciates that much of what has the outward appearance of manners is in fact – in a nation where litigation has replaced smoking as an approved stimulation – a personal-liability waiver. At Denali, most of the energy of legal protection is spent on preventing elderly American tourists being eaten by bears, the decision having been taken that the loss of even one, while aesthetically defendable, would be unwelcome in terms of bad publicity and compensation.

Hence all tour groups are exhaustively tutored in bear drill. On the coach I joined – again the only solo traveller in a party of interlocking package groups – the driver outlined procedure for dealing with an animated rug in a rage. The first step was to stand your ground. Luckily, it seemed to be the case that – when parent bears taught their offspring the drill for surviving against tourists – they told them to back off at the first sight of stretch nylon and a dangling Pentax. If, however, you came upon a bear who hadn't been listening during drill, and who charged you, the trick was to drop down, with your arms cushioning your skull, in a small ball.

'A *small* ball?' gasped a lady on the coach who was, by nature, a large ball.

We pulled out through the scrub, McKinley lazily playing peekaboo through the cloud in the far distance. We had been taught the watch-face system of identifying sightings, so that the right was three o'clock, ahead was twelve o'clock, six o'clock behind, and so on.

Soon, the driver said: 'Cow moose at three o'clock.' We peered to the right, where a large brown blur was chewing grass, its bulky head looking weighed down rather than lowered, as if its skull were stuffed with lead-shot.

The pink jump suit in front of me looked confused.

'A cow moose?' she asked the baseball hat beside her. 'Is that like a cross between a cow and a moose?'

'No, no, honey, "cow" means it's, like, a chick.'

'A *chick*?'

This illustration of the slipperiness of language would have thrilled Wittgenstein.

Animals were sparse all afternoon. At three o'clock, there was a caribou at six o'clock and, at four o'clock, a porcupine at twelve o'clock, but it was a long time between times and we began to plunder the boxed lunch included in the price.

After two hours, there was a drink-and-piss stop in a gravelled pit where prefabricated lavatories and army urns rose up like an industrial mirage from the tundra. It was here that I committed my crime against the tourist community.

The driver had hung two rubbish bags from the fender of the bus. Flattened picnic boxes were to be placed in one, food scraps in the other. I did this, but was left with a blue plastic drinking cup, with a special lid to prevent what the driver called motion spillage. Reluctant to carry a cheap beaker around Alaska and on to Canada, I tipped it in with the crusts and cores.

Two minutes later, one of the sixtysomething ladies stormed down the coach. Her jump suit should have been renamed a hopping suit. 'Can you beleeeve it?' she roared at her sister-in-law. 'Someone threw their cup away! How could anyone ever be so stoopid? This cup is gonna be so *useful*.'

I think she'd guessed that the transgressor was the English weirdo, because she glared at me so hard I began to pray that the cup would pass back to me. Also, she began to victimize me. The team-ethic of the package tour was clearly a powerful thing. As the homegoing coach route exactly reproduced the outward one, I lost myself in an English literary novel. I was just wondering whether or not the Tory MP would bugger the small boy he had met in a seedy London hotel when I was myself surprised from behind: 'How can you read when you've paid good money to see the landscape?'

The speaker was the champion of the special cup. I shrugged, left the MP on the brink, and watched the tundra for a while. There were more moose and caribou, but no bears.

Just before we got home, the man behind me, a tubby chummy Southerner, who had given me sympathetic eyebrows during the bad stuff over the cup, leaned across and whispered:

'See that lady in front of you, look at her next time she takes a picture.'

When there was a porcupine at four o'clock, she raised her camera and I watched. She had one of those flat, thin cameras the shape of a panatella packet. It was pink. The design was, however, irrelevant because she held the camera the wrong way round, squinting laboriously through the lens, with the viewfinder and number-strip of the film pressed to the coach window. Either this was her first time with a new camera or she had albums full of studies of her right eye. Or maybe she was an optical photographer, the next Manhattan craze, but then why shoot on location rather than in a studio?

The Southerner tapped me on the shoulder and whispered: 'You see? I sure wants to be around when she takes her first flay-ash!'

We both giggled and the keeper of the special beaker frowned at us in furious disapproval, the bad boys at the back.


Next morning, I bought Alaska's two daily newspapers as usual. The front page of one of them was funereally black-edged and said: FAREWELL! The *Anchorage Times* was closing down after seventy-seven years, ended by the recession. I had been wrong to be impressed that the economy supported two papers. This suffering among the world confraternity of journalists depressed me and I decided to skip the guided nature trek and catch the Greyhound bus to Fairbanks after breakfast.

I ate at a large hotel in the centre of the park. In the lobby, a harassed tour courier was having trouble with one of his charges. The name-badge on his lapel included a big yellow smiley-face, but his own was no longer remotely in competition with it.

'Jim, according to the printed literature, we have thirty minutes' free time here. Whatta we gotta do?'

'Well, Margaret, that's kinda up to you.'

Margaret stalked away, complaining that the brochure had said fully organized. In the hotel restaurant, I was reading the last *Anchorage Times* when someone said: 'Can I join you?'

I still reacted with culture shock. Even in the 1990s, most

British judges would readily grant incarceration under the Mental Health Act in the case of anyone striking up conversation with a stranger in an eating place. In America, though, you were most likely to attract legal attention for clamming up monosyllabically when harassed in this way.

'Hi, my name's Josie.'

'Er, Mark.'

Josie was wearing a purple *I Love Alaska* sweatshirt, decorated with a moose's head in felt. She explained that she was of Chinese origin, but now lived in Colorado.

'Good thing you don't try to buy that paper tomorrow, Mark.'

'Yes, I saw.'

'Same thing everywhere. Most jobs, you'd be silly to buy a two-year diary. Are things bad in England, Mark?'

'Yes. Pretty grim.'

'Are things so bad because Maggie Thatcher went . . . ?'

'Well, some people would say that Maggie Thatcher went because things were so bad . . .'

'Say again . . . ?'

In the circumstances, I decided not even to try to explain the events in Britain two months previously – which had occupied me between the Australasian and North American legs of the project – when Thatcher's successor, John Major, had won an improbable, and statistically unpredicted, victory in the election, therefore securing a fourth Tory term. Triumphing in large part by warning of the alleged tax burden under Labour, Major had promised: 'Vote Conservative on Thursday, and [economic] recovery begins on Friday.' There had so far been ten Fridays since he said it, to none of which the pledge applied.

'Listen, there's no one safe today,' Josie went on. 'My husband's in defence. Deep clearance. Eyes only. I said once: "If I were dying, would you tell me, just before I die, what it is you really do?" He said: "Not even then, honey." But, see, they're cutting defence. There were five hundred losses posted last month. We still don't know exactly how it will shake down. He decided he'd better not take this vacation. You leave the building, maybe they change the locks, right? So, I'm here alone. In my opinion, some genius – and, who knows, maybe Ross Perot, he couldn't do *worse* – needs to work out how to get all these defence personnel into other stuff. Me, I'm in the medical sector. Now, I hate to say this, but disease ain't gonna go away. I've a job for life. Law enforcement, that's the other one. I tell my kids, become a cop or a doctor. Jobs for life . . .'

Unless they get a disease themselves or get shot as a cop, I thought, but didn't say anything.

'I tell my husband,' she went on. 'You're so unlucky. Who'd ever have thought, ten years ago, that, defence, they'd be firing people . . .'

I had a sudden image of a human cannon in a circus.

'You smile, Mark. But I grew up in the fifties. Defence looked a solid bet . . .'

I marvelled at the way Americans surrendered so completely to whatever was the prevalent idea. A few years ago, they believed that the Soviets would march through Fairbanks at any moment. Now, they seemed just as certain that weapons were irrelevant.

'Oh, I'd have thought the market will pick up,' I said.

'Say again?'

'Well, you say there'll always be disease and, er, disorder. But surely there'll always be war as well . . .'

'You know something? You're right. I'll tell my husband when I phone him tonight. Cheer him up . . .'

I went to the rest-room and put the above in my notebook. The advantage for the exotic-world travel writer, I was realizing, was that the intestinal ailments which more or less went with the territory permitted regular retreats to keep your journal. In the quiet world, you had to risk the curious looks as you fled to the cubicle yet again.


As I waited to board the Fairbanks coach, the trekkers were leaving on their nature walk. Bear-drill for pedestrians, although including all the small-ball procedure given to coach passengers, also advised the wearing of bells round the neck. It was said that the creatures were more likely to stay calm if warned of your approach.

In fact, I suspected that this was comic apocrypha, resident

Alaskans' revenge on tourists. They walked off into the bush now, tinkling at the top, like human music boxes, the dull percussion occasionally drowned by the pleading of a watch alarm, indicating that it was time for the heart to have its helper. I imagined Alaskans sniggering behind the trees: 'They fell for the bell story again!'

Travel literature had a long tradition of interesting characters met on cross-country coaches, so I was mildly hopeful as the bus pulled in. I should have guessed that there would be an exclusion clause for Alaska. It turned out that I was the journey's only passenger. The ratio of drivers to travellers was 2:1. It was the tourist equivalent of being a child with special teaching needs. A few minutes in, the co-driver asked whether I wanted them to do the usual commentary on sights along the way. Looking out of the window, I saw only the possibility of a bravura arboreal monologue, so told them to skip it.

The bus company seemed to have a deal with shops along the route. If you shacked on a lavatory, the coach would pull in there for its two-hourly urination breaks. The driver would then advise the passengers, after voiding their bladders, to stack their bags with your knick-knacks. The driver stressed – in what was almost certainly an undue commercial pressure waiver – that we were under no obligation to shop. In fact, if you were the only passenger, it was hard to avoid a sense of moral pressure.

As I descended the bendy steel steps, the two drivers ready to take an arm each if necessary, four assistants were lined up outside the entrance to the shop. I had a brief sense of what it must be like to be the president arriving at a foreign airport. Except that the reception committee stared hopefully over my shoulder to see who else was coming, then, when no one did, shrugged and led me in. I had a brief sense of what it must be like to be the vice-president arriving at a foreign airport.

'Our speciality is fungus art,' explained the chief assistant. I wondered if this, like the bear bells, was another cruel spoof against tourists. If it was, the gag was elaborately backed up. I was told how fungus – also known as birch bread – was scraped from the bark, dried, and then painted. Such was the lottery of creativity. One man had looked upon mould and created penicillin; another had looked upon it and dreamed up fungus art. 'Very interesting,' I murmured. I felt a sudden sympathy for the British Royal family, who had to do this sort of thing as a career.

But I was equally sorry for the shop and a fungus art key-ring bulked in my pocket as we passed the signs for Fort Wainright – another of the US Army's Cold War redoubts – and tailed a single other car along the highway into Fairbanks.

To see Fairbanks was to take back what you had said about Anchorage. The clapboard houses were mainly painted fawn, rather than the bright white favoured in New England, so that the place looked like New Hampshire after a sandstorm. Make that a sandstorm and a riot, because downtown, even on a summer day, had a penumbra of neglect.

Even homogeneity was fading. There was no outward evidence of a production of *The Phantom of the Opera*. And, for the first time ever in America outside of New York taxis, I hit a language barrier.

At the reception desk of the Sophie Station Hotel, I replied to the standard insincere greeting with: 'I'd like to check in, please. I've got a reservation.'

'I'm sorry, sir?' said the clerk.

I blamed distraction or boredom for her incomprehension and repeated the sentence at the same speed.

'You want . . . er . . . Could you say it slower?'

I tried it at the pace of a wrecked record or an Englishman in Paris, with the only difference being that I and my confused interlocutor had been born speaking dialects of the same tongue. Perhaps it was more like being an Englishman in Glasgow.

Even at half-speed, the word-fog had not lifted for her. 'You stay there, sir. I'll get someone who's been down south a bit. See if they can understand you . . .'

This bilingual colleague, with bohemian experience of lower forty-eight, understood enough of what I said to let me in to the room I had reserved. It proved to be a suite, for the price of a single room in Anchorage, with a kitchen. The television gave you CNN, although with a lawnmower throb of interference running behind.

The viewer also had the problem of the noise outside. With Alaska's second largest airport and Fort Wainright both on the outskirts of a smallish town, it was often as if World War II and World War III were taking place simultaneously overhead. There was the drone and ticking of commuter propellor planes, which sounded like very big insects, and then the thunderclap of the latest Pentagon pets, which sound like very big storms. The Scout and Cobra helicopters made a noise more like beating rain. During summer, there were actual World War II planes, used by the fire department to water-blanket forest fires. Last decade, plane-spotters also had the chance of seeing Russian spy-planes, which would buzz over and be escorted back. When you bought property in Fairbanks, you didn't ask whether you were under the flight path.

I had grabbed some sightseeing leaflets in the lobby and after ruling out river-trips – Fairbanks had a long heritage of steamer boats – I phoned the number of something called Raven Tours, which promised escorted trips for individuals or parties. A man called Ralph not only understood my English perfectly but said he could show me most of Fairbanks in an afternoon.

Ralph was in his late fifties, with a droopy grey moustache and a soft voice. He was a native Minnesotan, but had graduated and married in San Francisco. He seemed to have been an early victim of the sixties: 'I was living in San Francisco, bust marriage, no work, all my friends killing themselves. I hadda get out. Came up here to work the summer as a firefighter thirty years ago . . .'

Alaskans seemed to divide between the missionaries, who with a sort of arrogant selflessness had believed they were needed in the new-found land, and the drifters, who had kept giving it another few months. Ralph was among the latter. He had worked as a teamster after oil was struck and then, more recently, had set up a mail-order book and antiques service. Recession had been cruellest to such indulgence trades, so Ralph had taken a business administration course, painted a raven on the side of his van, and distributed leaflets around the hotels. I was Raven Tours' second customer, in the first week of the season.

Ralph was a good example of the chameleon temperament – so how will I make money *today*? – which you needed to survive in a dodgy economy. I jeered as much as anyone else when British politicians and newspapers praised American can-do, but it was sometimes hard not to admire it.

'The fact is,' said Ralph, 'that Alaska's relatively wealthy. But 90 per cent of the economy is dependent on oil. And that's not going to last for ever. So where do we look now? Tourism is a renewable resource . . .'

On the drive out to the Alaska oil pipeline, Ralph taught me how to see variety in a mile of trees. A black spruce apparently had leaves of a much deeper green than a white spruce.

In the far distance was the local prison, which – in a *Playboy* feature written by two inmates who had tested a variety of jails – had just been voted the cushiest penitentiary in America. It was alleged that prisoners had eaten crab. To the Disgusteds of Fairbanks in the local paper, the prison authorities had replied that, by a quirk of the Alaskan food market, crab was somewhat cheaper than meat.

'But you wouldn't have much serious crime in a place like this?' I said to Ralph.

'Oh, more than you'd think. More than we had. Theft, mainly. But armed robbery now. It's sort of inevitable in a recession . . .'

We passed the local night-spot, the Howling Dog Saloon – which was a cow-shed with a blue roof and beer adverts nailed outside – and reached the fat steel centipede of the oil pipeline. While tourism elsewhere was relying on the high view (mountains, skyscrapers), Alaska was cannily offering the long view: its stretch of the two-thousand-three-hundred-mile Yukon River and of the eight-hundred-mile trans-state pipeline which was the trans-state lifeline.

I had expected it, as sightseeing, to be bathetic but, as a piece of capitalist arrogance, it was quite as impressive as the towering glass buildings – transparent cliffs – in financial districts. Six feet above the earth, it swept through the trees like a tin river or an anaconda's coffin. Heat-conductor rods flanked it at intervals on both sides, like pallbearers. Its exposed structure – in the summer, you could walk up and touch it – was a reminder that terrorism was the one twentieth-century barbarism never to have caught on in America. I said to Ralph that, in Britain, any such vulnerable industrial artery would be bombed within a week.

'Really? Oh, here, there's been a couple of guys aimed a shot at it. Bounced off. But that's not terrorism. You might say they were acting on behalf of their own heads . . .'

We drove away from the steel centipede and past the metal behemoths of the last remaining gold dredgers, no longer environmentally acceptable, which plough through the landscape, leaving a high spine of soil behind.

Driving back downtown, we passed a sustained spurt of churches which would have been thought to be flooding the piety market even in Middle America. There was the church of Jesus, a fawn-coloured barn; the First Baptist church, like a cheap ski chalet; tens of other huts and shacks and annexes raised at minutely differentiated doctrinal angles to heaven.

'An awful lot of churches,' I said.

'Too many,' said Ralph. 'Lotta fundamentalists up here. Because of it being the last state, and remote, and all that, Alaska's always attracted a lot of oddballs. Not to mention downright lunatics . . .'

I muttered something about the reported high suicide rate and expected to be rebuffed. Throughout the quiet world – particularly in New Zealand – I had brought some grim statistic about the nation into the conversation and it had been denied with a combination of foreigner contempt and country pride. If you referred to a suicide rate, you were told something about confusion caused by people accidentally cutting their wrists while trying to remove old watch-straps with scissors: a well-known local custom. Our relationships with our nations might be, on the whole, forced marriages but the loyalty, when challenged, was intense.

However, when I mentioned the reputed early death statistics in Alaska, Ralph said: 'I've read that. I've also heard that child abuse is above average here. Men hurting their wives too . . .'

'Why do you think that is . . . ?'

'Well, if it's true, then I'd have to say it was something to do with the life up here. You see, Alaska has a certain reputation. It is a place where men are men . . .'

His voice put a heavily distancing irony into the last three words. This continental footnote of extreme climates and terrain might indeed attract on-the-edge personalities but not all of the extremes were sinister. Ralph himself was a scholarly guy whose political sympathies were on the distant left of the Democratic Party.

I liked him, and rather hoped that the recession improved sufficiently for his antique and book service to pick up and leave Raven Tours as a hobby. For I doubted that even Ralph's energy could make Fairbanks a travellers' magnet. The problem with the idea that tourism might replace oil was that, up here, it was the oil – or, at least, the pipeline – which was the main tourist lure.

On the way back to the hotel, Ralph stopped and showed me some musk oxen in the pen of the university's animal research farm. Built like a truck with a brown hearth-rug thrown over it, the musk ox was perfectly adapted, in accumulation of hair and body fat, to survive Alaska's extremes.

Human evolution had been as thorough, although, apart from the typical beards and bellies, mental rather than physical. I thought of the various extra skins and layers which the state's human inhabitants had grown to help them cope: religiosity, masculinity, anarchism, eccentricity.

Then I left for what was – geographically, anyway – the most extreme place in Alaska: the edge territory.

The stewardess said: 'Welcome aboard Flight 43 to Barrow, with continuing service to Dead Horse . . .'

They certainly displayed a gruff and manly attitude to place names this late in the state. This plane alone was dropping in at one town named after a knackered nag and another – Barrow, my destination – which was named after either a handcart or a burial mound. I half expected to find, on the map in the airline magazine, conurbations called Shit and Shovel.

While the almost empty 737 taxied across the nearly deserted tarmac of what was called Fairbanks International Airport – so optimistic a description that there were probably landing arrangements for pigs – I reflected on how tough it must be for songwriters in Alaska. 'My kind of town, *Dead Horse* it is . . .' and '*Barrow, Barrow*, so bad they named it once' would always have lacked the catchiness of East Coast standards in the same fashion.

But the tourist is like a puppy who keeps friskily running up to a master who keeps kicking it. The next hotel, the next sunset, will be heaven. The names Barrow and Dead Horse already held for me a paradoxical romanticism. Admittedly, it was possible that I was suffering from the Alaskan traveller's equivalent of the prisoner's stir crazy. Maybe I had just seen too many trees: fir crazy. That morning, checking out of my Fairbanks hotel – the simultaneous translator having to be called in again for my query about the phone bill – I had watched a package group of US wrinklies saying their goodbyes (they were going home on different flights and coaches).

Amid the good wishes for imminent grandchildren or prostate operations – the dutifully remembered package chit-chat – one old couple went round saying: 'Enjoy the rest of your life!' Perhaps it was a standard tour-group platitude, but, spoken by septuagenarians, it held, for me, a terrible poignancy.

But perhaps I was just becoming a sissy. As an antidote, I read, on the hour-long flight north to Barrow, *AlaskaMen*, the world's most rugged magazine. A few years ago, an Anchorage couple, Susie and David Carter, had hit on another of the state's resources which might be exported as an alternative to oil. It was those other thick, rich geysers: the menfolk.

*AlaskaMen*, featuring photos and profiles of the local blokes, was aimed at single women, first across America and then around the lonely globe. The magazine's masthead creed growled: '*AlaskaMen* features an abundance of interesting and exciting men whose rugged individualism, spirit and vitality make them unique among men of the world.' In these politically correct times, the cited adjectives had the feel of a kind of agreed underground code for bit of rough or pre-feminist log-head.

It was a marital-misery responsibility waiver. Readers were being gently warned that, if you dangled a tea-towel hintingly in front of these men, they were likely to dry their dick on it and hand it back. Asked to change a diaper, they would probably mutter: 'Into what? I'm not a fuckin' magician.' These were outdoor men, which was to say that, if you were married to one, you would probably rapidly have decided that they ought to live outdoors. In short, it would probably not be a good idea to buy Gloria Steinem a subscription to *AlaskaMen* for Christmas.

In the edition I was reading, the cover guy was Ray, a twenty-five-year-old construction worker. Among Ray's hobbies were fishing, hunting, downhill-skiing, and drag racing, from which he liked to unwind by 'hot-tubbing . . . next to that special gal'. His gal of choice would be 'physically fit, active, non-smoking, and unafraid to try new things'. There may be those who wish to speculate about what the final element was code for.

Don, another offering, advised interested bodies: 'Life is a full-contact sport. Enjoy it!' The notes on Ron warned: 'Women who like cuddling beneath a stadium blanket and watching cars race should contact Ron.' Macho prose was generally accompanied by a macho pose. Michael was pictured playing with what appeared to be his pet wolf. Several of the suitors had elected to be photographed in snow storms, either to suggest hardiness or to disguise a serious dandruff problem.

Richer, and less prepossessing, men advertised in several successive issues. Occasionally, an exhibit – like Gary in the edition I read – won the accolade of having TAKEN stamped across his body in white capitals, the result of having been fixed up just before printing. The romantic pitches were interspersed with feature articles on general testosterone themes: 'The US Coast Guard', '50 Years of the Alaska Highway'. At the back of the magazine was a series of disclaimers: 'AlaskaMen does not assume any responsibility for investigating the background of any person depicted in the magazine in any form or manner, or for any form or purpose whatsoever, including but not limited to, health, wealth, emotional makeup, or how they treated their mothers.'

The publication appeared every two months but was keen to ensure that its connection with words beginning with the prefix 'bi' ended there. The matronly assistant at the Fairbanks Airport shop pursed her lips when I placed AlaskaMen on the counter and said: 'You know it's a magazine for women, sir?' I said that I'd seen a television documentary, and was buying one out of interest. Her look of disgruntlement seemed to mean: That's what all the queers say.

I was getting similar looks on the plane from the kind of outdoor types who might easily be featured in the magazine. I thought of explaining but then I decided: Bugger them.

I put aside the magazine when it was announced that we were

landing at Barrow, with continuing service to Dead Horse. The descent was one of nature's special effects. You dropped through heavy cloud and, after a lengthy period in clear air, were surprised to find another level of puffy white beneath, as if the cloud cover were false-bottomed. You started to go down through this layer too. But then there was a bump and you were on the ground. The second cloud was snow.

The arrival lounge would have been a lavatory at Kennedy. Outside were three battered taxis. Fodor's, with the diplomacy which seasoned travellers learned to read as innuendo, had said that everything of interest was within walking distance of the town. I wondered if I could walk to my hotel.

I leaned into one dusty, muddy vehicle. In the driver's seat was a thin hippy with hair and a moustache so long and wispy that you could have taken a dog for a walk with a snip of it.

'Excuse me,' I said. 'Is it worth getting a taxi to the Barrow Airport Inn?'

'Say again?' he said.

I tried the slow-motion approach, but, once more, I had the odd experience of lacking the right language in an Anglophone town. Finally, the driver said 'Airport Inn?' so often that I risked it and got in.

He ignited, accelerated, slowed, turned, braked. We had arrived at the Airport Inn.

'Four dollars,' he said.

'I didn't realize it was so close,' I muttered. He must suddenly have become tuned in to my accent, because he smiled.

The Airport Inn was neat and clean, like a decent big-city motel. The owner said the main doors locked at 10 p.m., but his tone told you that this might not be a tragedy for your social life. In the room, you still got CNN, but it was as if the newsreaders were having their teeth drilled while they were speaking.

I pulled on a second sweater, against the summer day, and walked downtown. I soon realized that the Airport Inn was the swankiest building in Barrow. I quickly decided that, on balance, the derivation of its name was more likely to be burial mound than handcart, but it was a close-run thing.

The main drag was a dirt track, its subsidiaries mud paths, with all the thoroughfares bordered by lake-sized summer puddles because of the absence of gutters. The utility buildings were usually of dusty tin, the domestic ones generally of dirty wood. I walked past one house which was a two-storey tin shed, extended by a wooden hut, the whole surrounded by punctured duck-boards. Outside was a holed boat and a battered caravan with broken windows. Antlers – apparently the trade of the occupant – were drying on the roof of the shed.

So Barrow looked like a shanty town. But, in two senses, this was another of Alaska's optical illusions. The first odd thing was that the grubbiness was confusingly finite. If you looked down the dirt track, you saw a blinding purity of whiteness. It was as if the frozen sea absolved the drabness but the incongruity was hard to get used to.

I saved the whiteness for later, staying on the tracks. A blue-painted shack had a hand-stencilled sign which read: Fashion Action. A felt-penned notice boasted: 'Rock 'n' Roll Shirts, Caps, Pins, Patches, Necklaces'. This was obviously the hot shop.

It was closed. There were few people out shopping. The problem about walking in Barrow, I discovered, was that every house had a large dog shackled to it. Not only did the hounds look uncomfortably vulpine, but each chain had a different reach. Therefore the trick was to walk down the middle of the track, guessing the length of the leash on the next few beasts and making sudden adjustments as the latest one lunged and slithered, growl-ing, towards you. It was like some souped-up game of hopscotch in which you put up your testicles as a stake.

Negotiating the last Baskerville alley – Barrow amounted to two separate groupings of houses and shops, a few blocks square, linked by a long mud road – I reached what would have been the beach in a resort where the sea was liquid. The guidebooks advised you to look out for traditional Eskimo skin-boats (*Umiaks*) but, in fact, what you saw lined up on the ice were mainly motorized snow-carts (*Yamahas*), those one-man Arctic transporters which looked like a cross between a big electric slipper and a dodgem car.

Even the purity of whiteness which had drawn the eye from the road, proved, on closer sight, to be misleading. The frozen water closest to the shore was disfigured by streaks of sewage and chemical discharge sealed by the cold, like chocolate and strawberry ice lollies you wouldn't want to lick. The effect added to the feeling, planted by the roads and homes, of an India on ice, Calcutta on the rocks. Except that the squalor was not the product of poverty. Almost everyone who lived in Barrow worked for the North Slope Borough Council, the Eskimo-dominated local government operation.

As North Slope's hegemony extended to the state's main oil fields at Prudhoe Bay – which brought it an annual income of $400 million – the council was generous to its employees. Doctors and teachers were also unusually renumerated, partly because their salaries included a sort of Dead Horse allowance, for relocating to such a harsh part. To the surprise of America's big city triumphalists, this wealthiness was common in Alaska, largely because of the oil business. In the 1992 US census, the state was ranked second in the table of highest mean incomes. The same survey found Alaska to have the highest proportion of high-school graduates in the USA. The latter statistic is perhaps attributable to the lack of distractions for the young.

The drabness of Barrow, then, was partly a matter of practicality. Why asphalt the roads when the freeze-and-thaw cycle would inevitably produce the bubbles and cracks of the tarmac acne which Alaskans called frost heaves? And if, for the same reason, your home and all your buildings must be raised on stilts and must withstand winter temperatures which looked like a spendthrift's bank statement, what was the merit in selecting materials for show?

There was also an element of cultural priority. The immigrant white Americans in Barrow would gesture to the byre-type housing around and tell you: 'The Eskimos don't care how they live.' But to say this was to assume shared aspirations. Eskimos, for whom residences were traditionally a matter of practicality, had never developed the heritage (or curse) of house-pride which was such a strong part of the modern industrial culture.

Here, in a fine rebuke to current Western values, a front door was something which allowed you to get into the house rather than a way of trumping the neighbours or hinting at what your income was. A wall was a windbreak rather than a canvas waiting to be pasted with expensive coloured paper. I could see the attractions of this attitude. Back in England, I had a house which had been on the market for two years and was still unwanted despite a 25 per cent reduction in the price. It had been purchased at the end of the Thatcher boom, which was now proving to have been cruelly illusory. People were being reminded that the word mortgage shared the same root as mortality and mortician.

But the Eskimos had not entirely disowned the white man's burdens. Barrow was now a dry town, because of difficulties caused by the locals' devotion to alcohol. Their thirst had reportedly equalled that of the Aborigines. People, though, were so relatively rich that they had beer and spirits flown up from Fairbanks. A buzz would go round the town when the word got out that, as it were, the illegal had landed.

Nor was drink the only big-town import. There was a danger in assuming that all the places in the quiet world – particularly its distant outposts – compensated for their lack of pace with absolute personal safety. In fact, Barrow's Department of Public Safety annual report – a document which began with the admirable sentiment 'Remember: safety doesn't happen by accident' – reported an average of nineteen adult rapes and eighteen child rapes in each of the previous three years. There were also an average of one hundred and forty thefts, although it was true that there had not been a single murder.

The previous week, however, there had been two deaths, from more ancient dangers. The residents had been out on the ice, pulling in a whale – two had been captured already, early in the season – when the rope snapped and crashed back across the ice like a motor-driven lash. Annie Bowen, a health worker of Eskimo descent, had been killed instantly. Daphne Perez, the wife of a senior doctor at the local hospital, had her arm torn off. She was briefly revived on the ice but, although they could not have known this, the locals pumping on her chest in resuscitation were flooding her blood out of the accidental aperture and making the revival self-defeating.

There was an expectation that men might die during whaling – although there had been no fatality for many years – but these were female by-standers, watching from the ice during what was technically the safest part of whaling: the hauling in to shore of the captured leviathan. In the modern world, there was a media style for sudden and terrible death – was dead on arrival at, the forty-eight-year-old mother of two, prayers were being said, tragic accident, a police spokesman said, an independent commission of inquiry – which provided a screen between the reader and reality.

On the front page of that week's *Barrow Sun*, the region's newspaper, the reaction was more elemental. Under the headline OUR JOY AND OUR GRIEF GOT ALL JUMBLED TOGETHER, editor Elise Sereni Patkotak contributed a page-one report which concluded: 'I like to think God sends many souls down to this Earth – some good, some bad, most of us solidly in the middle. I think He sent a few too many good souls out recently and got lonely. So He called two of his best back to Him to keep Him company, to keep Him smiling, to keep Him feeling like the human race was worth all His time and effort. I think Annie and Daphne were the two He chose.'

In the last decade of the twentieth century, most clergy in Europe, and even many in America, would have hesitated to preach a funeral sermon which so openly presented death as a blessing. The more favoured formula over the casket was one about humans not hoping to know God's purpose. But this eulogy for Annie and Daphne, it was worth remembering, came not even from a pulpit but from the front page of a local newspaper. If the plethora of worship structures in Peoria reminded you of the extent to which America was a Christian country, the report of the whaling tragedy in the *Barrow Sun* alerted you to the fact that, on the top edge of the nation, the piety – and explanation for pain and loss – was almost medieval.


My own feeling in Barrow was primeval. It was a desire to see the top-most piece of land in the USA: to stand at the geographical limit of this mad, maddening, vast but often claustrophobic, idealistic but two thirds ruined nation which was one of the century's most enthralling stories but also one of its most morbid. Or perhaps I just wanted to check that the monstrous entity really did stop somewhere, that it was not quietly accreting like a tumour, curling out across the Beaufort Sea to snare the Canadian islands and then Greenland.

I called a cab from the Airport Inn. All the firms listed in the directory had snow-joke names: Tundra Taxis, Arcticabs. I plumped for Tundra, where a female voice told me to be outside in five minutes. When I did, I saw, cruising towards me through the dust and dirt, a silver and black Cadillac.

The driver was a peroxide blonde in lilac knee-high boots, wearing sunglasses with lens as big as a beer mat and frames of green and purple stripes. The hands which rested on the wheel had lovingly grown fingernails the shape of shovels and varnished mauve.

'Welcome to the end of the world,' she said. Her name was Sheila.

We started out to Barrow Point – America's northern territorial climax – but it was soon clear that taxis in Barrow ran to their own rules. 'You're not in a rush to reach the Point?' said the driver. 'Because we might take a few calls on the way.'

The climate-driven problems of starting a car in the morning or keeping one on the road, and the cost of repairs in a place only sometimes accessible and then only by plane, meant that, in Barrow, taxis were a need rather than a treat. Sheila sometimes made $400 a night. So we would be half-way to Barrow Point and then the radio mike would crackle with a customer and we would double back to the hospital or a shop. One of the passengers from the hospital was an Eskimo woman who seemed grumpy and reluctant to get in and ignored Sheila's small-talk on the journey. When the woman got out, Sheila said: 'She wanted the other taxi company. That's native-run. They don't like the idea of a white woman doing well here. They tried to run me out of town.'

She fumbled in the glove compartment for some newspaper cuttings, which she handed over as corroboration for the story she now told, as we left, again, for the Point. Her name was Sheila Taranto. A forty-eight-year-old Californian, she had moved to Prudhoe Bay in 1979 to work for an oil company. Made redundant in 1986, she came to Barrow and bought Tundra Taxis from its Eskimo owner. She subsequently established a truck company, which specialized in rescuing vehicles dumped on the tundra by drivers who had partaken of one of the emergency bottle drops at the airport. She also had more romantic plans for a shop in Barrow selling silk flowers, the more usual bouquets and buttonholes being limited by topography.

In late 1991, she had discovered the existence of petitions, apparently written by officials of the North Slope Borough government, which accused her of prostitution and the smuggling of drugs and booze. The documents requested signatures from residents believing the allegations to be true. One of the petitions collected twenty native names in a few days. Rapidly applying the ways of lower forty-eight to this continental appendix, Taranto responded with a $1.1 million defamation suit. During preparation of evidence, it emerged that a gumshoe from Fairbanks had been employed by the council to pursue her. Claim and counter-claim were continuing, although the North Slope Borough had recently admitted its failure to find any evidence in support of its rumours.

'What do you think is behind it?'

'Look, this white woman comes here. And it's not that I'm exactly inconspicuous. They call me "Blondie". The women think I'm going to steal their men. The men are sexist as hell, anyway. And, suddenly, Blondie's running two businesses. Second, everybody here tries to start a cab firm, it seems the easy thing to do, but they go out of business like that. It's a tough fight. And here am I with the Cadillac, which gets me noticed, and I work nineteen hours a day if I have to. Also, the big thing you get in a small community is gossip, and, if it's a community where there are nearly three thousand Eskimos and a few white women, then who is the gossip going to be about? It's a classic small-town story . . .'

The Cadillac bumped to a halt. We had come to the end of America. Brown dirt shaded into the shining white of the paralysed sea. There was no statue or plaque, just four or five large lumps of ice which – if the first thing you had done on entering America was to order a drink – had a certain neatness, but otherwise seemed not enough. I thought there ought to be a statue of a large stone woman, in a green spiky hat, this time turned towards the shore, her inscription reading: 'Well, huddled masses, was it worth it?' And then I saw, lying on a the ground, a crushed Coca-Cola can. It was an accidental memorial, but not without aptness.

On the drive back, Sheila introduced a detour to show off her house. It stuck out like a rose on a rubbish dump. Objectively, it was a wooden hut, like the rest of the residences, but the planks were painted pink and there was a raised attic roof with a skylight. The whole house had a skirt of flower boxes. It was clear that the home – a monument to a quite different value system – would have done nothing to reduce Sheila's status as an enemy of the people.

Our next detour was for a chat with Roger, another continental immigrant, who was packing up that day to take his family back to their native Indianapolis. Roger was a labourer. There was a lot of work in Barrow but the Arctic cold was hard on his builder's injuries, his muscular souvenirs of old sites.

'Also, there's the politics,' said Roger. 'Too much politics. You can't just get on with it.'

Back in town, we passed the video store. 'A lot of people here, their VCRs keep them alive,' said Sheila. 'There's not a whole lot to do in the evenings.'

Her radio mike was filled with a pleading male voice. 'Please, Sheila, please, come and get me!' She laughed and told the voice she would get there when she could. This, it turned out, was a friend, arrested the previous night for drink–driving. He had been granted bail of $500 but didn't have it. He wanted Sheila to oblige. I wondered how this detail, once fed into the local defamation factory, would emerge in the campaign against the enemy of the people.


That night, I met another Barrow paradox. There were so many, in this town where it was still the norm that you shitted in a small bucket and bathed in a bigger one, but where people had money and VCRs.

And, in a restaurant that from the outside resembled an abandoned chicken shed, I ate one of the best Chinese meals I had ever had. The joint was called Sam & Lee's. The chef was Vietnamese. I thought of the bizarre translations which emigration brought: that you could be born in Vietnam and end up cooking on the brim of America.

In Sam & Lee's, you sat at a long table, with red plastic cloths, as if in a communal canteen. There were two other diners – American student backpackers – who had cautiously ordered the hamburger and fries which was listed at the bottom of the Szechuan specialities.

'Why you up here?' said one backpacker.

'Oh, I wanted to see the end of America.'

'So do I, man,' said the backpacker with some relish, and I wondered whether the remark was meant in an anarchist or geographical sense.

In the corner of the room, a television set was showing a documentary about the fall of Saigon, though whether this was a penitential gesture by the diners or a chastisory one by the proprietor was unclear. I ate lusciously plump prawn toasts and then chicken and cashew nuts, in which, unlike some big city eating experiences, neither element made you think you'd bitten a bullet.

A fortune cookie came with the check. It said: 'You will spend very many years in comfort and material wealth.' I wondered if all the fortune cookies manufactured for Barrow contained this motto, as a consolation.

At midnight, I sat outside and needed sunglasses to read a Canadian novel, which hymned the vibrancy of Winnipeg in Canada, where I would be in a week's time.

Next morning, I walked downtown at 11 a.m. and had the place to myself. Everybody was at worship. The bell tower of the Presbyterian church was still strung with loudspeakers from the memorial service for the women dead at whaling.

'"I am the Resurrection and the Life," saith the Lord,' boomed the pastor, his words floating across the dust and past the dog-wolves sleeping on the end of their chains and then out beyond the ice to nowhere.

# CHAPTER FIVE

# LOSING THE BAGGAGE

### Canada

Because my luggage failed to follow me from Alaska, I had an early introduction to the diligence, the application, the thoroughness, the abhorrence of hurry, the interest in tiny detail – for the moment we will call it nothing ruder – which is associated, in the popular imagination, with Canadians.

Some fifteen hours earlier in the day, at Barrow Airport – a medium-sized cupboard which was unlocked twenty minutes before each flight, thus abandoning to a frustrating skulk in the slush those who had observed international check-in conventions – the Eskimo bag-handler had attached the tags and cheerfully said: 'You won't see these again until Vancouver.' The safe traveller had the usual sinking premonition that only the first half of the sentence would turn out to be true and here I was, at a few minutes to midnight, left alone in the Vancouver International Airport baggage claim hangar staring forlornly at a carousel now empty except for a suspiciously corpse-shaped brown-paper package with FRAGILE stickers, which was intriguing but no substitute for my absent bag.

An Air Canada ground staffer, standing almost to attention and tautly uniformed despite the advanced hour, waited at a lectern marked HELP. I reported my bag missing and she hauled from a drawer a fat handful of forms. Half an hour later, I was beginning to reflect on what, if luggage got this fuss, you would have to fill in if you were applying for political asylum or quarantining a dog. Certainly, the attention Canada gave to a bag was dementedly devoted. If it was real leather, they needed the maiden name of the cow that had provided the hide. If it was a suitcase of tartan cloth, they wanted the name of the clan.

146

'Uh, what do you call your bag, sir?' said the valise police-woman. Even so close to America, I was surprised at the idea that people would be so attached to their holdalls as to be on first-name terms with them.

'I'm sorry?'

'I mean, what kind of bag would you say it was? Suitcase, rucksack, trunk, overnight bag, suitbag, carry-on, carry-all . . .'

Each of these portmanteau nouns had a code abbreviation which was to be entered in a box on the form. In fact, the missing item was one of those floppy canvas tube bags with a zip along its length.

'Oh, well, in England . . . well, in my house, we call it, well, a sausage bag . . .'

'A *sausage* bag, sir? Is that a manufacturer's description . . . ?'

And so, as midnight struck, we continued our philosophical symposium on the suitcase as the dead body in the brown paper bag edged around the carousel in the deserted terminal.


A trap of travelling is to see any incident in a distant place as typical. Even so, the methodical and ponderous cross-examination over my lost luggage – the absolute refusal to suggest that both of us might have better things to do at that time of night – confirmed my prejudice about the Canadian national character.

One option at this point would be to adopt a politically correct euphemism but perhaps it is better to come right out and say it: Canadians carry the burden of being widely regarded as the most boring people in the world. Perhaps this is partly because of the spreading of the poisoned testimony of their neighbours. The reputation of the most respectable person might be sullied by the accident of living next door to a malevolent gossip. And Canada undoubtedly suffered the geographical equivalent of a bigoted bitch across the garden fence.

Positioned beside the loudest and highest-energy culture in the world – and one which, furthermore, embodies an intolerance of other possibilities – the Canadians were always vulnerable to derision for their differences. The runt-culture, the gag national-ity, which the British made of the Irish and the Czechs of the

Poles and the Russians of the Lithuanians was provided, for Americans, by the Canadians. During a dull afternoon at the great New York publishers Knopf, the staff played a parlour game. The aim was to construct a catalogue for a new publishing house doomed to fail. The spoof lead title was: *Canada, Our Good Neighbour to the North*. This attitude had been remorselessly exported around the world along with all other things American.

And, certainly, in at least one way important to this visitor, the charge rang false. Canada had produced some of the most vivid and interesting English literature of the second half of the twentieth century. Margaret Atwood, Robertson Davies, Alice Munro, Brian Moore, and Mordecai Richler formed a team to give any Anglophone culture a tough game at five-a-side prose writing. And for the substitutes bench, we had Rohinton Mistry and Carol Shields. It could also be pointed out that Saul Bellow – a Nobel Laureate proudly claimed by literary snobs in the dismissive southern tribe – was Canadian-born. *The English Patient*, an intensely written and cunningly structured novel by Michael Ondaatje (Sri Lankan-born but Toronto-resident) had sustained me through the first three gruelling flights between Barrow and Vancouver.

And yet. Against this, I had to set the fact that the most boring man I had ever met *was* a Canadian. I understand the statistical fallacy here but the person in question was such an absolute crasher that the temptation to generalize from the particular becomes intense. An acquaintance of a friend, he was the world's leading authority on an aspect of art – Latvian gouache minimalism, let us say – in which nobody else on the globe had bothered to become interested.

Dogmatic without the possibility of contradiction, evangelistic without the hope of conversion, pedagogic without opportunity for instruction, he would, at parties, lecture for hour after hour on his speciality to glazed, panicked, sideways-edging faces. The stereotype was encouraged by the fact that he spoke very slowly – 'Now [*pause*] your [*drink*] mid- [*cough*] eighteenth- [*pause*] century [*breath*] gouache [*drink*] minimalists . . .' – and had a thick bottom lip, which he would suck, as carefully as if it were a vintage champagne lolly, as he considered his next thrust on the subject. Among terrified party-goers, encounters with him became known as the Saskatchewan Armlock.

Inevitably, as a journalist, I had met several more. Canadians had always owned British newspapers (the Lords Beaverbrook and Thomson, Conrad Black) but, in the eighties, they followed the Australians into the writing side. The chip of the Australians was intellectual – they were always learning Greek or quoting Chinese poetry – but the chip of the Canadians was cultural identity. They endlessly dropped their country or its history into conversation, as if their nationality was no more than a carapace of learned facts which would crack unless regularly aired. Their entire personality had become a defence of their birthplace.

A side-product of this neurotic historical awareness was an expectation that their detailed knowledge of the nation would be universally shared. In an earlier life, I had edited the copy of one of the many Canadian journalists on the make in England. His pieces would include governor-general jokes, which he clearly expected to be generally humorous. He would refer darkly in articles to the Constitutional Crisis of June 1971. After you had spent an hour ploughing through *Chronicle of the 20th Century* to match the reference to some forgotten controversy involving Edward Heath, you would tentatively challenge him and discover that he meant – of course – the Manitoba Income Tax Filibuster of that year.

I mention this because I think it is fair to declare the baggage which we bring to other countries. I declare it also to provide a context in which you can judge what seemed to me, on arrival in Canada, to be the uneasy shock of confirmation. After my midnight airport luggage seminar, I checked in to the Delta Place Hotel, where I fell into bed so sleepy that I woke next morning with a complimentary chocolate melting under my head, appreciating only then that the clean clothes, perfumes, squirts, and unguents of a man's morning toilet were all stranded in Alaska. The reception desk sold toothpaste and brush but, otherwise, I had to squeeze stale and sticky skin into clothes worn for a day and five flights, in order to shop for substitutes.

A crumpled skunk, I trudged down Howe, Richards, Seymour, and Robson streets – the pedestrian nature of the names (in honour of forgotten local politicians?) made a stroll round Vancouver a little like reading a school register – to buy an emergency shirt, stand-in knickers, and anti-perspirant. At the first glimpse of sleeves in a window, I went in. As I flicked through the shirt shelves searching for something big and cheap, an assistant – a beaming ginger-haired youth as big as a tree – appeared at my side.

'Need any help, sir?'

'No. No, thanks. The airline lost my luggage. I just need an emergency shirt until I know if it's coming back . . .'

'Well, yes, sir. But let's see if we can't choose you a shirt you'll want to wear again even if your luggage does turn up . . .'

A painful memory synapse pulsed somewhere in my brain. And soon I was caught in the Saskatchewan Armlock: 'Now . . . sir . . . this . . . one . . . is . . . a . . . superior . . . cheesecloth . . .' It was only a surprise that there was no denim imprinted with Latvian minimalist gouache. Eventually I rudely halted him in the middle of a monologue about the cooling qualities of cotton and dropped a big white cheap reduced-to-clear on the counter. He sold me underclothes without serious negotiation but, when I asked in the chemist's where the anti-perspirants were, the assistant said: 'Uh, what kind of skin do you have, sir?' and I began to think that maybe such pedantry and caution really were in the water.

Certainly, you had the sense of being surrounded by obsessively methodical people. At airports and in travel agents, they would spend half an hour questioning every aspect of a route on which they contemplated embarkation. Then, when the salesperson ripped the computerized itinerary from the printer and handed it over, they would study the piece of paper for several minutes – as if they were Gutenberg's assistant on the day of the first breakthrough – and suck their lips and say: 'Hey, what if I left on the 11th?'

But the baggage which affected the traveller in Canada was not just the received belief about national character. An additional problem could be the accumulation in the mind-library of other tourist sights. For example, Vancouver had the wide, clean feel which came to a city when it opened on to deep sea. Unlike Manhattan, it was a water-bordered city which had not forgotten its provenance. Downtown sits on a peninsula.

Accordingly, Vancouver boasted a harbour and bay, into which Captain Vancouver of the British Royal Navy had sailed in 1792, stayed for a couple of hours, and got the place named after him, the qualifications for civic immortalization clearly being somewhat looser in those days. Two centuries later, it remained a glorious expanse of water, made a mirror by the summer sun, bobbing with yachts and swirling with wind-surfers, reflecting an expensively and sensitively redeveloped pier complex: of shops, restaurants, boat clubs, walkways. It would have been completely startling. Unless, that is, you had seen Sydney.

Bizarrely, the identity problem was acknowledged by an act of what, depending on your charity, was homage, plagiarism, imitation, or subconscious influence. The Canada Place Pier – built for the city's turn at the global trade fair called an Expo in 1986 – was a handsome white construction with ten snowy gleaming shell-shapes on its roof. They looked like, well, to borrow a metaphor from an earlier chapter, they looked like a clutch of nuns with their heads bowed in prayer.

'It's designed to look like sails,' said my guide, a former colleague, a Canadian who had re-emigrated to Vancouver a few years previously.

'Well, yes. It's also designed to look like Sydney Opera House,' I replied.

'Mmmm. Perhaps there's a slight resemblance,' said my friend grudgingly. So I decided not to mention the big latticed suspension bridge which had just caught my eye.

But these optical allusions, as they might most politely be called, were symptomatic. There had always been a tentativeness about Vancouver's identity. In 1886, the entire young settlement burned down. It was almost wholly rebuilt within six years and perhaps it was this evidence of the rapidity of regeneration which had given the city, until recently, a cyclical rather than historical attitude to architecture. Only a late conservationist fuss saved the Pacific Railways Building, with its graceful colonnades, many of its sibling buildings having gone to the crusher in the rush to construct glass giraffes for business premises.

Even now, despite this shift from demolitionist instinct, the design dinosaurs huddled together around Hornby Street as if in an architectural zoo: the Gothic bulk of Christ Church cathedral was within singing distance of the old courthouse, with its domes, columns and stone lions, which had been preserved only because some relative municipal softy came up with the option of turning it into the Vancouver Art Gallery.

But, beyond this safe haven for weathered granite, the visual signatures were those of the anonymous modern city: the yellow Ms of McDonald's and teetering sheet-glass. It is interesting to consider the exact moment in the century at which the pragmatic justification for building high and thin in cities – the squeeze at sea level – gave way to the merely symbolic size and thrust of vertical architecture. Vancouver, for example, had starkly over-reached itself in that respect, with only 60 per cent of its tall walls occupied. The rest of the shining giants were forlornly 'to let' in a recession.

Vancouver's other modern icons included the BC Stadium, a sports venue where the roof is kept up by hot air (it became, inevitably, a popular political insult to suggest that an opponent should hold a rally there). There was also Sky Train, a computer-driven monorail which looped the city on a raised concrete doughnut. For the passenger, glancing at the empty cabin upfront, there was the eerie illusion of being in a ghost-driven locomotive.

I left this ghoulish tube and walked to two parts of town which, during the eleventh-hour fit of historical guilt, had been designated historical conservation areas: Gastown and Chinatown.

The Chinese had been the first modern exploiters of the region in the 1850s, drawn first by gold and then by fur. I reflected at this point on the role of animal-skin fashion in opening up Peoria and Alaska, my previous ports. For all its political and commercial pomp now, North America was built on haberdashery and millinery: a continent of coats and hats. But the contemporary Chinese community of Vancouver had absented themselves from the newest exploitation of the region: tourism. Visitors wandered among the bright red ducks and herbal pessaries but they were obeying tribal instinct rather than local invitation. In many shops, the only written or spoken language was Chinese.

The monolinguism of Chinatown was an accidentally ironic commentary on the rest of Vancouver and, indeed, of Canada. You noticed as soon as you landed *que demi de chaque signe publique était en français*. The half of every notice written in French was a result of legislation by the federal government designed to pacify Quebec, the increasingly French state which was flirting with removal from the Union.

In Vancouver, as in Toronto (the other main immigrant inlet), a large proportion of the population spoke another language. But it was almost never French, so the translations – or originations as Quebec preferred to think of them – hung uselessly around Vancouver as a monument to the sillinesses of political appeasement. It irritated businessmen – it was as logical as two-language signs in London as well as Cardiff, purely to make the Welsh feel better – and you could almost sense the whoop of joy when a manufacturer hit on a chance similarity of vocabulary so that, for example, makers of tourist baubles got away with 'souvenir of/ du Canada' on their labels.

In many shops and hotels, a third language had been added – Japanese – but this was from financial pragmatism rather than federal imposition. It was one of the late twentieth century's strange-but-trues that it was cheaper for keen Japanese golfers to fly to Australia or North America for a game than to pay out the tee fees back home. Money played strange tricks. In North America, the economy had become so weak that people could not afford to buy things. In Japan, the economy had recently become so strong that people could not afford to buy things.

But, without spending anything at all, I would soon be travelling to Tokyo on many different flights, captured as inadvertent background action on the numerous camcorders wielded by the Japanese, the lenses of which I crossed while strolling around Gastown. This was where Vancouver had begun, in 1867, with the arrival of Jack Deighton, who set up an inn. Deighton was known as 'Gassy' Jack, so the site of his hostelry evolved from Gassytown to Gastown.

According to all the guidebooks and tourist centres, Jack was called 'Gassy' because he was always talking. I am suspicious of this legend, given the tendency of municipal history to clean things up (I once attended an exhibition in Oak Park, Illinois, which detailed Ernest Hemingway's love for the quiet American suburb in which he was raised, despite all the evidence in his writing of hairy-chested contempt for it). I would guess that Jack Deighton suffered badly from flatulence and that the locals went around holding their noses and joking about the profligacy of his indigestion. Certainly, it would be a fitting little fable about tourism if the official translation of Gastown as a sort of Chat City in fact covered up its true past as a kind of Fart Town.

I met my ex-colleague, Julia, for lunch at a brasserie overlooking the beaches and English Bay, which were on the west side of the peninsula. There were several empty tables, so we chose one and sat down. A waitress came over. 'You've gotta wait to be seated,' she said, pointing to a sign which repeated this request in English and French. Grumpily, we stood up and went and waited by the notice. The same waitress joined us, looked around the restaurant with the care of a learner driver making their first right turn, and led us ceremonially to the table we'd come from.

'I'm afraid you get a bit of that in Canada,' said Julia.

After we ordered, she said: 'So, this book is about the most boring places in the world?'

I looked nervously around the restaurant, like an adulterer or spy. 'I'm not using the word boring,' I said. 'Quiet. Tranquil. Safe. Activity-challenged, differently interesting. Like, why do we throw the dice and end up with you here, and me in London, and not being shot at in Bosnia or starving in Somalia . . . ?'

'Right,' she said. 'Just, if you *were* writing about the most boring places in the world, you've come to the right country . . .'

'But, Julia, you emigrated here . . .'

'Yes. Sure, I know. But I grew up here and my parents live here. And I like being in a city with parks and beaches and sea. But I can understand why you guys might find it a bit dull . . .'

She had the North American tendency to address an individual as 'you guys', an alarming habit which made you wonder whether they had a serious sight problem or you had a serious weight one. I remembered that the most curious aspect of Julia's move to Vancouver had been that her husband was a war photographer, a noisy world expert who looked strangely naked if he wasn't in a flak jacket.

'What about Tom? Doesn't he find it a bit of . . . a contrast . . . ?'

'Oh, sure. He says the local newspapers are visually impaired. But he likes the outdoor life and, well, it's a great place to bring up a kid . . .'

For most of us, home was a compromise. After lunch, Julia drove me around Vancouver, in a charming but steely piece of surreptitious PR, like Cousin Claire's in Timaru. Vancouver's peninsula was shaped like a marble bust, so that downtown was the chest and neck. Atop it was a fat head with a bulbous nose and a long piece of snot hanging down from it. All of that was Stanley Park, a thousand acres of grass and flowers. I remembered a line from a guidebook: 'Many people come here just to see the hollow tree of Stanley Park . . .'

Julia couldn't find the empty trunk – 'I never heard of it. Are you sure you guys aren't thinking of somewhere else . . . ?' – but we passed the 9 O'Clock gun. Apparently (unless this was just some yarn spun to credulous visiting travel writers), people gathered here each day at 21.00 hours merely to hear an old cannon going off. Given the lack of variety in either timing or spectacle, this may say something about the entertainment possibilities of Vancouver. We drove up to Prospect Point, from where you could see the regimental line of thin uprights, which were the yacht masts in the harbour, and the equally strict parade of more substantial rods which were the tower blocks. On the docks, the vast heaps of sulphur were bright as buttercups.

Heading back downtown, we passed the Westin Hotel, where Howard Hughes reportedly hermited away several of his silent years. Suddenly, I understood the trick of his enforced seclusion. He had taken himself to places where there would be almost no other temptation to go outside. But then I remembered the reclusive billionaire's obsession with infection, and I understood another reason why he might have come there. It was a word you might easily use about Vancouver. Germless.

Back at the hotel, my lost sausage bag was in the room. The hotel had placed another small chocolate on top of it in consolation. I was increasingly astonished by this belief of the world's better hotels that people who could afford to pay their room rate were so sensorily deprived that they would go into a swoon for a sweet. It seemed to me the hotelier's equivalent of the male belief that sex was the proper return courtesy for women bought supper.

I also felt by this stage that, frankly, the Vancouver Delta Place could have better spent the money on elevators than confectionery. Raised astonishingly tall but incredibly thin – the Jerry Hall school of hotel design – the place could only accommodate two elevators within its wasp-waist. The result was that – allowing for the usual hotel phenomenon of septuagenarians suddenly spotting a former high-school class-mate in the corridor just as they were about to press 'Down' and wedging a case in the doors while they caught up for an hour or two – it took fifteen minutes to ascend or descend fifteen floors.

All right, this form of travel writing might have been short on poisonous snakes and hostile tribes, but it delivered its own terrors. Room Service Rage was, in its own way, as ruinous a malady as Dengue Fever. I stalked round the room, squashing underfoot another chocolate which had presumably bounced off the bed when I threw my bag on it, until I saw, on the desk, a manila envelope, which asked, in brown curlicue script: 'Please tell us what you think . . .' It was one of those four-page questionnaires which requested you, as 'one of our valued guests', to grade everything from the courtesy of the check-in staff to the orgasm-count of the cable porn movies in small square boxes graded down from Very Good to Poor.

I built a neat fence of ticks down the right side of the pages in the Poor column – even on the one about light fittings, a subject on which I had never previously held an opinion, I nearly went through the paper – until, wild-eyed, I chanced on the virgin expanse of manila headed: 'Additional Comments.' With recurrent recourse to that section of English vocabulary utilizing the prefix dis-, I wrote a brief and bilious dissertation on the subject of elevators which made *A Modest Proposal* look like a thank-you note.

Unfortunately, there was a flaw in this procedure, which was that, as you seethed on to the sheet, you were secretly thinking:

*If I sound really angry, maybe they'll give me a voucher for a free stay.*
But I fear that hotel complaints staff are wise to this paradox.
Clerk A: 'Ooh, read this one. Temper, temper . . .' Clerk B: 'I
expect he wants a free stay . . .' Clerk A: 'A free stay where . . . ?'
Clerk B: 'In this hotel he reckons is so cruddy . . .' Clerk A: 'Let's
not torture him then, eh?'

But, as therapy, it was excellent. Purged, I took a bottle of
beer, at the usual price of a crate, from the fridge and read the
Vancouver papers. In Sydney, Alan Bond, tycoon hero of the
first wave of Aussification, had got two years in jail for fraud. A
brief news agency item from Anchorage revealed that Mark Air,
the native airline on which I had flown from Barrow to Seattle,
had filed for Chapter 11 bankruptcy protection.

It was also reported from America that Dan Quayle's rehabilitation through his moral crusade had been undone by an unfortunate reversion to media type. Visiting a school, the Vice-President
had taken part in a photo-opportunity spelling lesson. Asked to
write 'potato', a small boy had chalked it up correctly on the
board when the deputy commander-in-chief had prompted him
to 'add a little something'. Scowlingly, he had affixed an e,
although it was clear that he had only done so from fear of being
shot by the secret service if he declined.

Quayle was now once more a national laughing stock. He had
made exactly the wrong mistake. In my experience of letters sent
to newspapers, moral intolerance and pedantry came from the
same circuit of the brain. People who wrote you twenty-page
rants about abortion and the raw tide of sewage through their
living rooms from the TV screen were precisely those who
(whom?) chided you over your use of who and whom. Still, if
this episode ended for ever Quayle's coveting of the Oval Office,
he might, I thought, have a future in tourism. It was the only
business in which he would get high marks for writing Olde
Potatoe Shoppe.

I switched on the television. On the channel I chose at random
from a USA-like range, there were three successive thirty-minute
news bulletins, their order providing an oblique commentary on
Canada's attitude to the beast which growled across its southern
border. In the early position, screened when people were finishing
work or travelling home, was Canadian news. It was followed

by, in the prestige time-slot, *NBC Nightly News with Tom Brokaw*, recorded earlier from New York, and then by local USA news, from a station in Seattle. It was either cultural humility or submissiveness, the same difficulty of distinctiveness which was represented by the architectural plagiarisms of the place.

Another example, to the outsider, was the attitude of the ruling Conservative government of Brian Mulroney. As far as I could tell from American television, on my visits there, he was always nipping across the border to shake hands with George Bush. His demeanour in these pictures was one of such awe and devotion that you could see why some Canadians believed that Mulroney was a double agent, George Bush's placeman in the North. Mulroney had even, bizarrely for a national leader, made a speech which asked: 'What's special about Canada? . . . We do not have a very good track record . . . what the hell makes us so special?' Yet, just that week, the federal government had been forced to start collecting tax on spirits, beer, wine, and tobacco at the boundaries shared between the nations. It was far cheaper for Canadians to drive down to their nearest town in the USA to stock up.

In its few genuinely national news programmes on the television that night, however, it was Canada's relationship with its old dominator and master which was under pressure. Only three months after an announcement of the separation of the Duke and Duchess of York ('Fergie' and 'Andy' to the tabloids), a book published in Britain – *Diana: Her True Story* by Andrew Morton – presented the marriage of the Prince and Princess of Wales ('Chas' and 'Di' to the small, square press) as a passionless sham, a story which Strindberg and Neil Simon might have written together. The royal couple – always an odd couple by virtue of age gap and intellectual interests – were reportedly no longer coupling. The princess was said to be a bulimic – a feast-then-vomit eater – and to have attempted suicide on several occasions. Her husband was reported to be in the thrall of a former girlfriend, Camilla Parker-Bowles, a horsy woman nearer his age. She and Charles were alleged to have employed the names of love 'Fred' and 'Gladys', while exchanging gifts and phone calls.

The US television networks covered the subject exuberantly, treating the British Royals as they do – and not without reason, given the projection of the defenders of the realm since the advent of Diana – as pop stars manqué. For them, the logical outcome of the story would have been not a British Republic but the opening of the Princess of Wales Bulimia Clinic. The Canadian press were more circumspect, whether from Commonwealth respect or a lingering fear that its Governor-General, Her Majesty's represent-ative, though only a figurehead, might deliver some kind of figurehead-butt. Their reporting of the story was anguished and mildly disapproving, stiffly remarking that the treatment and perception of the monarchy had come a long way since the days of Queen Victoria.

I released an internal yippee. This was one of those serendipi-ties of itinerary that travel writers crave. In the morning, I was going to Victoria, British Columbia, an island which was a shrine to the old sour-face. I was planning to take tea at the Empress Hotel.


'Are you for the flying cat, sir?' The question had a certain Lewis Carroll quality to the bleary traveller just after dawn. It didn't help that, by this stage of the trip, I was on drugs, not from any particular homage to the Dr Hunter S. Thompson school of travel writing but because of some air-conditioning bug which had set in overnight at the hotel.

I feverishly established that the flying cat was the wave-cutter trimaran that carried passengers between mainland Vancouver and Victoria. I had booked on the 6.30 a.m. I was a little late, because of having foolishly calculated that, so early in the morning, the snail elevators of the Delta Place would need only five minutes to drop eighteen floors. Infuriated by the disproval of this naïve belief, and dripping sweat from the bug, I won a gratifying wince of fear from the night clerk as I dementedly pressed into his hand the manila questionnaire containing my Denunciation upon the Elevators.

Calculating that I could still make the first flying cat, I dragged my bags towards the departure gate. I looked up. The clock above the dock digitally clicked to: 6:35. The flying cat no longer sat on the mat. I upended my sausage bag into a shooting stick and slumped on it against a wall, full of the double self-pity of the bad traveller and the chronic hypochondriac. So this was it. I would die in Vancouver and lie there for days, before anyone noticed that I was in a different condition from the rest of the population. Through smeared eyes, I happened to catch sight of the dock clock again. It now read: 5:41. I watched the numbers falling. 5:24, 5:23, 5:22. Time was running backwards. I wondered if it could be some chronological equivalent of an eclipse. Then, peering hard, my myopic, sweaty eyes made out a red line of neon writing above the sign. TIME UNTIL DEPARTURE, it said. I had five minutes left.

As the flying cat purred through the water, I caught up on the latest Royal revelations in the papers. I had managed to buy English and American ones, so got the full sleaze. Charles had more or less gone to his wedding night with his virgin princess wearing Fred and Gladys cufflinks. Among the first signs of Princess Diana's bulimia, it was claimed, had been her fainting at the Expo '86 exhibition at Vancouver. Synchronicity. I looked out of the flying cat and saw the Canada Place Pier, site of her swoon, now a station of the cross for Royal gossipers, fading into the distance.

The island of Victoria, an icon for monarchists, was still two hours away. As the loftier papers pointed out, even the widow Victoria had retained the services of a lover, John Brown, so that the latest Royal revelations belonged more properly in a history of the media than of the monarchy. The Queen of England had once ruled the world; now she was ruled by the *News of the World*. Even so, there was a poignancy in travelling through the Commonwealth to a monument to the Empire on a day when Britain seemed to have taken another twitch towards becoming a Republic or, at least, when Royalty had taken a further step away from authority and towards comedy.

There were a lot of school parties on the flying cat and the cabin was alive with the squeak of Nintendo machines and the shriek of teachers admonishing shrill and wriggly charges with improbable names: 'Madigan and Chloria, *stop* shouting!' But, with the help of the drugs, I was out of it until we reached Victoria.

\*

When I woke, I might have been asleep for forty years. Victoria was fifties, perhaps even thirties, Britain pickled. Cucumber sandwiches and Earl Grey tea were enthusiastically advertised at waterfront hotels with shaved lawns and oak panelling. Red double-decker buses purred the streets. There was the occasionally guilty nod at another inheritance – the Victoria Real Estate Society had funded a totem pole – but the first tourist attraction you saw after leaving the boat was the Royal London Wax Museum. Its first display as you went in was of the British Royal Family.

The waxworks were so bad that, if you had wanted an image of the Queen, you would have done better to buy a stamp. Elizabeth II was fawningly portrayed as young and smooth-skinned, but the Duke of Edinburgh mannequin was realistically wrinkled, so that the uninformed would have assumed that the Duke was a serial husband, currently established with a piece of jailbait.

However, the Prince of Wales, who actually had more or less married jailbait, was represented by a model of his younger self, so that he and his bride seemed to be of the same generation. The Princess of Wales, famous for having put the Di into diet, was unrecognizably busty, despite having, as we now knew, fainted from lack of nourishment just across the water at Expo '86. However, as the model of the late-seventies Elvis was pleasantly svelte, we could take it that wishful waxworks were the rule of the house.

The images were wrong, though, in more ways than one. The Prince and Princess of Wales were standing almost cosily close. Beside the podium was a kilted attendant, who I had at first thought was a waxwork but turned out to be merely a Canadian.

'What do you do when the marriages break up?' I asked.

'Right. It's a problem. You see Captain Mark Phillips and Princess Anne over there . . .'

I had wondered why Virgil from *Thunderbirds* sported a British Army uniform and why Lynda 'Wonderwoman' Carter wore a tiara.

'Well,' the attendant explained, 'Captain Phillips used to be gazing into the Princess's eyes. But, when they separated, we turned his back on her . . .'

It was true. The mannequins' death-mask grins now pointed in opposite directions.

'Luckily,' the attendant continued, 'we never for some reason got round to Fergie and Andy. We don't have Prince Edward either . . .'

'Eeeee, well, there's another story . . .' said another English visitor – a tubby little Geordie – who had been listening to the conversation. He was referring to another bit of the flotsam of Royal gossip which the New Elizabethans now learned in the nursery. The Geordie, who was with a similarly small round wife, turned to me and said: 'What about all this, then? We've heard some of the news, like. But are they separated, like?'

I gave a lurid précis of the papers I had read. Fred and Gladys. Vomiting. Several suicide attempts, including a bizarre one involving a lemon peeler rubbed across the wrists.

'Suicide with a lemon peeler?' gasped Mrs Geordie.

'Yes, well, perhaps you'd have to call that one more of a cry for help,' I conceded. I resumed the summary. Fall down stairs while pregnant. Cufflinks from Gladys.

'I wonder what she'd have made of it,' said the attendant, jerking her thumb at a waxwork further on in the exhibition. I wondered for a moment why the opinion of Roseanne Barr on this topic should be thought interesting, then I noticed the lace handkerchief on Roseanne's head and realized that this was Queen Victoria.

'Well, of course, she used to do it with her ghillie,' I said.

'Her what?' asked the attendant.

'Sort of a gamekeeper,' I said.

'Nivver! Did she really, like?' gasped Mrs Geordie, and she looked so shocked that I felt guilty and added: 'After Albert died.'

'And look at Henry VIII,' added the attendant. 'He seemed to get away with it . . .'

'Well, of course, he could rely on the press a bit more,' I said. A sudden fantasy came to me of a Tudor tabloid. HENRY AND ANNE RIFT. Or: HEADS WILL ROLL, PALACE SAYS. In blurred, snatched black and white charcoal, Catherine Parr, rumoured to be the New Woman in the King's life, would dash to her horse, hands raised to her face, through a scrum of engravers. Front page teaser

boxes would promise: Why King Must Diet – By Our Doctor –
p.6. Thomas More – the Voice of Reason – p.7. Holbein Cartoon
– p.8.

'Eeeee, well, happens in the best of families these days,' Mr
Geordie was saying. 'We had a son. Married a Catholic even.
Divorced now . . .'

'And 'im,' said Mrs Geordie, pointing at her husband. ''E
'ad four brothers. Three of them are split up. It's everywhere
nowadays . . .'

Shaking our heads in moral dismay, we walked on. In the US
Presidents' section, Richard Nixon looked like Jack Nicholson in
*The Shining*. But few of the other mannequins were so psycho-
logically accurate. Cleopatra, pert pink plaster nipples on display
as she bathed in real water, eerily resembled Cher. Her asp looked
like a *bratwurst*.

As I left, Mr and Mrs Geordie were at the Famous Historical
Figures display.

'Eeee, Napoleon were bigger than that,' said Mrs Geordie.

'No, he were a little lad, allus were,' her husband insisted.

As I walked across to the Empress Hotel, I wondered what
the future might be for Queen Victoria's descendants, if the
present bedroom farces proved to be a trend rather than an
interlude. Relatively quiet foreign exile – like the Duke of
Windsor and his American wife – seemed a solution from a world
of different media and commercial attitudes. A more appropriate
post-monarchy existence would surely be as a kind of theme park.
If you could get people to pay dollars to see the vaguely
approximate models in the Victoria waxworks, then what might
be the exploitative possibilities of the originals?

I imagined, somewhere in the United Kingdom, possibly in
the extensive grounds of one of the Royal palaces, a tourist
development called House of Windsor, that name to be trade-
marked. The members of the Royal Family would cut ribbons
and make speeches, even perhaps open a parliament of hired
extras; in other words, behave much as they did now, but be
funded not from the public purse but from the revenue produced
by those who paid to view them. In cases of severe marital
disagreement, one partner might be represented by a hologram or
model.

It was a perfect solution. After all, monarchists in Britain always deflected republican sentiment with the platitude that the Royals were good for tourism. Well, Disneyland and Disneyworld contributed a lot of dollars to the USA, but there was no suggestion that, every time the President wanted to pass legislation, he took the bill to Mickey Mouse for signature. After all, if British people and Canadian Anglophiles were prepared to stay in a hotel merely because it was called the Empress and adorned itself with Victoriana, then what might be the attractions of a hotel called the Elizabeth II, in which Elizabeth II actually lived, or a pub called the Duchess of York, in which the real holder of that title worked tables?

The Empress Hotel (est. 1908) was a once-handsome building which fussiness had made ugly. Essentially an imposing pink-brick oblong between two towers, it had been remorselessly touched up with green-lead cupolas, turrets, pyramids, jutting A-shaped attics, round white lamps like pickled onions, and a moustache and sideburns of thick ivy. Out of the Empress's backside, like a giant turd, protruded the long, glass, green-roofed tube of the Queen Victoria Conference Centre.

Most of the additions were taste-for-tourists, a Canadian's approximation of English tradition. In the lounges, Real English Afternoon Tea was served in relays, at half-hour intervals after lunchtime. There was also a Bengal Lounge, where, if you tipped them enough, they would probably drag a carcass across the carpet and let you pretend you had bagged it.

Downstairs, there was an exhibition of hotel memorabilia. A brochure from the 1930s boasted that it was 'tempered by the Japan current' and that 'This hostelry is the scene of an Olde English Yuletide.' I was beginning to see this as one of the most crucial rules for survival in the quiet world. If the spelling started getting like Dan Quayle's, get out.

Victoria was the place where Canadians came to die. It was a prime retirement venue, the continent's outcrop for the incontinent. Apart from that, it was a good example of a place which now existed mainly to attract travellers. It understood the two basic techniques of tourism: recreate the visitors' past and sentimentalize your own. So, in one corner of Victoria, you found Anne Hathaway's cottage, the thatched house which had, presumably, been used by the playwright William Shakespeare and his wife on their regular holidays in Canada.

This sentimental lie was part of something called an English Village Complex, including a variety of places for which Dan Quayle had painted the signs, such as the Olde England Inn and the Picadilly Shoppe, where linens were sold. The complex was full of English visitors, for whom this was the best form of abroad: another England, though not the squalid one of now but of the innocent past.

My project would end in the locations of the phenomenon of static travel, where the illusion of long-distance journeys was given on a single site in the quiet world. But Victoria was, for those from the United Kingdom and for expatriates, a form of static travel; like, for another type of tourist, the pubs in Spanish resort towns where paella and Rioja were never found, but only fish and chips and bitter.

And, in the other trick you had to work for visitors, Canada came sugar-wrapped as well. You could buy the maple leaf in milk chocolate, dark and white; in shortbread, barley sugar, syrup, marzipan, air-dried beef, and smoked salmon. You could get Mounties in all the same substances – as well as in the form of dolls and teddy bears – and mooses, in all of these species of food and toy. Souvenirs of/du Canada.

In the evening, before catching the last flying cat back, I had a drink at the Empress Hotel. The contemporary reason for the Anglophilia of Victoria was tourism. The historical explanation was that Vancouver and Vancouver Island had been built up by the British as a bulwark against American encroachment on the territory. And perhaps now, beyond the tourism, those old Canadians living here, proud citizens of the Commonwealth, promoted the ways of the mother country as a bulwark of their own against American cultural imperialism. The question which every Canadian had to answer was what attitude to adopt to the beast beneath.

You could tell the extent to which the Victorians of British Columbia insisted on resisting Americanization by the fact that, at the Empress, your drink came with only two lumps of ice.

★

In Peoria and Normal, I had idly wondered if there might be such a thing as Middle Canada. Because of the parallel presentation of the two North American nations, so that border states shared virtually the same terrain, it seemed not impossible that there might be. But, if Middle America was a duller version of America, then surely, in Middle Canada, you would just hear a gentle snoring, a human answer to cicadas, as you landed at the airport.

I had selected Winnipeg for this experiment. The place had a certain international renown as shorthand for Canadian drabness. Staggering away from an encounter at a London drinks party with the aforementioned expert on Latvian gouache minimalism, people would often hiss: 'He's probably regarded as quite exciting in *Winnipeg*.' American journalists, talking of their ambitions to be posted to Moscow or the White House, would say: 'But the way this story's going, I'll be lucky if they let me run the *Winnipeg* desk.' It was somehow just one of those place-names that sounded as if it might be Indian for shit-hole.

However, my foreboding was less than it had been. In Barrow, Alaska, as reported, I had read *The Republic of Love* by the Canadian novelist Carol Shields. Improbable as the idea might seem, the book, a comedy about the possibility of romantic love in the twentieth century, was the Great Winnipeg Novel. At the start of the book, admittedly, geographical baggage did sometimes distract from the author's lyrical descriptions. The sentence about 'the sunroom of the large three-storey stucco house in an old residential section of *Winnipeg*' (my italics) is somehow forced, on that final word, to return the interest payments it has taken from the reader. However, by the last page, I had been convinced that the city was, indeed, a teeming cosmopolis, a slightly more charming Chicago.

Well, after two days in Winnipeg, what I thought was that Carol Shields ought to get the fucking Nobel Prize for fiction for her achievement in writing up a paper Winnipeg so conspicuously more exciting than the bricks and mortar one. It was clear within hours that there was, indeed, a Middle Canada, a model of the American phenomenon, though smaller in scale in everything including fascination. If Peoria had been like New York run by the Mormons, Winnipeg was like Peoria run by the Salvation Army.

I spent the night at the Downtowner Inn, a motel intriguingly reminiscent of a mobile home. It was one of those establishments in which, as protection against theft or absentmindedness, the key was attached to a vast slab of aluminium, so cumbersome that only guests with a tin leg or a permanent erection could plausibly forget they had it in their pocket. It had occurred to me during my journey that there was potential for a set of internationally comprehensible pictograms designating hotel comfort. Cheap-and-clean would be represented by a drawing of the kind of key jailers could use in an emergency as a temporary ball-and-chain. The top end would use an etching of a chocolate on a pillow.

'Brings you to Winnipeg?' asked the clerk, as I hauled my key on to the desk on the first morning.

'Oh, I'm just trying to see as much of Canada as I can . . .' The second part of that sentence – *in as short a time as possible* – was spoken only in my head.

'Really?' he replied.

'Is there anything in particular I should look at here?' I asked.

'Well, there's a really neat mall on the next block,' he offered. 'A left and a right out of here, you can't miss it . . .'


The Portage Place mall was an aircraft hangar done out with fountains, marble floors, and elevators. Entering through a random door, the first store I saw was called 'Den For Men'. A testosterone shop, it sold beard trimmers, moustache clippers, prick-and-ball soaps, testicle chocolates, vagina ashtrays, antique revolvers, cigars, golf-ball holders, bastardizations of Scrabble in which players made expletives from their letters, and darts and bar accessories, including lewd optics in which the drink emerged from between a woman's legs.

This ballsy emporium was a clue that Winnipeg was not a place for political correctness, the confirmation being that not a single sign, in Den For Men or elsewhere in the mall, was translated into French. (There was a French sector of Winnipeg, in which the language was used, but there were also numerous other immigrant enclaves. It was more a place of parallel separatisms than multi-culturalism. Winnipeggers bought their cars, for example, in the Mennonite sector, this people having a reputation for integrity.)

Next, I did the mall's two bookstores. Here, as in the States, the 'New Books' table was laden with eleventh-hour texts. Scanning the apocalyptic volumes, I bought *The Betrayal of Canada* by Mel Hurtig, enticed by its ripely paranoid first line: 'Canada is disintegrating. The work and dreams of generations of Canadians are being destroyed . . .' I added to it *The Will of a Nation: Awakening the Canadian Spirit* by George Radwanski and Julia Luttrell, drawn by its wild-eyed title. My last purchase was less of a blind gamble: Mordecai Richler's *Oh Canada! Oh Quebec!: Requiem for a Divided Country*, an extract from which I had read in an American magazine.

I left the mall, and soon missed the quenching accidental spit of the numerous fountains. It was so hot that day that the precautionary Factor 45 sun cream I always wore on my summer travels was soon brimming in my eyes as acrid tears. At one point, I swallowed and the two sides of my dry throat scraped, like a car wheel catching a kerb. Admittedly, I was a traveller from a pale, damp nation. But locals too were telling each other how very hot it was and, crucially, discussing what the weather meant, environmentally. Thus they voiced the other recurrent concern, apart from sex and politics, of these strange years: that the world had turned on us. One of the by-products of the pre-millennial terror in the First World was that the universal standard pleasantry of discussing the weather had ceased to be merely a platitude.

The sun made shop glass flash like headlamps. Taking notes, my pen melted. An alien who had landed at that moment would have thought that humans fed through a strange conical or tubular organ, because a cool can or cone was pressed to every pair of lips. Refreshed myself by icy fizz, I trudged along a fat, leafy avenue to the Legislative Building. You knew you were in the Commonwealth when all the important buildings looked vaguely like the British Museum. The national architecture had been adopted along with British legislative practice as a kind of talisman.

The Legislative Building, office of Manitoba's premier, and seat of the state parliament, was another behemoth's wedding cake in local stone, with chiselled lions watching over teetering steps. The boldly swollen dome was topped by the symbol of Manitoba. Called, according to my guidebooks, Golden Boy, he was a statue clasping a sheaf of wheat under one arm and a flaming torch in his hand. The only thing which heat and grain made together was bread, but headier symbolism was apparently intended: a mystical invocation of Manitoba's agricultural past and its burning quest for technological progress.

The building also housed the Winnipeg tourist information centre, where I now sought a combination of inspiration and shelter from the heat. There were stacks of pamphlets and a couple of computer terminals, their screens offering menus of possible local excitements.

'You all right there?' asked a big-faced youth, whose features were as close to those of a moose as you could get while remaining human. There was often this solidity about Middle Canadian faces, which may or may not have been a mirror of their souls.

'I was, er, looking for some sight-seeing ideas . . .'

'Well, now. This building itself is interesting . . .'

'Yes. But I've sort of done this . . .'

'I guess you have. Do you like theatre . . . ?'

'Yes. A lot . . .'

'Well, there's a new Lloyd-Webber. Have you seen *Pha* . . . ?'

'Yes. Well, no, but I don't . . .'

'Pity. That's kind of the big show in town. Have you seen the house of Canada's first prime minister . . . ?'

I almost fell into that facetious school response *Why? What's happened to it?* but, I merely said, 'No. Is it . . . ?'

'It's neat. The guides wear historical costumes . . .'

'Really?'

'Yeah. Hey, hold a minute. What day is it?'

'Er, Monday . . .'

'I'm sorry. The first prime minister's house is closed on Mondays. So is the Winnipeg Art Gallery, I think, let me check. Yes. That's another place you might have gone . . .'

*And seen the Latvian Gouache Minimalist gallery*, my subconscious grumbled. 'I suppose the message is: don't come to Winnipeg on a Monday?' I said.

'That's right, sir,' grinned the moose. 'But you could always walk around a while. It's a great day out there . . . Oh, the city also has the windiest intersection in the world . . . that's on Portage and Main. I can show you on a map . . .' Reaching for a free Winnipeg street-plan, he suddenly looked glum. 'But I guess it might not be very windy on a day like this . . .'

So I walked around. As elsewhere in Canada, the buildings spoke more of facility than history. In their preponderance of young constructions, Canada's cities sometimes reminded you of Japan's, although what had been done there by the atom bomb had been achieved here by town-planners. Apart from the British tinge of the civic buildings – and the thick grey tradition of the preserved Bank of Montreal site – the predominant influence was American. There were malls and skyscrapers downtown; ranks of used-car lots as you went east to Portage Avenue towards the river, and a west side on which beggars played the entrances of shabby thrift stores.

Traipsing back across the city, I bought a frozen yoghurt from one of the street stalls cleverly exploiting the greenhouse effect, and slumped under a tree with my set of cry-the-beloved-country books about Canada. I spent the afternoon cooling myself with their gloom. Mel Hurtig, author of *The Betrayal of Canada*, was described on the dust jacket, with ominous pomposity, as 'a man of many achievements as a publisher, speaker, writer, and political activist'. Readers were advised that 'common to all his efforts, however, is his consuming passion for Canada'.

This was reminiscent of the self-promotional tone of Ross Perot, and the book was a similar mix of volcanic pessimism and national re-affirmation. There were attacks on the planned Free Trade Agreement with the USA and Mexico (charged with raising unemployment) and the legislative generosity shown to giant corporations by the Mulroney government. The most intriguing section was on health-care. A right-wing columnist had apparently described Canadian health-care costs as a 'cancer on the state', a piece of bravura insensitivity which met more welcomes than it might from legislators. Hurtig argued that, just as the USA began critically to examine its lack of medical insurance, Canada was beginning critically to examine its possession of it. The author viewed this as an irony. Yet, once you compared the country not with America but with its mother culture, the development was not ironic but logical: an echo of the argument in Britain and New Zealand.

In the pivotal chapter, Hurtig asked: 'Do we want to become Americans?' He answered negatively, but feared that the magnetic attraction might already be irreversible. The best answer he offered was a quote from a newspaper article by Margaret Atwood: 'We would like to think we're about to get the best of both worlds – Canadian stability and a more caring society, as well as US markets – but what if instead we get their crime rate, their health programs and gun laws, and they get our markets, or what's left of them?'

Atwood had written this in 1987. Five years later, there was even more reason to suggest that this might not be the perfect time to be applying for membership of the United States. I wondered if Prime Minister Mulroney appreciated, as he tetchily dismissed the eleventh-hour polemics (the phrase 'the last chance for Canada' reverberated through Hurtig's text) being published in his own country, that eerily similar works crammed the bookstores of the nation he viewed as his aim and inspiration.

For someone like me, born into the middle class of a comfortable country, and continuing in both cocoons through education and work, the phrase 'Third World Crisis' had become a standard piece of cultural snobbery, liberal sympathy. But to travel through the English-speaking world in 1992 was to understand the possibility, far stronger than any politician would acknowledge, of a First World Crisis. Perhaps they cannot properly be compared – for the latter was an agony of loss of plenitude, the former a more or less continuous absence – but the feel of lean years, of the seeds of upheaval, was inescapable. I briefly toyed with retitling this book *The Battle of Capitalism Creek – The First World Crisis* to catch the market.

Prostrate in Winnipeg, I turned to *The Will of a Nation: Awakening the Canadian Spirit*. You could tell how widespread the genre was, because the jacket pledged that this book was 'not just another cry of anger and fear'. The most useful chapter was the one in which the authors asked the question: 'What's So Special About Canada?' This section was a response to the implication in the Mulroney government's deliberate movement towards America: that there was not much great national tradition to abandon. What was cunning about Radwanski and Luttrell's work was the way they turned Canada's historical baggage into cherishable values: activity-challenged, as it were, substituted for dull.

For example, the authors argued: 'Other key aspects of what makes Canada special also revolve around values that have come to characterize our behaviour as a nation. For example, when people in other countries describe their perception of Canada, one of the words most frequently used is "tolerant".' Well, yes, *one* of the words most frequently used. Ingeniously, the writers posited this tolerance as the explanation for the nation's low global impact: 'Perhaps it is an offshoot of this tolerance, this mistrustfulness of extremes, that makes us tend to be so diffident about our national identity. We Canadians are always reluctant to speak of Canada, out loud, in terms of being superior or exceptional, even though there are many respects in which our country is both.' Shy as well as tolerant, then.

The sun was bashfully descending over Winnipeg's Golden Boy when I reached Mordecai Richler's *Oh Canada! Oh Quebec!*, in which he memorably described his compatriots as 'history's couch potatoes'. The book also quoted Andre Laurendeau, Quebec nationalist hero and newspaper editor, on a visit, in 1964, to Winnipeg: 'I wish I were somewhere else . . .' Synchronicity. 'From my window I see a discordant urban landscape, with absolutely no beauty: a few modern buildings, some flat roofs, a tiny badly fenced patch of green.' Synchronicity.

I was already familiar, from the magazine extract of the Richler, with the details – comic to those outside, sinister to those in – of Montreal's word-police, prowling the city's streets, photographing the '*Ploughman's Lunch*' sign outside the pub, then following up with a fine and a thundering injunction to advertise *Déjeuner d'Agricole* or nothing. This was the result of Bill 101, which banned bilingual signs. The legislation was a banner for Quebec separatism.

As I read on, a boy flopped down beside me on the grass.

'Civics student?'

'Sorry?'

'All those books on "The Threats Facing Our Great Nation"? You must be cramming for a paper, right . . . ?'

'No. I'm just travelling round. I'm sort of interested in

politics, it's my area as a journalist, so I tend to buy this kind of stuff . . .'

Rick – who was doing literature at the University of Manitoba and working in the Legislative Building for the summer – was a stocky youth with sandy hair and a trainee beard of a slightly darker shade.

We got through the Are-you-English?-really?-oh-London's-great-my-granpy's-Scottish stuff. Then, 'What do you make of it?' he said, gesturing at the glossy fan of eleventh-hour texts beside me.

'Well, it's this tone of fear, of last chance, everywhere you go at the moment. "Help, help, the sky is falling . . . ?"'

'*Right*. You know, here anyway, what that's about?'

Canadians said *aboot*. It was one of the few vivid differences between the North American accents. (In John Updike's *Rabbit* books, the American Everyman Harry Angstrom is irritatedly reminded of the dubious roots of the ABC news anchorman, Peter Jennings, by this rogue vowel.)

'Well, recession, as everywhere else . . .' I began. Conversations with natives of another nation were as queasy as vivas. You kept worrying that you would upset the examiner, or that he would move to a subject outside your revision. 'Then, here, specifically, the question of Americanization, by default or design. Then, I suppose, the, well, cohesion of Canada. Can it be held together . . . ?'

'*Right*. Hey, for a tourist, you seem to have really thought about Canada . . .'

I wanted to reply: *There's not much else to do in Winnipeg*, but I kept quiet. Rick said: 'How much do you know about the Meech Lake Accord . . . ?'

One of my mental early-warning systems screeched at these words. If the Latvian gouache minimalism expert didn't get you in a corner about Latvian gouache minimalism, what he got you in a corner about was the Meech Lake Accord. In our hysteria, we had bastardized, or codified, it to the Meech Beach Agreement. Staggering away from his company after pleading emergency appendectomies or sudden deaths in the family, party-goers would mouth 'Meech Beach' to the next potential victim.

'Well,' I said, 'for most of this century, Canada had been

trying to end the system of effective control from Britain. The problem was that, while almost everyone was pulling in the same direction – away from Britain – Quebec saw the negotiations as an opportunity to pull away from Canada . . .'

'Right,' said Rick. 'Wow, I wish all tourists took this kind of interest in the Canadian Constitution . . .'

'Oh, well, I sort of sat through a course in it once . . .' I explained, my mind suddenly filled with an image of the great, slow-moving lips of the LGME. 'Anyway, that's about as far as I go . . .'

'Good enough,' said Rick. 'Where it goes from there is, in 1982, Pierre Trudeau . . . hey, do·you know his gag about the elephant?'

'Yes. Someone once . . .'

It was a normal part of human discourse for jokes to circulate among communities. The only real difference in Canada was that there seemed to be only one joke. It was a speech by former Prime Minister Pierre Trudeau in which he had said that living next door to America was like sharing a bed with an elephant. All Canadians eventually told you this. It had attached to the national central nervous system in the same way as some of Churchill's rhetoric had to the British. They usually added that he received a standing ovation.

'Trudeau,' Rick resumed, 'eventually got together the Constitution Act of 1982. That gave the finger to Westminster, but there were all kinds of squiggles for the western provinces – about being able to ignore the bits they didn't like – and Quebec wouldn't sign, despite the fact that the Charter of Rights made French and English the joint national languages. Which plays for phooey in Quebec, because they've already ruled French only . . .'

The difference between Rick's rendition and the LGME's was that between Pavarotti and a concrete-mixer. But, even so, submerged traumas surged to the surface as he summed up. 'So you have a kind of permanent bubbling constitutional crisis, which nobody takes much interest in. In the late eighties, Mulroney stitches together the Meech Lake Accord, which recognizes Quebec as a "distinct society", and so on, but, because of that, it's not acceptable to the non-French provinces. So it collapses. It should be called the Meech Lake *Discord*, really!' I reflex-smiled. 'Right now, he's putting together a new one. *Oui, oui*, again, to Quebec, but, this time, more representation and self-determination for *all* the provinces, plus perks for the Native Canadian Peoples . . . They reckon on a plebiscite in October this year . . .'

Apart from Canada, India was the only other place in the world in which I had known people to talk so intensely about politics, languorously bathing themselves in constitutional language like 'accord' and 'plebiscite'. Both were nations on which British structures and practices had been imposed. I wondered how aware the Canadians and Indians were of the irony that Britain itself had neither constitution nor Bill of Rights and housed a people essentially indifferent to political ideas.

Rick had finished. It seemed that something was needed from me.

'Do you think Mulroney can get it through?' I said.

'Mulroney couldn't get through a *door* without falling over . . .' Rick giggled. Everywhere you went that year in the quiet world, prime ministers and presidents were buffoons, scapegoats, jokes.

'I write about America a lot. It's weird there at the moment. Angry, confused. Ross Perot as messiah and all that. These books seem to be the same kind of thing . . .'

'Oh, *sure*. We even have our very own Ross Perot . . .'

'Yes, of course. Preston Manning?'

'*Right*.'

I had picked up on Preston Manning in the Canadian papers. He ran the Reform Party, a gathering force in Canadian politics. Like Perot, he stood on an Augean Stables ticket, presenting himself as an honest patriot who was uninvolved in the ambitions, slithering, and self-aggrandizement of politicians. In fact, it was arguable, as with Perot, that to lead an outsider's crusade required more megalomania and ego than to rise to the top of an established party.

Manning was a neo-Conservative, who believed in a one-language Canada, meaning that Quebec should either leave the confederation (a solution he seemed to favour) or start speaking plain Canadian English. He also supported welfare cuts. Crucially, he was, like many but by no means all of his supporters, a fundamentalist Christian (and, consequently, some alleged, anti-semite), who roared against abortion and promiscuity. (He even used that giveaway phrase 'the Canadian family'.) Manning, however, differed from Ross Perot, or other populist dema-gogues, in not being an isolationist. Nor, though, was he an expansionist. He was what you might call a submissionist, liking to refer to Canada as 'the northern part of the North American continent'.

Perot used the slogan 'Take it back!' Manning's was more 'Give it back!': to God and to George Bush. This was an illustration of what a complicated matter Canadian patriotism could be. Nationalism in the USA was a simple business: our-selves alone and hell to those that get in the way. But Canadians like Preston Manning and the Latvian gouache minimalism expert – who were outwardly massive patriots, talking about *Canada* all the time – were really, in a sense, pretend Americans. Their patriotism was, oddly, a desire for their nation to be swallowed.

'Reform Party plays well in Winnipeg,' said Rick. 'Conserva-tives who think the nation's lost its way . . .'

'People talk about Middle America,' I said. 'Is there such a thing as Middle Canada . . . ?'

'There probably is. And you're sitting in it. Winnipeg's a kind of strict city . . . You familiar with the work of Robert Lepage?'

'Yeah.'

Lepage was a young French Canadian theatre director, associated with visual radicalism towards classical texts, whose re-interpretation of *A Midsummer Night's Dream* as a piece for mud-wrestlers was one of the media talking-points in London that year.

'Lepage,' explained Rick, 'gets all of his worst reviews in Winnipeg. The last one, one of the critics said, "Far too much French." That's Winnipeg . . .'

So, Middle Canada seemed a reasonable supposition: a region like Middle America, or the edge cities of the USA, in which people had remained, or to which they had fled, partly as a statement against the direction of their nation.

'Nice talking to you,' Rick said, standing, and slapping the grass off his jeans. 'You don't find many people you can chew over the Great Constitutional Crisis with, even in Canada . . .' I didn't say, *I bet*. 'Say hi to Great Britain for me. Did you know? Richler points out in his book that when the North America Act was passed in your British parliament in 1867 – this is the legislation that effectively creates Canada – the House was 75 per cent empty . . . !'

Surprisingly high turnout, I thought to myself, when he was out of sound. Then I looked briefly at a statue of Rabbie Burns – there was a lot of Scottish blood in Winnipeg – walked downtown to the Downtowner, and packed.

I have so far resisted in this book descriptions of non-Anglophone cab-drivers, largely because, in the English-speaking world these days, they come with the weather. However, my driver on the day I hoped to leave Winnipeg was remarkable in lacking even the parrot noun 'airport'. He did possess one phonetic English word but, distressingly for the visitor, it was 'Directions!'

'Airport, please.'

'Dreckshuns!'

'I'm a visitor. I can't . . .'

'Dreckshuns!'

It was a humid evening and both rear windows were wound down to their limit. This allowed me to extend both arms and to attempt an impersonation of an engine which, because of my dry throat, emerged as a groan. Enlightenment brightened his face, and I feared he had mis-read my impression and was taking me either to an aviary or to the Church of the Crucifixion. But, at length, the sweaty air took on an edge of kerosene and we had made the airport.

The canned music in the cabin before take-off was 'The Music of the Night' from *The Phantom of the Opera*. Lloyd-Webber seemed now to be the soother music of choice for the world's airlines. It was a depressing thought. If anything went wrong, your ears would be sealed for eternity on a pseudo-Puccini show tune. During the three hours speeding east, I ate a chicken breast so tepid that the cooking process could only have consisted of a stewardess breathing on it. Landing at Toronto, I picked up a driver, a Sikh who, a huge improvement on Winnipeg, knew numerous words of English, but, unfortunately, not the one chosen by the owners of my hotel. This was their fault more than it was his. A commercial nonce-word, Novotel existed in no language, but sounded disturbingly as if it might exist in several.

'Novotel,' I said, from the back of the cab.

'A new hotel,' said my driver. 'Many new hotels, sir.'

Never having moved in circles where charades were played at parties, I was becoming alarmingly adept at the art. But how the hell did you mime Novotel? Any charade of the first syllable would inevitably introduce the word 'new', increasing the confusion which already existed. (Whatever Quebec believed, a pessimist would say that persuading Canadian citizens to speak *French* half the time was only the second challenge facing the government.) At length, I found the address and encouraged the driver to head for that, in isolation from any name. Soon, we rolled up outside the Toronto Novotel.

'Not new hotel. *Old* hotel,' the drive smilingly corrected me.

Toronto was a revelation, or, at least, a consolation. You would have to be bleakly determined to pursue a thesis about the tedium of the nation to include Toronto in the condemnation. This, though, was merely to agree with the conventional wisdom. The guide books recounted how, after a long period of unfashionability (the write-ups actually confessed that the town had been a butt of the 'First prize, one week in ——', 'Second prize, two weeks in ——' joke), downtown Toronto had become established as Canada's Manhattan, a place for smart talk and art, chic eateries and vibrant nightlife. Once, the books said, Torontonians had driven south for the weekend; now, New Yorkers roared north. My natural scepticism about this had been encouraged by the narrator of the novel *Cat's Eye* – by the Toronto author, Margaret Atwood – who had been witheringly wary about this transformation.

Even so, encouraged by these claims, I decided to go to the theatre that night. Scanning the pages, I saw that Lloyd-Webber was already there in bulk, as was an English trouser-drop comedy, and Ustinov's one-man show was on the way. The only really surprising title was a musical based on the novel, play, and movie *The Kiss of the Spider Woman*. Even here, though, closer examination of the theatre boards established that the authors were the

Broadway bards Kander & Ebb (*Cabaret, Chicago*) and the director Hal Prince, another member of New York theatrical royalty.

In short, Toronto was being used as an out-of-town try-out for New York. (One of the city's arts writers speculated about the possibility of Kander & Ebb, who had written the anthem 'New York, New York', coming up with one called 'Toronto, Toronto' during their visit, although it was clear that extreme vocal clarity would be required to stop such a song sounding like a discarded theme tune for *The Lone Ranger*.) A similar cultural clue was that Toronto was regularly used as a stand-in for American cities by Hollywood movie directors. No one could dispute that it was a cleaner, kinder version of a US metropolis – and managed to be, multiculturally, more melting-pot than tinder-box – but it therefore also followed that its surface similarities to an American city were another instance of the difficulty of Canadian distinctiveness.

These latest examples of imported, or surrogate, culture somewhat undermined the claims made for the city as an engine-house of Canadian culture. Protestations of the city's beauty, at least of the more modern kind, were less tendentious. Heading towards the lakefront from the Novotel old hotel in the morning, the first impression was depressing. Pedestrians walked under an oily concrete bracelet – the Gardiner Expressway – which circled the city above head level, supported by regular concrete arches, disfigured by smuts and bumps. In the morning and evening crushes, the arches were like a guard of honour for a wedding of cars, moving slowly in twos.

Once through this murky circle, you encountered another perimeter fence. This time it was that contemporary equivalent of the city wall: the line of high and wide apartment blocks and hotels like barricades, though placed, in the twentieth century, not to expel invaders but to attract them. However, beyond these two circles of relative hellishness, you saw the waterfront and the sweep of Lake Ontario.

When I had told people I was going to Canada, those who had not been immediately negative (rolling out the activity-challenged allegations) had said: 'Oh, the lakes. The lakes are great.' (This was presumably why they were called the Great Lakes.) Generally, those who were upbeat about Canada cited the

Lakes. This somewhat worried me, for, while I well understood the primeval appeal of sea and of big rivers (I lived on one side of the Thames and worked on the other, and walked across it most days with a small lift of interest each time), I was equivocal about lakes. It seemed to me that, among the ways you could take your water geographically, lakes were a little, well, wet.

The water just lay there looking pretty, often unable to offer even the sense of infinity in one direction or the other which a sea or river can. I found it hard to imagine Hemingway having written *The Old Man and The Lake*, or Iris Murdoch *The Lake*, *The Lake*, or the solid Christians of Winnipeg belting out, at worship, the hymn 'For those in peril on the Lake'. Well, perhaps it was just that I was visiting in summer – and sun on water is one of nature's most reliable confidence tricks, the light bouncing up like diamonds on the jeweller's cloth of the deep blue water – but the lake and waterfront at Toronto enthralled me so that, for the first time in Canada, I resolved to return there one day.

And the common currency of architecture around the First World at that time was the tarted-up harbour, the jaunty wharf, the dolled-over dock. In London and Liverpool and Glasgow and Sydney and Vancouver, the places where the working classes had earned their money, until progress intervened, were being re-imagined as places for the middle classes to spend their money. Toronto's, though, was one of the smartest. The harbour-front development stretched across a mile of restaurants, cafés, performance and exhibition areas, and, inevitably, shopping malls. (The warehouses where raw ingredients had been stored wholesale were now partitioned into chintzy salons where treated ingredients were sold retail.)

But the development at Toronto had, like the remortgaged waterfronts elsewhere around the world, experienced fiscal difficulties, either because of the quiet revenge of the economic cycle or the cackling ghosts of old dockers. The bankers and media types expected to come and play on the harbour had been limited by the global cash-flow problems. Canada's famously complicated funding arrangements – by which nation, province, and district invested in different proportions in various projects – had meant that belt-tightening was a complex manoeuvre.

That summer day, though, there was a ruck of sunbathers and

tourists in most available spaces. In the exhibition tents, there was a Holiday and Leisure Exposition. From the loudspeaker above the tents came the announcement: 'In a few moments, we will be beginning a video entitled "*The Magic of Nova Scotia*".' The Torontonians laughed hugely. The bully-runt syndrome again.

I took a harbour cruise. Just off-shore was the show-off oddity of Toronto Island Airport, a landing strip built on landfill and bordered by water on four sides. Planes skimmed across the lake like seagulls. Toronto's skyline wasn't Manhattan's but the comparison was not as mad as some made by tourist boards. The skyscrapers had a similar constructional range, so that, from the water, you looked along a line of spangly and pastel boxes – oblong, square, and cylindrical – like Christmas presents stacked under a tree.

The two most striking sights from the water were the Sky Dome and the CN Tower. The former was the sports venue, a shiny white sphere like an astronaut's helmet, the roof sliding back like a visor for baseball games. It was the home of the Toronto Blue Jays, a baseball team which regularly beat those from the USA. Yet, again, this source of national pride needed to be qualified. Playing an American game, the team competed in a North American League, for the purposes of which it was joined to its big brother territory. Most of the key players were Americans. There had reportedly been embarrassing moments when they were asked on TV sports shows: 'What do you love about Canada?' The thing I kept thinking in Toronto was that, placed next to perhaps the most aggressively magnetic democracy that had ever existed, Canada kept coating itself in iron filings.

Along from the Sky Dome was the CN Tower. If you sought to generalize about sightseeing, then European tourism highlighted age (the oldest limestone church in . . . , the site in 437 of the signing of the famous . . .). Denied this, North America stressed size (the deepest, the highest, the longest). But then tourism consisted of turning history into money. Britain and France could rely on a steady income from old investments. Canada and the USA needed the frequent boost of new issues.

The selling-point of Toronto's CN Tower, for example, was that it was the tallest free-standing structure in the world, a more massive and habitable version of Canberra's flagpole. Its one thousand eight hundred and fifteen feet and five inches formed a rapier which jousted with the clouds. Some see high-rise architecture as phallic. But, if so, then the CN Tower was, strictly, phallic-kinky, its long, smooth shaft interrupted half-way up by a thick ring fixed round the middle. This was the Skypod, the home of the hardware – some civicly practical, some militarily sinister – which was the real reason for the big tin prick.

Back on shore, I went literally downtown to Underground City. Burrowed under Toronto was a three-mile glass-and-marble cave, a non-bargain basement of shops which – in another example of the selling on dimensions which was a feature of New World tourism – was billed as the longest pedestrian walkway in the world. In the event of Armageddon, Torontonians would be able to go on shopping and dining out in this customer bunker for a period of several months. (A new application of that consumer-boom phrase about shopping until you dropped.)

There was a British souvenir shop – called the Leicester Square WC2 store – from which packets of Rowntrees jelly babies had recently been banned because they were not half-labelled in French (*enfants tremblants*, presumably.) As I wandered around the book-stores and flower shops and delicatessens in these overlit depths, I wondered if such ground-scoopers would replace the sky-scraper as the buildings of the future and, if so, what, in a million years – if the planet survived – archaeologists would make of the remains of this sunken mall.

They would probably conclude, extrapolating from the fragments and books and newspapers of the period, that North Americans (*c.* AD 2000) shopped underground because they were frightened of the harmful daylight or scared to purchase goods in full-frontal view of those beggars and malcontents who roamed the streets above. By then, of course, either or both of these surmises might be right and civic planners will have congratulated themselves on the accidental foresight of underground development.

I walked up to and through the city's Queen's Park – which was an almost successful attempt to do a smaller Central Park without the semi-naked excrement-smeared weirdos singing cabalistic hymns to themselves up trees – and spent the afternoon and part of the following morning in the Royal Ontario Museum.

North America's biggest relic house apart from MOMA in New York, the ROM was significant for its cross-disciplinary policy, accommodating bones, pots, paintings, inventions, musical instruments, antiques, and stuffed animals on a single site.

The place was particularly famous for something called the Bat Cave. This was a serious exposition, with models and soundtracks, of the evolution of the small black winged mammal, and so I was impressed to find a huge queue of Canadian youth, from toddlers to teenagers, waiting for admission to it. It was only when, during my tour, two children just behind me began sobbing and whining, 'Where's Catwoman?' that I realized that, for this generation, the main cultural association of the term Bat Cave was with the *Batman* movies. (The latest, starring Michael Keaton, Michelle Pfeiffer, and Danny De Vito had opened on the North American continent the previous week.)

But at least that particular ambush of a Canadian cultural asset by an American one was unplanned. The establishment as a whole, though, did little to weaken my prejudices about the territory's more general difficulties in this direction. The ROM was an intelligent and illuminating museum but, even here, my prejudices were not entirely dampened. Any national museum or art gallery must reflect the culture of other nations as well as collect the national heritage. Economy trumped geography in the heritage business. For example, some of the best stuff by Seurat and Rembrandt hung in Chicago, despite their minimal personal connection with the city of the big shoulders.

Yet the impressive panoply of the Toronto collection – its colonization, through cash and intelligence, of exhibits from the key eras of civilization – could be read, at its harshest, as an avoidance of a void. The civilization of which the place gave you the weakest sense was that of Canada. The nearest I got – which was by no means close – was in a non-permanent exhibit called 'Teenagers In Toronto'.

Sandals, parkas, and Grateful Dead T-shirts were solemnly displayed on felt-covered crates, like Etruscan jugs elsewhere in the building. A pair of scuffed Doc Martens bulked in a display case, above the grave explanation: 'In some youth circles, the size of boot-heel corresponded to the wearer's social standing.' Visual display units and captions explained that the city's youth was divided into a number of peer groups, identified by dress, appearance, and attitude. These were Hippies, Rockers, Preppies, Punks, B-Girls, and B-Boys. (Also known, because the exhibition was culturally sensitive, as *Les Hippies*, *Les Rockers*, *Les Preppies*, and so on.)

The exhibition ended with the results of a poll in which young Torontonians had been asked to list their priorities. The answers were: (1) Environment; (2) Family; (3) Racism. In videotaped comments expanding on the third answer, the teenagers revealed the old dream of global social coherence, that 'the peoples of Canada and of the world will live together in harmony'. That this sentiment was then translated into French – not for the benefit of visitors but supposedly for Canadians themselves – was a reminder of the reality which was encroaching on this dream, even in this famously safe place.

Late on my last evening in Toronto, the line outside the CN Tower finally seemed bearably brief. During my short wait, I noted that the elevation was a member of something called the World Confederation of Towers (in North America, as I said earlier, there is a support group for everything), of which Blackpool Tower was another scion. An elevator which accelerated like a plane taking off carried us to the Sky Pod, where, in ten languages, fathers were cracking the joke about what happened to little boys who misbehaved up there.

I peered down at the Sky Dome twelve hundred feet below, where the Blue Jays were playing – back-stop turned into a full-stop from this height – and thought about the curiously durable appeal of the high view in tourism. The origins of the phenomenon were incomprehensible enough. When human beings spent their lives on their feet, the clomp up the stone steps of the tower was a rare chance for an elevated perspective. When planes were rich types' sport, the skyscraper's elevator was the cut-price way to the godly downlook. Yet most of those tourists at the CN Tower had seen Toronto from the same remove, and higher, merely arriving, and were lodged in glass-giraffe hotels. Many of the locals with them worked in teetering offices.

Why did the plunging point of view remain so appealing when, objectively, most of what you saw from the CN Tower was pointillist car parks? A tower, I supposed, offered a freeze-frame rather than the fast-forward you got from a plane. And, on a flight, you were distracted by the calculation of the odds of crashing. (Take-off being, remember, one of the two most risky periods. But, then, even up the CN Tower, the safe traveller was working out the chances of the windows splintering under the air pressure.) Presumably, then, it was an in-built human need, in all except those with vertigo, to lose the angle we were landed with.

I looked down at the baseball stadium and the drab concrete bald-spots on the top of the mirror-glass towerblocks of Toronto, a city which had resolved the great Canadian problem of looking down – the fact that, at the country's feet, lay the most influential culture of the century – through impressed reflection. And then I flew a short distance east to a part of the confederation which had commendably declined to ape America, but which could still not properly be called Canada.


In my Montreal hotel, the staff answered the phone with a compound hello: '*Bonjourgoodmorning!*' In the restaurants, waiters glided smilingly between 'Enjoy!' and '*Bon Appetit!*' generally, but not always, guessing the tongue of the diner from their cut. But these were impromptu decencies: an underground resistance to the feared effect of Quebec's speech laws on tourism. (And, on the menus which offered translations, hamburger was given, perhaps pointedly, as *hambourgeois*.)

On the streets, as Richler had advised, all state-owned information, on road signs and the Metro, was flatly Gallic, while private commerce opted for bolshy bilingualism or, more normally, cosmetic alterations: Eaton's, the Canada-wide department store, had been required by what Richler called the tongue-troopers merely to drop its giveaway English possessive and become Eaton, which could be pronounced *aye-tonne* and therefore taken as respectfully French. Meanwhile, the *Commission de Toponymie* was labouring, map in one hand and Larousse in the other, to redesignate any streets, hills, or rivers with Anglophone associations. I feared, as I strolled around, for Rue McGill and Rue Duluth.

I appreciated Richler's sarcasm about some of these procedures but, as a visitor rather than a resident, found it hard to share his wider anger. After weeks among the parched architecture of North America, it was a lift to be among buildings which had done time. There was a clutch of the steroid-fed telephone kiosks of modern corporate dwelling, but the heart of Montreal was a pretty city, rolling down from hills to river. The place was as tight with churches as Peoria, but these, at least, were stone and called after saints who died horribly, rather than Perspex and named the Eighth Temple of Christ the Chiropodist, or whatever.

About as far from the latter as you could get was Montreal's basilica of Notre-Dame, a twin-towered edifice of sooty stone so broodingly Gothic that, to be seen to its best effect, it would need not light but lightning. Broadly speaking, the history of church architecture reflected the journey within organized religion from the idea of God as a fussy traveller who demanded five-star hotels to the idea of a matey deity who would settle for the sofa bed downstairs.

Whatever the theological attractions of the latter – a functionalism partly produced by the view that Christianity might more usefully provide buildings for the poor to live in rather than for the rich to worship – twentieth-century tourists benefited from the five-star château phase. And Notre-Dame of Montreal was the product of a period when God was believed to be a very picky guest indeed. The vaulted ceiling above the altar was an explosion of gold; the altar-piece resembled a vast hand-carved fort with six watchtowers; the organ pipes were as long and formidable as a prison fence.

Tourism here was European rather than New World, the selling line not height or depth but length of existence. For example, beside Notre-Dame was a seminary, the city's most venerable building, and supporting, according to the guidebooks, 'the oldest public timepiece in North America', an elegant white-faced clock with a carved bell-shape above it. As the clock struck, it struck me that, since historical tourism was an attempt to recall lost time, staring at, and photographing, a clock in operation for four centuries was possibly the ultimate symbolic piece of sightseeing. Even so, as I stood among the crowd gazing up at the timepiece because their guidebooks told them to, this was one of the occasions on my journey when I had a strong feeling of the emperor's new clothes, of the enforced enthralment which tourism is.

Even in *Vieux Montreal*, not everything was the frozen past. In the place Jacques-Cartier – where the Frenchification of the city had not yet faced up to the embarrassing presence of a statue celebrating Nelson's victory at Trafalgar – the traditional pavement salesmen were using portable phones to warn each other of police presence, and the traditional homeless men were sifting the litter in the bins. There were also tourist stupidities, like the careful preservation of the old Olympic stadium. Tramping around a shell, of which the only interest had been events which were long past was, I always thought, like showing dinner guests the empty packets of the ingredients from the great meal you cooked the night before. The old Olympic complex also apparently boasted 'the world's tallest inclined tower'. Having done the world's tallest upright tower in Toronto, I was not inclined to see it.

Yet this was, in general, a city with a memory. It was true that Montreal's preservation of its past was a recent enthusiasm, and motivated by political self-interest more than altruistic preservation of the heritage. Yet Montreal was still the first place I had visited in Canada which gave the impression of both remembering where it came from – its foundation by French missionaries in the seventeenth century and subsequent defence against the Iroquois – and knowing where it wished to go.

And even my first experience of a state with mandated language rules – I do not count the politically correct impositions of America, where the penalty for slips was dirty looks rather than fines – was less eerie than I had feared. In a single respect – of daily conversation – Montreal was not like France at all. In Paris, for a visitor to speak French badly was interpreted as an act of cultural vulgarity, political hostility. In Montreal, for a visitor to speak French badly was interpreted as a vote of cultural support, political sympathy. English tourists at the railway station or a shop, dragging their minds back decades for a declension or conjugation, would meet encouraging nods and even interrogative offers of the elusive French words. Hostility to visitors was restricted to the insistently Anglophone, of whom the bulk seemed to be Americans. And, on the Metro, only those both monolingual and colour-blind would have faced serious difficulties, as a different primary shade was allocated to each route on the map.

I had been taught French by Francophone Canadians, members of an American-based missionary teaching order which had ended up in Hertfordshire. We had seen them as more softly spoken Yanks, who read more books. I had never detected separatist ambitions in them, but then – if Scottish and Welsh nationalism were any comparison, and they seemed a reasonable one – the zeal of a constituent country to be free rose and fell in relation to external irritants (recessions, unusually dogmatic federal administration) and the prominence of politicians willing to kick it up.

An argument which I had heard in Glasgow during the 1992 British election, from a Scottish Nationalist Party candidate, was echoed frequently in Quebec. Asked how Scotland might manage financially alone, the candidate had snarled that her economy would flourish when it no longer had 'the weak British pound dragging it down'. The audience had applauded and roared. I had thought then that it was dishonest rhetoric. It was reminiscent of the speeches of populist demagogues during the break-up of the Soviet Bloc, but at least most of those peoples' leaders had advised that freedom would mean a period of tough economic re-adjustment. In this case, the implication was that the re-ordering of borders would unlock cash.

A variation of the same phrase – denigrating the Canadian economy for holding down Quebec's – was popular with the French separatists. Quebec was a large and rich province, a transport and financial hub, but the logistics of independence were still jolting: the new French-Canadian nation would need its own passports and currency, army and police, would have to negotiate terms for trade with either the small Canadian rump or the vast American lump. It was doubtful that these realities had been faced. But then the USA's large percentage of revolting voters had not properly contemplated what a President Perot would mean. Practicalities were not the point. Anger and national re-affirmation were. In the quiet world that year, the countries were reshuffling, more peacefully but no less seriously than in the wreck of Eastern Europe.

To me, breezing through, Montreal seemed an appealing remake of Paris, in which the architecture and cuisine survived, but bad French was permitted to be spoken and the pedestrian had a higher life expectancy because of strict traffic laws. Yet to feel this was to see another factor in the Canadian nation's fundamental incoherence. To paraphrase a famous French expression, *c'était magnifique, mais ce n'était pas La Canade.* It was – forgive me, tongue-troopers, a translation – magnificent, but it was not Canada.


Going home, I changed planes at Halifax, Nova Scotia, a fishing village on the outer eastern edge of Canada. And, in the airport bar there, I experienced a coming to terms. Sadly, it was not the nature of Canada to which I was reconciled, but that of the USA.

Canada was the second largest country in the world (although most of that space was as uninhabitable as, well, space), but it could not make sense of its dimensions. The USA had made its remorseless topography logical through geo-political influence. The problem for Canada, as for Australia, was being vast but marginal. Australians, though, had managed to establish a distinctive spirit and personality. But Canadians were widely perceived as sedated Americans.

It was a place defined by its neighbours and progenitors. Canada equals America minus $x$. Or, depending on where you went, Britain minus $z$. Or France minus $y$. Vancouver and Victoria were winsomely British, Toronto pretend American, Montreal insistently French. Only the centre – Winnipeg – held to a vision of what to be Canadian might mean, and even that was a spin-off of the Middle American mentality.

This should not be read as colonial triumphalism. Britain, undoubtedly, was now an international irrelevance, but it traded, for tourism and residual influence, on past associations. Canada lacked either former significance or present importance.

America was a young country, but it had accumulated cultural and political history with dizzying speed. After seeing Canada, I also understood, if liked no more, the aspects of American life which had always appalled me. The fanatical patriotism, the veneration of the flag, the furious obsession with the Constitution, were the product of an organized attempt to impose a coherent identity on a pan-cultural sprawl of a people, born in civil war. Canada had failed to impose such coherence. In the USA, it spasmodically looked as if the glue was melting – the Los Angeles riots had been an example – but Canada had never even managed to fix some adhesive in the cracks.

Canada, unarguably, was a cleaner, kinder country. But the USA was like a tennis player who had all the shots but also a terrible temper. People said: 'Oh, if only he could learn self-control, he would be quite glorious to watch.' But the talent and the tantrums were linked. In the same way, people said: 'Oh, America would be swell, if it wasn't for the violence and the military expansionism and the gun laws and the gut-stuffing cuisine and the religion.' Yet all this – the things which made America a difficult country to live in or to live next door to – was inextricably linked to all that made it a thrill to visit or read or write about. America was unlucky but wonderful. Canada was lucky but dull. Canada was the tennis player with Corinthian manners, who always got thrashed by John McEnroe.

My own luggage hopefully now flying with me, I wondered if Canada would ever lose its baggage of imposed or imported identities. Weeks before, when I was heading for Peoria, the transatlantic 747 had made landfall at Labrador. Now leaving behind the lost Empire and the more or less surrendered Commonwealth, we topped Labrador again and ploughed through the night towards the new emergent empire of Europe.

# PART THREE

# EUROPE

# CHAPTER SIX

# TAKING THE PISS

---

## *Luxembourg and Brussels*

Luxembourg is one of only three European countries – the others being Monaco and San Marino – which, when mentioned, produce a soppy smile of the kind which adults give to tiny children. The dismissive reputation of its northern neighbour might be 'plucky little Belgium', because of that country's endurance during World War II, but Luxembourg's cachet in the popular European imagination is even more patronizing. Sweet little Luxembourg.

Even its official name as a nation – the Grand Duchy – has a cuteness which makes you think of one of George Bernard Shaw's chocolate soldiers. The political system as well speaks of an almost comic inconsequentiality to the affairs of state. The government was formed from the two most successful parties in the general election, not from cynical smoke-filled negotiations for a coalition, but by statute. I fantasized about the same rule being imposed on the main parties in Britain and America who had recently, or who were about to, fight a campaign of mutual character assassination.

If you were English, the only time you really came across the place was during the annual Eurovision Song Contest when Luxembourg's entry generally consisted of a Heidi-like girl with a guitar and plaits singing a song called: 'Hah! A bird! Ha ha ha!' When you laughed at the Dutch entry – usually two ageing hippies with a rock number called 'Zip zop! Zap zip!' – or the Swedish – normally a blonde, semi-dressed in Lurex, belting out 'Loff me, don't liff me!' – the laughter was harsh. But, to the girl from Luxembourg with the guitar, you gave the baby smile again. Useless but cute.

Even so, in the business of tourism, insignificance was not necessarily a negative, provided the negligibility was dressed in romance and saccharine. Monaco and San Marino earn as large a proportion of their GNP from visitors as the obvious sightseeing leviathans of Europe and North America. There is a curiosity about nothingness. And a significant number of obvious non-residents – students with backpacks, Americans with mono-grammed luggage – got off the train on which I arrived in Luxembourg City.

I had boarded in Paris. On the train, one of those unfortunate European culture clashes had happened. The young French guard ushered three attractive English backpackers through to first class and explained that, the carriages being empty today, they were welcome to sit there. There was, I thought, an implication that they might wish later, in gratitude, to sit on him, but they shrewdly took his gift but not his hint.

Every thirty minutes, he would walk through saying 'Comft-ubble, lediz?' and they would smile and say they were. Unfortu-nately, at the border, he was replaced by a stooped Luxembourger with a greying walrus moustache, who demanded that they pay ten years' pocket money directly to the Grand Duke for fraudulent transportation in first class. It was another small example of the bizarrely disparate mentalities which were theoretically due to be united as Europe.

If you looked at it on a map, the country of Luxembourg was just a gout of toe jam wedged between the extremities of France, Germany, and Holland. But, once you squeezed in, the setting of Luxembourg City itself was dramatic. It rested on two hills, with a deep valley between them, crossed by a viaduct, as long and humped as a mythical sea monster, called La Passerelle. Houses, tiered like stadium seating, edged down the sides of the valley, so that the effect, when you looked from the bridge, was of some neat and undestructive landslide.

The first hill held the railway station. It had a bell tower and high vaulted roof and seemed generally more the kind of place to which people made their final journey than their thousand daily ones. It was a tempting traveller's generalization that, in Europe, the railway stations looked like old churches while, in the USA, the churches looked like modern railway stations. In Luxembourg, most of the hotels crouched around the station in the hope of catching trade. I chose the President, where, in yet another refinement of bedroom confectionary etiquette, the chocolate on the pillow was glued to a piece of card which bore a pretty picture of the city.

On the train, I had made a diligent list of the places I would visit on the first afternoon. The Cathédrale Notre-Dame, I supposed, was a must; and it seemed that I could not reasonably miss the Musée National and the Musée Pescatore, the second of which seemed to hint, linguistically, at containing either fish or body-builders. But, on this sixth leg of the trip, I was becoming increasingly aware of a condition which could afflict travellers: sightblindness, a product of too much sightseeing. So, after dumping my stuff at the President, I thought: Tomorrow will do for the museums. I indulged myself with the revised light programme of a stroll across La Passerelle followed by dinner and a couple of hours with the new Ian McEwan novel.

Just over the bridge, at the heart of a hillside park, an eternal flame burned within a three-faced steel sculpture, so that the general impression was of a rusty tricorn hat on fire. This was Luxembourg's tribute to the dead of the Second World War. Unlike certain other countries where French was spoken, which will not be named here in the interests of European unity, Luxembourg made a touching fuss of acknowledging its moral debts from the Second World War. Boulevards were named after Kennedy, Roosevelt, and Patton; the English visitor was greeted with politeness and helpfulness.

If only there were more reason to go there. The next morning, I woke and looked out of the window. It was like watching a grey suit going round in a washing machine. It was true that heavy rain became few cities, but it was equally the case that some became unbearable in it. Southern European cities with a fondness for building in grey stone were particularly vulnerable on this score. I thought: After breakfast, I will trudge through the rain to the Cathédrale Notre-Dame, then the Musée National, and, after that, the Musée Pescatore. I paused and then I thought: And, when that is done, I will get on a train and go to Brussels. Well, if you put it like that. I stood at the window for a very long time, watching the grey suit being rinsed. That time in Luxembourg was the closest I ever came to repeating the crack-up at Seattle.

I will have to admit it. Reader, I skipped the museums. Or, rather, I reached the first room in one of them – in which a sign said: *Many interesting ancient coins have been discovered in the City of Luxembourg* – and decided to settle for an impressionistic pedestrian assessment of the place.

There is little pleasure in being rude about Luxembourg. So let it be acknowledged that its buildings impressed. The old-folks home in the Municipal Park, for example, was a vast château. If you were going senile there, you might well be forgiven for thinking you were Napoleon. There was also a huge Japanese-owned golf course, established for the employees of the Tokyo electronic companies which had invested heavily in Luxembourg in recent years.

And Luxembourg was friendly, clean, and neat, a good-natured place which seemed – meticulously and non-moralistically – to feature one of everything: an emporium of sex aids and pornographic material, a shop selling devotional and evangelical religious objects. It was a country of exceptional political stability, and one in which the papers still wrote nice things about the Royal Family.

But what is it for? Luxembourg lacked either resonant history or contemporary significance. The guidebooks and museums tried to do a PR job on John the Blind, an early ruler, but he had not really caught on as a historical icon, a failure perhaps explained by the fact that he was immortalized for his eye trouble (he was not, you noticed, John the Great or John the Wise or John the Conqueror). This lack of identity was apparent in the tourist shops. There was no strong association to exploit except the name of the place. So glasses, sweatshirts, teaspoons, chocolate boxes were perfectly routine except for the name of the city. Dolls held pieces of silk imprinted with: LUXEMBOURG. Obviously someone had decided that the agonized features of John the Blind were not sufficiently souvenir-genic.

So his country had ended up as Luxembourg the Nice, failing to achieve the national stature for which its breathtaking setting seemed to mark it out. It was as if, in the original divine geopolitical blueprint, Luxembourg was down as a hub town of history, and given the scenery to match, but then the wily French slipped God some kind of sweetener or backhander and historical significance was switched to Paris.

Luxembourg also represented perhaps the most tragic example of the bully-runt and penis envy syndromes, the particular severity of its condition being that, whereas New Zealand was awed by cocky Australia and Canada by the rampant USA, Luxembourg was in the shadow of . . . Belgium.


On the train from Luxembourg to Brussels, I finished the Ian McEwan novel, which juxtaposed rationalist and spiritualist explanations for an encounter in post-war France between a honeymooning couple and two large fierce dogs. That year, everyone was writing about Europe. Every other book concerned the Second World War or was set in Germany, Italy, or France.

It was as if the End of Empire novel – the classic British fiction of the 1980s, set in India, Pakistan, South Africa, Australia, New Zealand – had been replaced by the Start of Empire novel, in which British writers grappled with the prospect of European nationality and subsumption into a pan-continental structure. Many of the books, like the McEwan, balanced the continent's 1990s wave of freedom against its inheritance of past terrors. McEwan asked: 'What possible good could come of a Europe covered in this dust, these spores, when forgetting would be inhuman and dangerous, and remembering a constant torture?'

It was a pertinent question. Even Belgium – plucky little Belgium, racing towards my train – had voted in uncomfortable numbers for parties of the extreme right in the recent elections. Denmark had voted no in a referendum on European unity. The French would be balloted in September, with a close result expected. On the brink of submission, the proud singularities of Europe were pulling back from the union which their politicians had been presenting as their historical destiny.

Part of the peculiarity of the process was the way in which 'Brussels' – always formerly English and French shorthand for boredom – had become a word of Satanic associations. People worried aloud about 'government by Brussels', using the phrase not, as before, to suggest an eternity of worthy speeches by turgid men, but to mean dictatorship by unelected bureaucrats and the erasing of native tradition. In its way, this change in a place's reputation was as improbable, for the post-war generation, as Moscow's graduation from military monster to economic victim.

I left the train at the Gare du Nord and the first surprise was the mood. This was mucky little Brussels, the walls bending beneath graffiti of which the only word you needed to understand was 'Immigrés'. Though distressing, it was not surprising to find Belgium involved in the foreigner-hostility which was a product of the reshuffling of Europe. (The Maastricht Treaty proposed weakening border controls, at the same time as a tide of refugees from disintegrating Eastern Europe.)

Yet hating strangers was already a Belgian tradition, because of the ancient unpleasantness between the Flemings and the Walloons, the two linguistically and intellectually inimical resident peoples. Belgium was Northern Ireland run by the Swiss. A civil war of social iciness not violence had produced hidden intensities. Events in Europe had provided an excuse for their release.

There was an undertow of menace on the streets, so that, in a comparison I would never have thought possible, Brussels reminded me, at times, of Detroit. Admittedly, the Gare du Nord lay in a sleazy region, the streets featuring the throb shops and strip bars, but the impression of a new unpleasantness seldom relented throughout my time in the city. In fact, it was in this place, of all I visited, that I felt closest to physical danger. From the station, I had followed a sign saying 'Taxis' down a littery, deserted street, at the end of which a ragged, dirty youth was about to get into a ruined saloon.

'Taxi!' I shouted.

He straightened and turned, dishevelled and tense. I realized that the only evidence that this might be a taxi had been the sign at the beginning of the street. The word appeared nowhere on the vehicle. It seemed far more likely – now that I twitchily reviewed the visual clues – that he was stealing the car and had been interrupted by me.

'Taxi?' he grunted.

'Er, oui,' I improvised. He stood and looked at me for so long that I feared my bad accent had accidentally produced a phonetic rendition of some French perversion or insult. Finally, he said: 'Où? Wheh? Wheh yugo?' I mentioned the Metropole Hotel and he quoted a sum greater than the train fare between Paris and Brussels via Luxembourg.

'OK,' I said. He relaxed. I was fairly sure by now that he had broken into the car, but had seen the possibility for some opportunistic extra earnings as he took the goods away. I tried not to think about the other explanation, which was that he had spotted an opening for what you might call a drive-in mugging. While I waited by the passenger door, he walked round to the rear of the car and stood looking at the licence plate for several minutes. I guessed he was memorizing the number, in case of being stopped by the cops.

He came back round to the door at which I had disturbed him, shook it free and flipped up the lock-stalks at the back for me to get in. The first key he tried would not fire the ignition, but he pulled a second from his pocket and we were away. Five minutes later, he pulled up outside the Metropole. I paid him and arrived at reception elated that the worst had not occurred. Actually, when I reflected on the sum he had won for a short journey, I realized that he had effected a bloodless mugging. But, if there had to be one, that kind was fine by me.

In the hotel, the safe traveller experienced another peril of his chosen latitudes. It was my severest, and most humiliating, outbreak of Room Service Rage. At the desk, I filled in the inevitably thorough three-page Brussels questionnaire on my eye colour, blood group, licence plate, and reason for travelling. Then the clerk handed me a dirty white plastic oblong. From years before in a stuffy classroom in Hertfordshire, I managed to recall the French expression *avoir besoin de*, to have need of.

'*J'ai besoin d'une clef*,' I tentatively said.

The receptionist smiled and pointed to the card in my hand. The lifts weren't working, so I stomped up two flights of stairs with my hundredweight of luggage, mainly books. I reached the door supposed to be mine, but could find no slot for the plastic oblong. I was squeezing it forlornly in the jamb-crack when a morning-suited manager tapped me on the shoulder.

'Yes, excuse me?'

'I don't seem to be able to open the door,' I hissed.

'No, indeed. Well, this is because you do not have a key. I advise you to enquire at reception,' he said, with language-school flatness of tone.

I stormed back along the corridor and down to the lobby, dropped my bags of Europhobe fiction on the marble floor with a satisfying bang and jump of dust, slammed the plastic card down on the counter, and shouted, like the kind of Englishman abroad I had never wished to be: 'I think I need a key.'

'Oh, I am sorry, sir. You must exchange this token at the concierge's desk for your key,' the receptionist said soothingly. 'I am sorry if you thought it was the key itself.'

Admitted to the room, I cooled down with a heavily chemical orange juice from the mini-bar. It was late afternoon, with driving rain which further reduced what few beauties Brussels had. For a while the gloom suited my mood, but eventually I decided to switch on the light. There was a lifeless click and no light. The television was just as dead. I grabbed the telephone and thumped the numbers like someone throttling a chicken.

'Yes, hello, can I help?'

'I don't,' I steamed, 'seem to be able to . . .'

'Ah, Mr Losson. You have got into your room all right now, I hope . . .' the concierge crooned. I was sure I could hear laughter. The Englishman, who tries to open his door with his plastic key voucher, now he has another problem!

'What is your problem, Mr Losson?'

'The lights – and the television – don't seem to work . . .'

'Ah. Have you pressed the on switch?'

'Yes, of course I've . . .'

'I shall send someone up to assist you . . .'

Herman Melville may have thought that whoever has but once dined his friends has known what it is to be Caesar. Well, whoever has but once stayed at the Metropole Hotel in Brussels has known what it is to be a seventies rock star. Never before in my life had I wanted to trash a hotel room. I was wondering how the lightstand and the mini-bar would look on the pavement when a concierge arrived. He peered knowingly at a switch by the door, depressed it and then, with maddening little flourishes like a children's magician, strolled round the room, illuminating every light and operating the television.

'You see, Mr Losson. Only when the main switch is depressed will the others function. It is a conservationist measure. This is indicated in the notice beside the switch in languages including English . . .'

In remorse, I tipped him nearly as much as my cab fare from the station. I was almost beginning to wish my project had taken me across the desert on a pogo-stick.

Brussels was famous for only four things. A statue of a small boy urinating, the manufacture of the kind of chocolates which gave weight-gain a good name, an empire of exquisite restaurants around the Grand Place, and, more recently, the creation of a federal Europe by stealth. Beyond this, it was not a nation of historical resonance. A few years before, a British newspaper had run a competition, in which they printed the answers and the trick was to guess the questions. The one that everyone got was 'René Magritte'. It was pitifully easy. Clearly, the question was: 'Name one famous Belgian.'

However, in the matter of tourism, there was a lot that other small excitement-disadvantaged countries could learn from Brussels. Think about it for a moment. The city possessed a single unusual sight. It was the statue of the cheeky toddler peeing. It is called the Mannekin Pis, its fame helped by the fact that the second word served the same purpose in most languages, being a rough onomatopoeic notation of the stream released. Even so, it did not immediately seem promising material for the attraction of travellers. Indeed, it was possible to imagine a Bob Newhart sketch in which the head of the US advertising agency charged with raising the global profile of Belgium put in his first phone call to the Brussels *Touristführer*.

'OK, Hans, whatta ya got for me?'

'Vel, ve haf a splendid statue of a little chap, uh, going to the lavatory. Ve think that perhaps ve make models of . . .'

'Hold it there, Hans. You're telling me that people are gonna buy reproductions of his weener in twenty different fabrics . . .'

But they do. In the foreigner-coveting shops around his perch, the little piddler did his thing in bronze, copper, charcoal, silver, clay, plaster, and probably Latvian gouache. There was a representation in lace, a strange combination of vulgarity and delicacy. He pissed from cups, glasses, coasters, toby jugs, clocks, watches, barometers, thermometers, and spoons. He micturated in silhouette, in one dimension and in three. There was even a merchandising line in statues of the cheeky leaker wearing different professional outfits – tennis player, soldier, prince, policeman – each with an outlet for his famous function. It was a sort of Hand-Action Man.

Other urinary souvenirs included one of those plastic domes you shook to make snow-flakes scatter on the Mannekin's head as he emptied himself. There was a plant bowl which he stood over, watering your flowers if you attached him to a hose pipe, and a teapot, of which the spout was his knob. Ringo Starr had once said of Lord Archer – then merely Jeffrey and the organizer of a charity event featuring the Beatles – 'That man would bottle my pee and sell it, if he could.' Well, Brussels had achieved an equivalent feat of commerce. A penis was for reproduction, but no penis had ever been so often reproduced. Were they taking the piss?

If they were, people swallowed it. The statue had become the most famous urine sample in history apart from Ben Johnson's at the 1988 Olympics, the most celebrated leak since the Pentagon Papers. Apparently, in the Latin quarters of Belgium, that act of urinary masochism called a golden shower was renamed a mannekin pis. (How do I know? All right, I realize that there are travel writers who would have discovered this information because they were down there in the red-light district being widdled on. I got it from a book about the sex industry I was once given to review.)

A large crowd was gathered around the pisser's plinth in the early morning, so that the scene resembled a shrine. The boy even wore a crown of flowers, like a urological Mother of God. The religious metaphor failed only with the faces of the congregation, which wore half-embarrassed smiles. Before taking a picture, people would wander around looking studiedly uninterested, as if they were pickpockets, before suddenly pulling up their cameras and stealing the scene. Then they would glance sideways and shrug, as if to indicate that *their* photography, if no one else's, was ironic or post–modernist.

But who was I to be superior? This was my fourth pilgrimage to him, and the first on which I had the excuse of professional observation. The little chap was made of a bronze more blackened than I remembered from earlier sights. I was unsure if this was a result of the degradations of time and climate or if there had been a racist element in the fame of the statue which I had not previously appreciated. I had also remembered him nude, but, on this day at least, he was kitted out in miniature blazer, flannels, and cap.

As I left, another coachload of pisser pilgrims was clambering across the cobbles, their eyes excitedly fixed on the open flies of Belgium's great inanimate ambassador. It was, objectively, ridiculous. The first oddity was that a sombre city had connived in the evacuation of a bladder becoming its international symbol. The second was that the world's tourists so enthusiastically encouraged the cult.

I wandered off around the city, reflecting on why this should be so. Within a few minutes, I knew. The city was not a country in which you could afford ascetically to deny yourself the obvious sights, preserving your time for the less advertised delights. Brutally, in terms of tourist opportunities, there were the restaurants, then the widdler, and then the art galleries.

So, with my plaque of the Mannekin Pis in my pocket, I wandered up the Mont des Arts, the cultural strip of Brussels, a wide slice of park and galleries and palaces which hung like a bright and expensive tie between the shabby grey lapels of business and industrial Brussels. But even here, in 1992, the undertow of unpleasantness could not be escaped. On the steps and fountains approaching the Palais des Congres, the graffiti was so deep as to have produced an accidental mural. Nor did the events unfolding on the artistic boulevard all belie the place's reputation: a large banner boasted that the 'First European Fluid Dynamics Conference' was taking place. I tried to imagine what it must be like to be a delegate to such a gathering. 'How's tricks?' a friend asks. 'Oh,' he replies. 'Exciting. I'm off to a fluid dynamics conference at the weekend. In Brussels!'

My destination, though, was the Musées Royaux des Beaux

Arts, the pair of galleries at the top of the hill. On one side, signs directed you to *Art Ancien/Oude Kunst*; on the other side to *Art Moderne/Moderne Kunst*.

Looking at the signs, I realized that I felt stranger and shakier than could be properly accounted for by the height of the Mont des Arts and my detailed research on Brussels cuisine the previous evening. There was a slight breathlessness, a sense of adrenalin and blood pressure being up.

Then I realized that I was suffering from the condition which could afflict travellers anywhere in the world at any time, an affliction of the nervous system far more likely to strike the average tourist than Legionnaire's disease. It was called Memory. Or, to give it the full psychological name, association of place.

My first trip to Brussels had been in 1980. I was eighteen and was one of fifty students touring Europe – 'Fine Young Minds' was, I think, the optimistic description in the competition literature – as the prize in an essay competition for school leavers organized by Barclays Bank.

In the first round, you wrote a four-page essay. My chosen topic was 'A short story set in the year 2001'. (The alternative, as I remember, was 'If I Were Chancellor of the Exchequer for a Day . . .') My favoured reading at the time was the novels and stories of Kafka and the plays of David Hare, Howard Brenton, and Howard Barker. Accordingly, I wrote a brief dystopia in which a man was confined to a squalid cell in a Britain which had become a police state. (Mrs Margaret Thatcher's first administration had begun the previous year.) I fear that there were also dark hints that the man was Jesus Christ, a second time on Earth, and murdered by the British government, which was under the impression that he was just some long-haired dissident.

The story's central premiss was that money and materialism were a bad idea. Indeed, the is-he-Jesus was wiped out for spreading such heresy around. Either Barclays Bank was determined not to judge the stories from a corporate perspective or there were students elsewhere in the country typing out *Das Kapital* and sending in that as an answer to 'If I Were Chancellor of the Exchequer for a Day'. Whatever the explanation, I survived the essay stage and was invited for an interview in London.

One of the panel of the three seemed happy, indeed eager, that the man in the cell should be Jesus, and there was no further enquiry about the anti-capitalist drift of my submission. Two weeks later, I was called to my headmaster – a monk from a basketball-playing order of American missionaries now operational in Hertfordshire – and told that I had won a place on the Fine Young Minds tour of Europe.

It was a seriously generous deal. A two-week trip, with first-class accommodation, in France, Belgium, Germany, Switzerland, and Italy. It may also have occurred to many of the eighteen-year-olds selected that there was the possibility of proximity, in hotel rooms, without parents, with one or more of forty-nine fine young bodies; or, anyway, young, or, anyway, bodies.

I needed to be a few years older before I appreciated the reasoning of our benefactors. At that time, every undergraduate arriving at a British university was handed a leaflet from the National Students' Union urging them not to bank with Barclays, which allegedly had extensive investments in South Africa. The European Tour had been, I now assumed, counteractive propaganda among the young. An account was opened for each winner and, twelve years later, I was one of the few people who felt a small warm feeling of gratitude every time they walked past the branch where they banked. I would probably have discovered sex, dissolution, and existential despair anyway, but that I discovered them at that time, and with someone else paying the bills, was entirely to the credit of Barclays Bank.

Before we left London – where there was a send-off lunch with the bank's barons – I was besotted. She was called (or I will call her) Isolde, a result of her father's passion for opera. She had green eyes and a snub nose and light brown hair which she wore in elaborate braids, so that, if you stood above her and looked down, the top of her head resembled continental bread. It was my dearest wish, from early on, to stand above her and look down.

As soon as I was introduced to her at the drinks before the London lunch, I was calculating the romantic odds. Of the twenty-five males – the party was exactly co-educational – I was sure that two were gay, a few were even more gauche than I was, and several seemed to have made close liaisons with other girls in the party already, presumably at the interviews or through neighbourhood connections. But, against this, an experienced bookmaker would have balanced the fact that I had never yet even kissed a girl and that Isolde had an air of sexual sophistication which I knew only through Eric Rohmer and François Truffaut.

It was then that God (or so my adolescent self took it) intervened. At happy random, the bank had placed me next to Isolde at the lunch. I knew, as a fine young Roman Catholic, that it would be a dangerous historical and theological precedent if God were actually to let anything happen between me and Isolde, but for the moment it was enough that He had seated her next to me. It was even more generous of Him that she laughed at my jokes, sat next to me on the coach, and – after the group dinner in Paris on the first night abroad – suggested that we gave the party the slip and went for a walk along the Seine.

I walked slowly, and very slightly doubled over, from the effects of a condition common in young males. Symptoms increased, although an involuntary alleviating leeching also threatened, when Isolde suggested that we bought a bottle of wine and went back to the hotel, before the return of the others, who were being given a night tour of Paris architecture by one of our bank chaperones, a foreign commodities dealer, who could be earnest in eight languages. At this stage, I wondered if I was the beneficiary of some petulant resignation note from God, who was jacking it all in and abandoning Catholic morality in a last night of doctrinal mayhem in which the secret prayers of young men formerly obedient to Rome would actually be answered.

My belief in this divine reversal was only increased when, on our return to Isolde's room, it was revealed that, amazingly enough, her room-mate had not quietly left the architecture viewing group because of the onset of Parisian flu and was not propped up in one of the beds reading a book. After a few diplomatic swigs of the wine which was the official reason for our return, we kissed and I moved my hand between Isolde's legs, in a manoeuvre for which the careful study of modern American novels had prepared me.

'It's my period,' she said. 'And I've got a boyfriend at home. Just hold me.'

So God was still consistent, after all. Even so, by the time we reached Brussels, our next city, in that summer of 1980, I was in a state of excitement perhaps greater than is normal for first time tourists to Belgium. The next morning was free time, although the foreign commodities dealer let it be known that he was willing to lead a guided tour of the older churches. Isolde suggested that the two of us took in the art galleries. She caught hold of my hand on the Mont des Arts – a confusing move after the previous night's reference to the boyfriend, but not to be refused in my condition – and I began to wonder if God had pulled his resignation note out of the wastepaper basket and might yet reconsider posting it.

It was then that Satan intervened. As we reached the door of the Musées Royaux des Beaux Arts, we heard an English voice.

'Well, fook me, if it's not the Happy Couple!'

This was Void. A Northerner christened David, he had symbolically demolished his parents' nominal imposition as part of his devotion to punk rock, then current. He now preferred to be called Void. In fact, it might have been argued that his parents would have got the message of rebellion from his hair, which he had cropped tight and dyed green. He had a loud voice and laughed at his own frequent would-be jokes but, perhaps because of this, he tended to be on his own, so could not be completely eliminated from my list of potential rivals for Isolde.

'What are you two fooking up to, eh? Apart from fooking?' leered Void. He winked on the innuendo. This was fairly typical of his approach to conversation. I fully expected Isolde to tell him that it was her period and that she had a boyfriend at home, but – writing this, I see that being eighteen again would not necessarily be sheer pleasure – she consolidated my confusion by taking my hand again and telling Void: 'Wouldn't you like to know?'

'Aye, well if tha've room for another on top, let me know!' roared Void. 'What I'm after is, bloke told me it were somewhere down here tha gets dope . . .'

'Well, we're going to the art galleries,' Isolde explained.

'Fooking coolture vooltures!' said Void. 'But, OK, you've persuaded me. I'll come with you.'

I see now, grudgingly, I suppose, that his manner was the thick overcoat of the lonely, but, at the time, I was making a list of useful household objects to be constructed from his testicles.

'Well,' yelled Void. 'Where should we start? Old cunts or modern cunts?'


The whole of that film of experience had unscrolled just because of seeing the signs beside which I now stood again, twelve years later. This way: *Art Ancien/Oude Kunst*. That way: *Art Moderne/Moderne Kunst*.

On that occasion, at least, Void's scatology had not been merely habit, but mildly inventive, or at least multilingual. We had begun, as I did again now, with the modern cunts, the moderne kunst, the contemporary artists.

As I went, I was followed around the gallery by three eerily vivid ghosts: myself as a Fine Young Mind, Isolde, Void. Ideally, travel was discovery. Yet, inevitably, simply because of the international business circuit and the small roster of places favoured for romantic weekends and annual vacations, half of the journeys you made involved being ambushed by the past. I wondered if those widowed, or divorced or left against their will, had to black out sections of the map, establish no-go zones for trips in new relationships. Of course, there was also the other aspect of association of place: the deliberate bath in the past. Couples who were still together booked tickets to places where they had once been happy. And that went either way. The ghosts could give a blessing or a curse.

In this case, they were merely laughing gently at the demented romantic intensity of the youth in the gallery more than a decade before. At the entrance to the first display, there was a large poster visually explaining the museum rules. A drawing of a bag with a line through it advised the checking in of luggage. A crossed-out camera prohibited photography. A cake with an X through it ruled out eating. And so on.

'Fooking 'ell! I laike them. 'Ooo painted them, then?' Void had enquired. Isolde and I exchanged a look which established our superior maturity.

In Cubism, Isolde suddenly excused herself and headed for

the *Dammen/Femmes/*Ladies. This pleased me, as it suggested that her claim of menstruation the night before had not been merely strategic. Void hit me very hard on the back.

'Well, are you fooking her?'

'Well, er . . .'

'She'll come through in the end. Classy type like that, you want to give her a bit of the Irish airline . . .'

This was a reference to a mildly feminist joke of the time: 'My boyfriend thinks Cunnilingus is an Irish airline.' As Void noisily celebrated the wit of his innuendo, my main worry was that the sight of this foul-mouthed green-haired youth hanging on the back a pale reserved one in a light blue nylon shirt would be taken by spectators as a surrealist exhibit.

When Isolde came back, we went into the Magritte section. The country did well by its one famous son, although the call for his work around the world thinned out the exhibits.

'Oh, great, I love Magritte,' I had said.

'Magritte is the kind of artist you like if you don't like art,' said Isolde.

Now, this strikes me as both shrewd and, in my case, true, but, then, I was devastated. 'I know what you mean,' I said quickly, in one of those cowardly renegotiations of romance. Void made an exaggerated *Ouch!* face at me behind Isolde's back, which served to worsen the defeat.

''Tain't art. Joost like fooking *Monty Python*,' said Void.

The me of 1992 was far more reconciled to liking Magritte, although *Une Panique au Moyen Age* now had a charge which escaped the three of us in 1980. On this visit, I also noticed that, if you spoke English, several of the Magrittes carried a pleasant little additional joke. The galleries' formula for 'gift of' was *'legs de'*. On a picture like *La Magie Noire*, in which a half-blue nude stood beside a window, the body was cut off just above the knees, beneath which lay the words *'Legs de Mme Georgette Magritte'*. Lucky Renée, if they were.

Isolde, Void, and I had moved on to *art ancien*, the *oude kunst*, the old cunts. 'Good name for a fooking band!' said Void in front of a Hieronymus Bosch. Afterwards, outside, Isolde had insisted on taking a photograph of Void, and I had been gloomy, assuming that she had been impressed by his views on modern art, but then she said, crisply: 'This photo is after Magritte. I'm going to caption it: This is not a human being.' Void didn't get it, but Isolde held my hand on the way back to the hotel and a panic of young age subsided again.

But, in 1992, I had a flight to catch. With a postcard of *Une Panique au Moyen Age* in my pocket, I took a taxi to the airport, still unsettled by the intensity of the presence of the ghosts of Isolde, Void, and the once-me.

I had never expected Belgium to have this effect. Even in the safe world, you were not safe from memories. But, as Proust proved with his lump of sponge, the strangest things can set us off, and I was overcome in Brussels. Yet at least those memories were essentially happy. It was Switzerland which held the demons for me.

# CHAPTER SEVEN

# UNEXPLOSIVE PACKAGE

## Switzerland

One of my more disastrous relationships – not the one with Isolde, on which you and I have just commenced, but another one – went wrong because of the obsession of the other party with 'spontaneity'. Her entire life was organized around the unexpected.

Our outings were mainly to plays or to restaurants. However, though sharing these interests, we differed in approach. I paid a fee to be an Advance Booking Member of all the major subsidized theatres – a privilege which permitted the purchase of tickets before the scenery was painted – and my diary was filled with notes first to book our favourite restaurant and then, on the day of the date, to telephone to confirm.

She – 'Let's be spontaneous' – preferred to start merely with a meeting time and then, over a preliminary drink, flick through the newspaper and say: 'I think I'd like to see *Hedda Gabler*,' or 'That new Italo-Thai place in Covent Garden sounds interesting.' In my experience, this meant that neither seats nor tables were available and so we would end up at *Oi, Where's My Trousers?*, an English sex romp in its eighteenth year, with fast food (or food fasting) to follow. Eventually, on the nights when the itinerary was my pick, I started to fake it. Plucking a drama and a brasserie apparently out of the air at 6 p.m., I would in fact have made bookings days before. On arrival at the venue, I would say, 'You pay the taxi while I dash in and see if they can fit us in.' By the time she arrived at the box office or reception desk, I had secured our pre-arranged reservations and was turning with a relieved: 'Yes, looks like we're OK.'

I mention this because the same philosophical divisions existed among travellers. There were those – a species currently prevalent among the young professional classes – whom you heard saying: 'Holiday? We're taking the ferry to Boulogne and then we'll drive where the spirit takes us. We haven't booked anywhere. If we see a gîte we like around about sundown, we'll stop and hope they've beds . . .' Well, fine, but my fear would be ending up with the accommodation equivalent of *Oi, Where's My Trousers?* and the speedy pizza. There were those of us whose mental equilibrium was best underwritten by hotel reservations guaranteed by credit card for late arrival and plane tickets with onward portions of the ticket reconfirmed at least seventy-two hours before departure.

But, there was a level of traveller's sandbagging beyond even that. In Alaska, I had suffered some exposure to package tours. In my view, the only other way of assembling such a collection of anal retentives would have been to put superglue on every seat of a train. Those scenes stiffened my belief that a project of safe travel should include one piece of detailed field experience in that line. Adding braces to belt, I decided that the safest form of travel should be through the most chronicledly innocuous of nations: Switzerland.

My package was the Swiss Panorama Express, offered by Thomson in its *Lakes and Mountains Summer 1992* brochure. To adapt a scale of comparison from culture, in the world of the package holiday, Thomas Cook was Mozart and Cosmos was Lloyd-Webber. Thomson was sort of Puccini. The first extended to escorted trekking in Nepal. The second descended to teenage gang-trips to the Costa del Hell. Thomson was the conveyor of the affluent but cautious middle classes.

The Swiss Panorama Express was a seven-day trip promising an opportunity to 'see the scenic heart of Switzerland and experience the romance of rail.'

To go alone would be to invite suspicion. The package holiday was the province of the couple or, at worst, the pair. But my wife was saving up her money to go to New Zealand again. There was a tradition in travel-writing that the author is accompanied by some exotic eccentric: a dyspeptic poet, a brace of randy débutantes, a Latin American mistress, an alcoholic ex-para-trooper, a spoiled priest, a characterful dog, an elephant. All of these would have been too conspicuous on a Thomson holiday – and, anyway, I don't seem to know any – so I persuaded my father to be my guest. Born in the north-east, near Stephenson's birthplace, he had a lifelong interest in trains. Our cover identities would be those of an eccentric retired telecommunications specialist and his shabby and clumsy son, a teacher if anyone asked, spending some of what the Americans called quality time together.

DAY ONE: UK–ZURICH–LUCERNE.
*Fly to Zurich (journey time 1¾ hours) where your representative joins you for the 1st-class rail journey to Lucerne and the Hotel Monopole (TTTT) where you'll spend the next two nights. During the afternoon, there'll be time to explore the town and perhaps to visit the Transport Museum, with its collection of steam engines and old railway carriages.*

Detailed advance descriptions of each day were an important feature of the package holiday. They allowed the tourist to complain about any deviation from the schedule. For the package traveller, complaining was at least as important as the weather and the scenery, perhaps more so.

In an exceptional demonstration of this phenomenon, the roots of mutiny were present in our group even before any event had taken place which could be measured against the prediction. Owing to a computer problem at Head Office, several of the party had been accidentally bumped off an alternative tour, the William Tell Express ('A superb journey by rail and lake through Switzerland'), and offered the Swiss Panorama Express as compensation for the error when it was discovered.

At Zurich Airport that July morning, these refugees were already discovering the comraderie of discontent. 'Did I overhear you saying you originally booked on the William Tell Express? . . . Yes, yes. So did we. Computers, did they tell you? Mmmm. I shall be *very interested* to see if this trip is an adequate replacement.' The last phrase was the classic foreplay of the tourist consumer: the first move towards the hoped for climax of the formal letter of complaint.

But this should not have been surprising. Some people, undoubtedly, chose this kind of holiday for the possibility of company, but my father, who went with my mother on several such tours every year, was notoriously self-contained. He – and the majority of the customers – went, I assumed, because they were the kind of people who liked rules. My father was the only person I had ever heard of who once wrote to the Inland Revenue complaining that he had been under-assessed. Returning from family holidays, he would troop us through the red channel to declare his undrunk half-inch of tooth-mug Scotch.

'You're cutting the train connection a little fine,' he warned our personal Thomson representative at Zurich Airport. Others murmured in support. The other constant on a package holiday was the terror of missing connections. People arrived three hours early for a flight, one hour early for a train. If Christopher Isherwood had written a book about package holidays, it would have been called *Mr Norris Worries About Changing Trains*. An alternative title, of course, might have been *I am a Camcorder*, for the other uniting factor in such groups was that they videoed everything which happened, with a zeal previously seen only in the KGB.

My father, rather irritatingly, turned out to be right to have fretted about the connection. A queue at the ticket office – where the rep bought all the tickets, just like on school trips – meant a platform dash for the Lucerne train. Several of the party were in what we were now asked to refer to as the Third Age, and running for a train was something which now happened to them only in dreams.

We collapsed into the carriage – with its sign satisfyingly announcing 'Reserved For Thomson' – with one whistle-blow to go. The chase had dangerously taxed some travellers. A husband was burrowing in luggage, while his wife, spreadeagled on the seat, wheezed like a cheap heater. He fumbled out a tablet and pressed it under her tongue.

'Her doctor said she wasn't to run,' he said.

Our personal Thomson representative was Zoe. She was a

giggly East Londoner just out of school. In a white blouse and blue culottes, with a scarf in the company colours, she would accompany us throughout. The company's recruitment, reported to be furiously competitive, depended on the lure of foreign travel. But the truth was that the job was a combination of teacher, orderly on a urology ward, and railway station manager on a morning when indefinite delays on all services had been announced.

Zoe's group that week – apart from the retired telecommunications specialist and his clumsy shabby teacher son – comprised the Borrowbys, a Liverpudlian couple in their late sixties; the Leonards, a retired husband and wife from Romford; the Todds, a seventyish father and fortyish son; the Misses Durham, teacher sisters just retired; and the Keens, a Midlands couple in their forties, who worked in local government.

What, as they say in detective novels, had brought together this disparate collection of individuals? By the end of the week, I had pieced together that Mr Borrowby had been a train driver and Mr Leonard and both Todds were steam-railway buffs and locomotive spotters. Borrowby even still dressed in the dark serge trousers and light blue epauletted shirt of the British railway employee. The Misses Durham had been motivated by interest in Switzerland and had booked the William Tell Express, attracted by the greater element of cruising. So had the Keens. This was the nagging sadness of these couples. They were complaints waiting to happen.

But little of this, beyond opening pleasantries, was known as we checked in to the Hotel Monopole (TTTT), which was opposite the railway station in Lucerne, with a view of the lake if you were lucky, which we weren't.

The afternoon was scheduled as free time. I read the *International Herald Tribune* by the lake, with a beer. Ross Perot had dropped out of the presidential race, complaining of Republican dirty tricks. Among his allegations was that the party had computer-enhanced a wedding picture of his daughter to suggest that she was pregnant.

My sense of dour duty in being away was at its lowest since Australia. One of the mysterious physics lessons of tourism was that the combination of water and alps in Switzerland achieved a kind of natural air-conditioning. Beside the lake, a squealing school party from England was making the delicious discovery of the reliance of German signs on the word *Fahrt*. A man in a coloured tuxedo and bowler hat, with a monkey on his shoulder, was winding an organ. A bloke in *Lederhosen* was blowing the vast and bizarre Alpine horn, looking like a Magritte painting called *The Pipe Smoker*.

For dinner, our party was arranged at one long white-clothed table. The food was works canteen with attitude: a generalized broth, meat in cream, vegetables steamed to screaming point. Conversation was faltering and Zoe was forced to fall back on professional prodding: 'Is this your first time in Switzerland?' The necessity of this skill was the single point of connection between tour reps and princesses.

An American tour group raucously occupied the rest of the restaurant. They were lamenting the departure of Perot: 'Hell, we've had politicians. And what've *they* done?' Two of the couples were celebrating big-number wedding anniversaries. 'Tell you a story about marriage,' yelled a man who looked like one of those oil types JR used to fool in *Dallas*. 'Couple on their honeymoon in a hotel. She sits on the edge of the bed, looks down at his, uh, parts, and says: "Oh, God, it's so big!" Twenty-five years pass, they have a couple of kids, they decide to celebrate their jubilee in the same hotel. He sits on the edge of the bed, looks down at her, uh, parts, and says: "Oh, God, it's so big!" That's the story of marriage for ya!'

'Oh, Harrison, you are ders-gusting!' said his wife.

Until this moment, our table had been the mess of resentments which any English social gathering was – the Liverpudlians finding the Southerners snooty, the Southerners thinking the Midlanders chippy, everyone flinching from Liverpool wit – but suddenly we were briefly united in disapproval of the Yanks.

'If you think that's bad, try sharing a campsite with them!' said Mr Keen. Everybody shivered. But then they agreed the Germans were worse.

During coffee, Zoe stood up with a clipboard.

'My job is to make this simply the best week's holiday you've ever had,' she said. 'Or the best two weeks, if you're taking the option of an extra week in a regional centre after the Panorama Express. The hotels, like the one we're in, will be of the superior standard which we call a 4T hotel . . .'

'I ordered tea and they only gi' us one!' cracked Mr Borrowby. He had elected himself the clown of the group.

'But, seriously,' Zoe went on. 'If you need anything at all, I am available twenty-four hours a day . . .'

'Waaaaar-haaaaay! You said the wrong thing there, pet. What's your room number?' roared Mr Borrowby. The Misses Durham looked uncomfortably reminded of parents' evenings. Mrs Borrowby seemed to have learned to close herself off from these moments.

'Lucerne was first written about in 840 – so it's been around quite a long time!' chirped Zoe, then gave us a Swiss Railways half-price travel pass and a voucher for a free souvenir silver spoon at a local jeweller's.

### DAY 2: LUCERNE.
*A day at leisure in Lucerne, with its famous covered medieval bridges and quaint pedestrian old town. Many visitors join the scenic boat trip to Weggis and Vitznau and take the cog railway to the top of the Rigi Mountain (approx. £14 with half-price travel card).*

I was the first down to breakfast, because, on this day without organized excursions, I was going alone to Zurich on the train, a piece of rebelliousness from the schedule which raised eyebrows from every member of the group I told. My father had refused to countenance joining such a departure.

On the table, between the silver coffee pots, was a wicker basket of rolls and one of croissants. I had two of the latter. By the time I was leaving, the rest of the party was down, and I heard Mr Keen say: 'Hey! Some bugger's had two croissants.' Dismay swept the table. (I later asked my father how I was to know this rule. 'People that go on these things just know,' he said. 'One roll, one croissant. It's a sort of folk knowledge.')

I had chosen to go to Zurich because I doubted that Lucerne was a whole-day place. Oh, and all right, the Heritage Secretary

David Mellor had been reported to have an actress mistress, and the English newspapers were available on the same day at Zurich Station.

Leaving aside the regional influence of France, Germany, and Italy on different cantons, there were four Switzerlands, each of them somehow antiseptically separate from the others. The first was tourist Switzerland, the clean cute region through which we were travelling on the Swiss Panorama Express, its symbols the cheese, the chocolate bar, and the cuckoo clock. The second was political Switzerland, the place of the oldest democracy, international neutrality, the Red Cross, eleventh-hour peace conferences, the airline of choice for the traveller fearing terrorism during the Gulf War, its symbol the cruciform of white on red or red on white. The third was business Switzerland, the country of industrial efficiency and financial prosperity, its symbol the jewelled hand-tooled watch.

Political and diplomatic Switzerland was understandably regarded with real warmth by dissidents and prisoners of war. But the attitude of other Europeans towards this – and towards tourist and business Switzerland – was a somewhat chilly admiration. Perhaps this was because of the perception of a fourth Switzerland, only spasmodically glimpsed beneath the other three.

This one was a country, in which one canton had only recently given women the vote, of legislative pedantry – the lease of a block of flats, according to one report, requiring males to urinate seated after 10 p.m. because of the splash-factor noise. More sinister judicial powers included the alleged removal to mental wards, without the approval of their families, of women suffering post-natal depression, or the castration of male psychiatric patients, again without relatives' consent. Political neutrality, often taken by outsiders as an executive expression of decency, could also be seen as moral abdication, a paradox best expressed in the way in which those tyrants whose victims were being assisted by the Red Cross in Geneva themselves stashed their loot in Zurich. The symbol of this Switzerland was the numbered bank account.

I had travelled from Lucerne, which was tourist Switzerland, to Zurich, which was business Switzerland, but also the hidden one, a world capital for both clean and dirty money. The massive digital clock on an office building opposite Zurich Station read 19:50 at ten o'clock in the morning. Was it a subliminal declaration of the superiority of clockwork? For if New York was, as Tom Wolfe had called it, the billion-footed city then Zurich was the city of a billion hands. They moved silently towards each other in whole parades of jewellers' windows, joining but never applauding.

If you wanted to be rude about Zurich, you would say that even the buildings wore grey suits. On the outskirts, it was true, there were some impressive old stone fortresses, now largely turned into restaurants: cannonballs into salad bowls, as the Bible nearly said. But the central architecture had a sombre uniformity. The Borse, a concrete block, was as cold and bald as a jail, a connection perhaps made from direct experience by some of the country's shadier depositors. There were banks of banks and insurance companies flocked like vultures on the prime lakeside real estate. In and out of them padded dark-clad men, being polite to each other in five languages.

A majority of the restaurants and bars in Zurich – as in Switzerland generally – were named after Willhelm Tell or his dramatic chronicler, Schiller. I read the latest Mellor stuff – his mistress had apparently liked to give him what the tabloids neatly called a 'toe-job' – over an apple juice in the Willhelm Tell Café. In the old days, the waitress would have placed an apple on your head, speared it with an arrow from twenty metres, then crushed the resulting pulp for your drink. Now, she opened a carton. Such was progress. On the dumbly punctual train back to Lucerne, I got into a confusion with the ticket collector, and a schoolboy of about seven interpreted, moving effortlessly between German and English. 'He is asking you whether you have shown him your ticket before,' he beamed, nervelessly accomplishing one of his second language's real safety-net tenses. I was grateful, but he was a literal example of a metaphorical perception: the Swiss as the class swot of Europe.

Back in Accommodation Centre 1, I strolled round the lake to the Lucerne Transport Museum. The aviation section rubbed in the rapidity of the aeroplane's history, with a display of models and dates, moving from a bicycle with a plank strapped on to the

747 in less than seventy years. I thought again of poor Richard Pearse of Timaru. In the history of tourism section, a display recalled the time when travellers were carried individually in sedan chairs: an early version of the package holiday. Another exhibit was a dusty guest register from a turn of the century Swiss resort. There was a column for name and a column for place travelled from. But most of the names were also places. The first travellers had been aristocrats. You could be as snobbish as you wanted about mass travel, but the democratization of the holiday, of knowledge of the world beyond your own, was another of the century's revolutions.

Before dinner, I criss-crossed the River Reuss, taking in the stone *Spreurbrucke* and the stone *Kapelbrucke*. These two fifteenth-century bridges were fine examples of the seventeenth-century art-form of gable-painting, in which scenes from a story were depicted on the triangular spaces inside the roof. (The Dance of Death on the first bridge, lives of the local patron saints on the second.) If a Swiss in 1680 said they were going out for a bridge evening, this was what they meant. It may even have been a precursor of television, in which you ran across the bridge for moving pictures, walked slowly backwards for action replay, stopped dead for a freeze-frame. Right-wing burghers probably complained about the possible psychological damage resulting from bridge-crossers' daily exposure to gable-paint nasties like the Dance of Death. An alternative theory was that the concertina of triangles anticipated the design of the Toblerone, Switzerland's most exotic chocolate bar.

While I was dressing for dinner, my father appeared, splenetically, at my bedroom door.

'They thought we were queers,' he said.

'What?'

'At breakfast this morning, after you'd gone, that one from the Midlands said, with heavy innuendo, "So your *friend* is going off on his own today?" I told him, that's not my friend, that's my son . . .'

The last remark would, I thought, have given hours of enjoyment to a family psychologist. At dinner that night, my father sounded like a language cassette on family relationships, speaking with exaggerated clarity sentences like 'I will ring your *mother* after dinner' and 'Did you telephone your *wife?*' Keen and Borrowby blushed.

The dessert was *crème brulée* for the second night running. Borrowby and Leonard made entries in the notebooks they carried, again as foreplay to a final outpouring of complaint.

'Cases outside doors by 7 a.m.,' said Zoe brightly, over coffee.


### DAY 3: LUCERNE–INTERLAKEN.

*Today you travel by 1st-class train past the picturesque lakes at Samen and Lungern and over the Brunig Pass into the Bernese Oberland. At Brienz you take the cog railway, powered by its vintage steam engine, up the Rothorn Mountain for some spectacular views over Lake Brienz and the mountains of the Jungfrau Region. Your journey continues by steamer across Lake Brienz and ends in Interlaken where you spend the next three nights at the Hotel Royal St Georges (TTTT).*

On the third day, we rose again, ate one roll, one croissant, and caught the train to Brienz. Everyone fussed and ostentatiously scuffed their feet while I put my half-price rail pass through the automatic machine. I realized that all of them, my father included, had been to the station before breakfast to mark their cards. It had not been part of Zoe's orders. It was package folk knowledge: never risk delay.

There was a modern fashion for television channels on which therapeutic pictures – of water, grazing animals, hills and trees – were played in front of classical music. They were usually called the Landscape channel or the Harmony channel. The window of a Swiss train or boat gave you this for free.

'You can tell which cows are the best milk producers by the size of their bells,' read Zoe from her clipboard.

'Eh? Oh, *bells!* I didn't hear you for a minute, luv,' Borrowby exploded. His wife went facially AWOL again.

On the full-colour weather map in my *USA Today* – a placebo because English papers had not reached Lucerne before we left – Switzerland was a country so small that there was no space for its name. A slightly fatter Luxembourg, it sat like a clump of moss between the boulders of Italy, France, and Germany. Wedged among ancient aggressors – like a European Israel, but one whose neighbours at least accepted its right to exist – its espousal of neutrality, you realized, was as much smaller-than-thou as holier-than-thou.

During the journey, a mutiny began to brew. Keen – to the enthusiastic support of Leonard and my father – suggested that the food in Lucerne might not have been of '4T standard'. He was particularly surprised that 'they wouldn't give me an extra crois-sant when some bugger'd had two'. One of the Misses Durham had heard of another Thomson holiday, taken by a colleague, on which the hotel had employed an 'Animator', who organized communal games and quizzes. She wondered if we might not have benefited from such an arrangement. Borrowby made another note.

From Brienz, an atmospherically asthmatic steam engine hauled us up the Rothorn. It was a nearly right-angled climb, so that all the way up you feared engine failure, while brake failure obsessed you all the way down. At the top of the mountain was a viewing station, an exorbitant café and a tourist kiosk. As the group queued for coffee, Mrs Borrowby sat down suddenly, puce and panting. Borrowby dived for her handbag and tried to be nimble with arthritic fists.

'I think we're going to lose the wife,' he hissed. 'Thin air. The doctor . . .'

'Oooh, that's a bit of a larf!' said Zoe. I wondered if she had cracked under the pressure of the potential mutiny, and forgotten all her training courses. But then I realized: *She thought it was another of his gags.* It was the equivalent to Liverpool humour of the story about the boy crying wolf. By the time she realized that he was serious, Mrs Borrowby was mainlining angina tablets and seemed likely to survive.

On the viewing platform, the Camcorders sucked in the mist, plunge, river, moss, and cow stuff they had come for. Leonard was videoed by his wife pretending to yodel. Of all the stops on my project so far, Switzerland was the first absolute tourist standby. The feeling I had had in Australia of its surviving visual originality now returned in the opposite connection. Travellers to a popular location, I thought, were like policemen or the parents of missing children, wandering around with a photograph until they got a match. Discovery was confirmation. The word 'picturesque' had achieved a new literality. It meant somewhere you had seen a picture of, and to which you now travelled to take one of your own.

The two-hour cruise to Interlaken offered another programme on the nation's natural Landscape channel, but, by now, I regarded it as a repeat. I was reading Malcolm Bradbury's *Doctor Criminale*. Suddenly, in the middle of the chapter I had reached, the characters went on a cruise around a Swiss lake. I looked from the page to the lake, from the descriptive passages to that described. It was a jolting moment. I mean, if you weren't safe from post-modernist experiences on holiday, then where were you?

The Hotel Royal St Georges in Interlaken at first seemed to appease the dissidents. After the shabby functionalism of Lucerne, it offered smart rooms, with power showers, mini-bars, and CNN on the television. But, at dinner, the revolutionaries were re-ignited. The printed menu card promised: Cream of Cucumber Soup, Kebab Zingara with Fondant Potatoes and Vichy Carrots, and Caramel Pudding with Whipped Cream. Well, Zingara, wherever it was, obviously had a lot of supermarkets as the kebab named for it consisted mainly of convenience cocktail sausages. Fondant potatoes were roast spuds. As for the Vichy Carrots, I distantly remembered that some war-time atrocity had taken place at the town of that name. Well, they were obviously taking it out on their vegetables now.

My father mentioned in a loud voice that the brochure definition of 4T accommodation was a hotel which offered a choice of dinner menus. Borrowby made a note.

'I mean,' said one of the Misses Durham. 'What if the only thing they served were something which one could not eat?'

'Exactly,' my father agreed. 'If I eat fish, I swell up and need to be taken to hospital . . .'

Zoe said she would call her area manager in the morning.

Days 4 and 5: Interlaken.
*Set between the lakes of Brienz and Thun, Interlaken is one of Switzerland's oldest and most stylish resorts. The view from the*

*Hoheweg of the Jungfrau peak is legendary and no visitor should miss the mountain train excursion via the Lauterbrunnen Valley and Wengen to the Jungfraujoch and the Aletsch glacier and down through the 'glacier village' of Grindelwald (approx £24 with half-price travel card). In the evening, you can visit a folklore show at the century-old casino and try your luck at the gaming tables (maximum stake SFr5).*

On the first day in Accommodation Centre 2, only the Borrowbys decided to ascend the Jungfrau. One of the country's main attractions was mountains for people too frightened to climb them. The rest opted out, because the sole point of travelling to that height was the sights, and the morning weather forecast was morbid, with the mountains which surrounded Interlaken already obscured by a bread-mould mist.

In the morning, my father and I walked around the town. This was Tourist Switzerland at its most industriously yukky: the kind of national town that nationals stayed away from. It was like being trapped in a music box, as the thousands of different-sized cow bells in the hundreds of gift-shops tinkled in the wind. The two most tell-tale signs of the town's motivation were the British-style red telephone boxes and a large number of amenities named after the old Empress, although the Victoria Jungfrau Hotel at least had the originality of commemorating the old grump as a young girl. Interlaken had been an upmarket Victorian resort, the kind of place British men went for their chests, but it had become a downmarket New Elizabethan destination, the kind of place British men exposed their chests.

The guidebooks recommended the local funicular railway, a vertigo locomotive, common in Switzerland, which was a cross between a train and a cable car, rolling up and down a slope on steel ropes. The carriages were like portable Victorian living rooms: yellow curtains, wallpaper, paintings, flower-shape lamp-shades. It took two minutes to get to the top, then the same length of time to come down, which was all there was to do once you got there. I began to wonder if the guidebook I was using was a rare ironic excursion in the genre.

In the afternoon, I became convinced of it. We went by boat to Thun. The guidebook swooned over an 'unusual detail'. In this town, apparently, the roofs of the lower-level shops were the pavements for the upper-level shops. I walked up and down, thinking, Wow! This is a shop's roof I'm on, but I could not get as excited as the previous writer. The local museum contained the old town drum of Thun, and ancient plates with scenes from village life. My father stood rapt before the captions, while I sullenly consulted my watch. It was like family outings of old. But such is the inevitable generational divide. I knew that I would one day drag my own unwilling offspring into medieval castles, gushing, 'They've got the old drum of Thun in here!'

Following a day of summit meetings and inter-cantonal phone calls, a tired but triumphant Zoe emerged to announce that the hotel had agreed to provide a substantial hot and cold buffet. After sampling this, the revolutionary forces – headed by Borrowby, Keen and my father – agreed that progress had been made.

Mr Borrowby reported back from the Jungfrau: 'We couldn't see anything at all at stage one. We saw a bit at the second, but it was a blizzard by the time we reached the third.'

'But just going up it is part of the experience,' Zoe consoled them in her brightside role.

The Keens had taken a cable car up Mt Pilatus, a journey done by Queen Victoria by mule in 1868. This peak overlooking Interlaken was an interesting example of the parochialism of the medieval view of the world. The mountain's name quite clearly derived from the Latin *pileatus*, meaning covered with clouds, as the thing usually was. Then some local preacher put it about that the hill was dubbed Pilatus because the devil had dumped the ghost of Pontius Pilate there after death. The fog around the top was his dirty disembodied conscience. It was an interesting example of the national compartmentalization which existed before mass media and travel that for centuries no one questioned the theological premiss that the ghost of a Roman ruler of the Middle East would see out eternity in Switzerland.

That night, I had an anxiety dream, in which I was being driven through Zurich by taxi at 1 a.m. When I reached the hotel, I had only Portuguese *escudos* in my wallet. The driver pulled a gun, which he aimed as I woke up. What did this mean? I had never knowingly given Portugal a thought. People attempting to end an addiction – cigarettes, drink, food – often had dreams in which they are still indulging what they have abandoned. Perhaps, in the same way, in Switzerland, I was dreaming of danger.

On the second day in Accommodation Centre 2, the rain came. In Toronto, I had reflected on the way in which water – collected in rivers, seas, lakes – increased the appeal of a place by about 50 per cent. Now I was discovering the corollary. Water falling to the ground in sheets or drops was deleterious to the same degree. Interlaken could not afford the loss of half its charms. I read in my room all day.

DAY 6: INTERLAKEN TO MONTREUX BY PANORAMA EXPRESS.
*It's all aboard the 1st-class train again today via the elegant resort of Gstaad, set in mountain pastureland and surrounded by forested mountains. There's time to explore and enjoy some refreshment here before the scenic ride through the Sarine Valley to Montreux on the Panorama Express. You will travel in classically elegant restored 'belle époque' period carriages. You'll stay the next two nights at the Hotel Villa Toscana.*

'Why doesn't the Hotel Villa Toscana have a T rating in the details?' demanded Borrowby and my father of Zoe on the train to Gstaad.

'Because this is the first year we've used this hotel and T-ratings are based on previous performance. You'll be given forms at the end of your stay, which will allow *you* to help fix its T-rating . . .'

It was a clipboard answer, but smart psychology. For many package holidaymakers, filling in questionnaires was at least as important as the weather and the scenery. Borrowby and my father glowed with anticipation.

Nearly three hours were allowed for Gstaad, which, outside of the skiing season, was probably about 90 per cent too generous. It amounted to a street of sod-the-poor shops and surrounding hillsides which – with their cropped grass interrupted by chalets – resembled golf courses with eighteen clubhouses instead of eighteen holes.

At Gstaad Station, the mutiny put down new roots. The

classically elegant restored *belle époque* period carriages were not in operation. Zoe protested that travellers had been informed by letter, but this did not prevent cold-eyed notes being made in pocket books.

'And, anyway, at least you've got the panoramic carriages,' she chivvied the group. 'It's a really beautiful ride round to Montreux.'

Poor Zoe. When the train arrived, it became apparent that the panoramic carriages – which had a second tier of seats above inside a sort of large glass turtle-shell – were not in operation either. Even I – who had wedged myself like a Swiss diplomat between Zoe and the group moaners – could see the objection here. The Swiss Panorama Express Tour without the Swiss Panorama Express seemed dangerously like the package holiday equivalent of *Hamlet* without the prince.

It was a quiet, brooding journey to Montreux.


### DAY 7: MONTREUX.

*Lying at the foot of wooded hills and vineyards on the edge of Lake
Geneva, Montreux enjoys a mild climate and some spectacular views
across the lake to Mont Blanc. The lakeside promenade, with its flower
borders and terrace cafés, is the perfect spot from which to watch the sun
set over the lake. In the afternoon, you can take an excursion
to Blonay and travel by steam train to Chambray (approx £10
with half-price travel card).*


The Hotel Villa Toscana turned out to be a French-run hotel with home cooking for which they would not have spat at you in Paris. But I feared for its T-rating. There were sour faces at dinner when salad was served as a separate course. Deviations from the English way caused dismay.

Montreux differed from Interlaken in being a Swiss holiday spot in which the Swiss actually took vacations. It was glamorous without the film-star naffness of Gstaad. It had a dreamy quality, the vast lake always in soft-focus, either from mist, or from sun-shimmer, its fairweather twin. The surface looked glassily placid, but this was a trick of the light. Up close – in a boat or on one of the overhanging jetty restaurants – it was full of pouts and sucks, mottling and popping, caused by currents or the jumps and dives of fishes.

It had also attracted a better class of artist than Gstaad, which peaked with Julie Andrews and Roger Moore. Montreux had Nobel Laureates and near ones. This cultural community was partly explained by the twentieth-century phenomenon of political exile. Stravinsky wrote the *Rite of Spring* in Montreux; Nabokov lived for nearly twenty years in the Montreux Palace Hotel, with its distinctive buttercup blinds above each window, like vulgar eyeliner. An American political exile, Charlie Chaplin, had seen out his days at Vevey, a little further round the lake.

But the soulful and romantic feel of the place alone had also drawn free artists. Byron, on a drinking holiday, had called at the Castle of Chillon, the ominous Savoyard castle of towering keeps and plunging dungeons, which jutted out into the water close to Montreux. The poet wrote *The Prisoner of Chillon*, about the nonconformist François Bonivard, who spent the years 1530–36 chained in a dungeon by the ruling duke. Whatever the comfort of the dungeon, the place deserved, on the view alone, to be known as the Savoy Prison. Graham Greene – whose film *The Third Man* and novel *Doctor Fischer of Geneva* were prominent among considerations of Switzerland in modern literature – had holidayed and later died at Vevey, and was buried near by. Another of Vevey's literary stations of the cross was as the location of the headache and feeling of lassitude suffered by Anita Brookner which was to inspire *Hotel Du Lac*, her award-winning novel about a woman having a headache and a feeling of lassitude beside a lake in Switzerland.

My dismissiveness about that plot was partly personal defensiveness. For me, too, Switzerland was associated with emotional self-indulgence. It was by the lake at Montreux that my Fine Young Minds relationship with Isolde, begun so promisingly in Brussels, had ended, without consummation.

From shock at the new possibilities, I had become too possessive, arriving silently by her side at every meal and outing, like a politician's bodyguard. One lunchtime on the Swiss part of the trip, she had given me the slip and dashed away to join another group, which included – crushingly – Void. I spent the whole of that afternoon staring at Lake Geneva. I was impressed by how much it helped. Years later, pointlessly in love with a married woman, I knew what to do, and spent a week on a Montreux hotel balcony in an unusually but suitably stormy July, drinking white wine and listening to requiem masses on a Walkman. Switzerland was nature's version of Valium. It was the best country in the world for narcissistic introspection, a lake being, in certain lights, a mirror.

My other previous visit had been less happy. I had once attended the European festival of television comedy, held annually in Montreux. Tourists snootily attracted by the shades of Stravinsky, Nabokov, Chaplin, Greene, and Byron also had to consider that the place was haunted by a million old sit-coms. If you listened carefully by the lake, you could hear the ghostly echoes. 'Why don't you get it out now?' 'I thought we'd have this wine first.' 'I *mean* the wine.' 'If I ask you nicely, will you give me one?' 'Sure – I'll just eat this chocolate.' 'I meant, will you give me a chocolate.' This debris of innuendo, this rubble of puns, must by now have cancelled out Byron in the cultural fabric.

On our only full day in Accommodation Centre 3, my father was back at the hotel, working on the first draft of his letter of complaint to the tour operator. I had a fish lunch beside the lake and then took the train to Vevey. Visiting Swiss towns, you got some sense of what it must be like to be a dignitary, political or Royal, who never went to any place where the streets did not seem just swept, the benches newly painted, the hedges recently trimmed. Visited on a random day, Vevey looked on best behaviour.

It was true that there was not much to do there. But I spent a pleasant afternoon at the Alimentarium, a sort of planetarium of digestion, sponsored by Nestlé. There was an enjoyable interactive computer game, available in six languages, in which the player was asked 'to find a balance of diet and exercise to maintain Mr Smith at his present weight'. Mr Smith was a graphic man. You ticked two daily snacks on a list (ranging from cream cake to a stick of celery) and two bouts of exercise (from a range between piano-playing and marathon running). The correct answers were so obvious, although I could not claim to have applied them in my own life, that there was no challenge.

Then it occurred to me that, with this computer programme, you could play a kind of alimentary battleships. I selected for Mr Smith two daily nibbles of beer, cream cake, and German sausage, followed by leisure pursuits of forty-five minutes piano-playing and thirty minutes choral singing. The machine beeped peevedly. 'Mr Smith would gain 45kg in one year. That is too much,' the console scolded. Warming to this nutritional pinball, I put Mr Smith on a regime of apple and celery, sixty minutes speed-swimming and forty-five minutes running. 'Mr Smith would lose 45kg in one year. That is too much!' the computer fumed. For a few more minutes, I moved the cartoon human between Sumo-size and baby-weight. In such an anal place – the nation, not the Alimentarium – there was a special satisfaction in breaking the rules.

Then, an attendant said: 'I think you have enjoyed yourself for long enough on this equipment. It is principally for the education of children.'

### DAY 8: MONTREUX–ZURICH–UK.
*Today you'll have the morning free for shopping and sightseeing in Montreux before leaving by 1st-class train for your evening flight.*

But everybody left long before lunch, just in case of delays. My father chose a Montreux–Zurich Flughafen train which allowed us eight hours for the three-hour journey. At breakfast, the Borrowbys and Leonards exchanged addresses and threatened to get in contact with each other when their holiday videos were developed. Borrowby and my father handed over their Holiday Questionnaires to Zoe with a glow as if they had written a poem. The second draft of my father's letter of complaint to Thomson was in his luggage. One way and another, the literary output inspired by Lake Geneva had put on several more leaves.

# CHAPTER EIGHT

# GREY FLAMINGOS AND CONCRETE COWS

## *Milton Keynes*

The week I went to Milton Keynes I read a story in the British press. It went like this. Why are flamingos pink? Because they eat shrimps. The hue produced made them attractive to mates. But Britain – reluctant to shell out on fish for its birds – had traditionally fed them a reddish dye. This additive had now been banned by the European Community in Brussels, as it was permitted to do under legislation providing for uniform standards in a united Europe. The result was that British flamingos would now be grey and unproductive. Unless Brussels relented – or, an angle the patriotic-indignant press was reluctant to pursue, money was found for the fish – the last grey unloved bird would eventually lie down in an English stately garden and die for want of dye.

The anecdote seemed to me to be a miniaturized history of modern Britain. You could read either (in the banning of the additive) increasing European interference with British sovereignty or (in the long use of the additive) the great British tradition of shoddiness, deceit, and muddle-by.

I took the latter view. Natives or fans of nations visited so far – who had assumed that the chapter on my own country would exonerate it or raise it smugly above the failures of its colonies – can now relax. I had never before spent so long away from Britain in one year. Coming home, it looked a poor, deluded place.

In the late-September week I went to Milton Keynes – and read the story about my poor nation's grey flamingos – Britain's government, economy, and monarchy seemed to be playing after-you down the garbage shute.

231

On September 16th, Prime Minister John Major and his Chancellor of the Exchequer Norman Lamont had lost £3 billion of Britain's currency reserves attempting to maintain the value of the pound in the Exchange Rate Mechanism, under which it had a fixed target against other European currencies. The gamble failed – so that the government's action was equivalent to putting £3 billion on a horse which fell over – and Britain left the ERM, abandoning the pound to float or, perhaps more appositely, sink.

The Major administration's only two firmly held policies – artificially maintaining the value of the pound and moving towards closer ties with Europe – had evaporated. Having won the election on a pledge never to raise taxes, the Prime Minister now presided over a bankrupt country. No minister or government advisor felt it necessary to resign or apologize over this ill-fated accumulator on the Brussels Handicap. When a Tory did go, it was David Mellor, who got the boot not primarily because of his toe-jobs but because he had put his foot in it as well over family holidays paid for by the daughter of a leader of the PLO.

The toe as an erotic zone had been the British public's main learning curve that summer. The previous month, the Duchess of York, estranged from her husband, had been photographed with a lower digit in the mouth of John Bryan, a Texan supposedly her accountant, at a Riviera villa. Avoiding prying eyes, the Princess of Wales had succumbed to nosy ears, featuring in a tabloid newspaper transcript of a mobile phone conversation in which a male friend called her 'Squidgy' and pledged his eternal affection. Worries over the methods by which this information had been collected – a network of snoopers able to rely on newspapers to purchase what they picked up – were supplanted by a perception of the possible consequences for the monarchy. In the seventies and eighties, there had been talk of the monarchy lifting the veil. Now it was the swimsuit and the bedsheet.

So I went to Milton Keynes. I could have chosen Clacton or Bognor – British internal joke towns, the spiritual twin towns of Timaru – but Milton Keynes held a special attraction. It had been deliberately invented, twenty-five years before, as a safe, clean, happy town for the late twentieth century, a capital of the quiet world. I wondered how it was bearing up in the now bankrupt mother country, the constitutional monarchy in which neither half of the equation looked very secure.

On February 3rd, 1965 – one month after the death of Winston Churchill and in the same week as British Rail announced the halving of British rail services under the austere Beeching Report – Richard Crossman, minister of housing and local government in Harold Wilson's first Labour administration, announced to parliament a New Towns Bill, intended to address 'London's overspill problem'. Overspill accommodation was that time's politically correct phrase for what had been known as slum clearance.

Two years later – Wilson having increased Labour's majority to ninety-six in an intervening election – his second administration introduced the North Bucks (Milton Keynes) New Town (Designation) Order. Under this scheme, twenty-two thousand acres of prime farm land was to be urbanized as a planned town.

In the seventies, the idea would grow up in Britain that the new town was called after the surnames of the poet John Milton and the economist John Keynes (the other option would presumably have been John John). Articles about the place expanded on this symbolic marriage of money and culture. In the eighties, a decade in which money had the upper hand on culture, it was commonly believed, and published, that the place was named after *two* economists, Keynes and Milton Friedman, early and late adherents of monetarism, the then ascendant economic discipline.

In fact, the name Milton Keynes had been co-opted from an existing pub-and-steeple village (pop. 150) within the development area. The housing minister of the time, Anthony Greenwood, believed it would lend a rural tang to a futuristic town. The theft of the name, however, merely encouraged protests of despoilment. The *Daily Mail* reported from the existing hamlet on 'Fear in Milton Keynes: The Village London Is Swallowing'. A local newspaper headline covered hunters' worries: NEW CITY WILL BRING PROBLEMS FOR WHEDDON CHASE.

Captain Robert Maxwell MC – in one of his earliest and relatively honest public manifestations as Labour MP for North

Bucks – telephoned the local newspaper from Calcutta, where he was on business, to lament the threat to local farmers. The *Daily Telegraph* accepted the loss of countryside, given the extent of homelessness in the British capital. A leading article commented: 'Hard upon the shock administered by *Cathy Come Home*, the BBC's exposé of the misery endured by the homeless in great cities, comes news of the most ambitious single project for providing the sufferers with homes. Not that it offers alleviation of the immediate problem: Cathy's grandchildren have a better chance of living in Milton Keynes than she has . . .'

Milton Keynes was the dream of a Socialist government and the venture represented unashamed state intervention in people's lives, social engineering. Housing and employment would be available within the same grid, reducing travel and thus congestion and pollution. With precocious environmentalism, each of the location's first householders was given two tree tokens, exchangeable for a free sapling to plant in their garden. By the sixties, an Englishman's car was his castle, but early visions of Milton Keynes concentrated on alternative transport. A monorail was considered.

From the old town of Milton Keynes to the new one of that name was seen as a rapid progression from village wells to H. G. Wells. In the finished plan, it was envisaged that, by the eighties, there would be an innovative computerized bus route, in which vehicles would be directed to occupied stops by the passengers' use of a kerbside terminal. Architects designing houses were expected to take account of the probability that the average British family in the last decade of the century would keep a boat as well as a motor car.

The clear public assumption of that time was of fluent moral and technological forward movement. A 1967 *New Statesman* competition inviting extracts from a novel set in Milton Keynes in the year 1997 reflected widespread expectations of a four-hour working week, electric cars, Community Cannabis Centres for chemical leisure. The belief of a generation only twenty-two years away from a global conflict that post-war life would become progressively better – that the world had done its worst – is clear to see.

Turning the first sod of the new development in 1967, Lord Campbell of Eskan – the establishment panjandrum who ran the

Milton Keynes Development Corporation, the state-created civic midwife – openly boasted that the design of the town was intended 'to make life better'. Campbell was upbeat, although the recession then affecting Britain had led him to consider toasting the enterprise in beer rather than champagne. But Milton Keynes would, he believed, be part of Britain's recovery from its industrial and economic troubles.

'In thirty years' time, purely manual labour will have disappeared,' said Campbell. 'Higher incomes and more free time will create leisure activities . . .'

The excitement had seemed justified at first. An architect's remark that Milton Keynes would be 'a stretch of Los Angeles in the midst of the gentle Buckinghamshire countryside' had been meant as a compliment – in 1967, LA was shorthand for glamour rather than urban collapse – and had met with general approval. So had the remark of Lord Campbell that 'some visitors who have seen Australia say that Milton Keynes reminds them of Melbourne . . .' I pass on his perception without comment.

But another comparison with Australia may be seen as the turning point in the public perception of Milton Keynes. In the seventies, as the town settled down, someone had called it 'the Australia of modern England', meaning that it was where the misfits and malcontents and drop-outs now went instead of the colonies. Milton Keynes became an easy joke for comedians and newspaper feature writers. This was partly because of the reflex snobbery the English middle classes had about town planning, at least in their own generation; perversely, they gloried in Edinburgh and Bath, neither of them accidental cities.

But it may also, in the case of Milton Keynes, have been because this last and most ambitious of the British new towns invited hostility through its evangelical individuality. There was the experimental housing, some of it with precocious solar panels, much of it blush-red boxes, built for speed and cheapness, and lacking the expected residential headgear of chimney or television aerial (Milton Keynes being cabled from an early age).

Yet the houses, whatever their shape, were dry and clean. It would have been snobbish to the point of psychopathy to expect those moving from the London slums to have remained at their drab capital addresses merely on the grounds of their greater historical character. The problem was that the Development Corporation no longer presented the development as functional – a response to slums and homelessness – but as a shining city on a hill. Inflating their language to match the bullshit spirit of the eighties, they would put out press releases speaking of 'Milton Keynes now being widely referred to by its residents as MK, an almost deliberate echo of LA'. A television legal drama series called *MK Law* was confidently expected.

So a view that it was futile to attempt to manufacture happiness was the serious core to some of the national sniggering. In both its planning phase and its eventual realization in the eighties, Milton Keynes had the air of a state holiday camp for daily living, though for two quite separate visions of the state: first for Harold Wilson's gentle collectivism and then for Margaret Thatcher's vision of a 'property-owning democracy' which 'stood on its own two feet'. During her tenure (which, at her departure, accounted for nearly half of MK's adult life), the Development Corporation liked to use the word 'self-starter' to describe the kind of new-town pioneer they sought.

There was something surreal about the zeal of the town fathers. In 1989, I had been one of the journalists sent to cover the state visit to Milton Keynes of the military ruler of Nigeria, President Bobangida. He had been persuaded that Abuja – the new planned overspill capital of his nation, supposed to replace Lagos – would be an exact reproduction of MK. With splendid insensitivity, the Development Corporation arranged the president's photo-opportunity in the mock jungle of the town's leisure centre. He didn't seem to mind, going away with his eyes ablaze with the vision of a corner of Nigeria which would be for ever Milton Keynes. I mentioned to a Nigerian journalist that Milton Keynes was something of a joke in Britain. 'That's fine,' he said. 'So is Abuja. It's a network of roads going nowhere . . .'

What did Milton Keynes care? In the mid-eighties, it had been declared the most prosperous town in Britain.

In 1992 – five years before the deadline Lord Campbell of Eskan had set for a Britain devoid of manual labour, where people had higher incomes and more leisure time – I walked up Midsummer

Boulevard from the Forte Crest Hotel, an international Esperanto hotel of marble and glass and overweight potplants which a brochure claimed as 'the favourite local setting for weddings, christenings, and other celebrations in Milton Keynes'.

Downtown MK, in its maturity, was a town – to its fury, HM the Queen had just refused a charter making it a city – of fat boulevards lined with plane trees. A building height restriction of seven storeys gave it spaciousness. Mock onion-shape gas lamps lined the roads, so that, at night, there seemed to be torchlit processions spreading from the centre.

As I crossed Midsummer Boulevard, to my left was the shopping colossus, a mile-wide buying complex, the British mall of them all, which was what the words Milton Keynes summoned up for most Southern Britons. Inside was another example of a phenomenon I had noticed in most British malls. The more futuristic or American the complex was, the more free-standing stalls appeared on the marble walkways between the stores, selling opportunistic approximations of the British past.

The MK mall had fast and modern bakers, but a wheelbarrow marked Traditional Baking did business in the interstices, selling cakes and bread which looked home-made and were wrapped in cellophane with a bow, instead of printed cardboard. There was also a stall selling log-section house signs – varnished pine lozenges with blackened edges – with titles like The Priory or The Stables. The conventional shops were either extending their summer sales or advancing their Christmas ones for, in late September, all items claimed to be a bargain. That year, in the quiet world, the retail business had become a kind of formalized equivalent of a Third World bazaar, in which, if you looked like walking away, the stallholder knocked a bit more off.

Back on Midsummer Boulevard, I walked across to the Point, the town's entertainment complex. A mirror-glass pyramid with a red-painted steel exoskeleton around it, it looked like what the aliens landed in at the end of those B-movie sci-fi films called *Red Dust from Planet Tharg*.

Behind the Point was Britain's first ten-screen cinema. Milton Keynes had become something of a pioneer in cultural colonialism (or receptivity), also hosting Britain's pioneer drive-in Kentucky Fried Chicken restaurant, its first Buddhist peace pagoda, and its début Japanese boarding school. This bizarre mess of references was one of the things that gave the town the cutely menacing feel of a David Lynch film. Another was the concrete cows. In fact a witty gift to the town from a departing American artist-in-residence at the local college, these four fibreglass cattle, standing in a field beside the railway track, had been read by commentators as implying either a sad acknowledgement of the place's lack of pastorality, or an arrogant declaration of industry's superiority to nature.

But I could see why people projected malice or menace on to Milton Keynes. It did have an eerie feel. At best, it was emptiness; at worst, malevolence. This was partly the absence of people. You could walk for minutes without seeing anyone. Conceived with an eye to the demise of the car, this metropolis was now automopolis. There were spaces at the mall for ten thousand vehicles. A dual-carriageway grid system linked the shops, offices, and housing estates. The roads indicated crossing points, but there was no help for the pedestrian in the form of lights or markings on the tarmac. Indeed, signs around the shopping centre stressed: *Pedestrians Do Not Have Priority*.

Another aspect of the isolation was created by the landscaping. There were more pedestrians than you thought. It was deliberate that you did not see them. In order that a person looking around from downtown would view only trees and green, a rural illusion, the surrounding planned parkland dipped and peaked. This meant that the Redways – miles of reddish asphalt pavements winding away from the town, beneath flyovers and bridges to the houses – were a series of deliberate blind-spots.

I walked down one of them towards the houses. One of the small pleasures of visiting an established town was to guess the derivations of the road names: the history and literature ones were easy (Balaclava Terrace, Dickens Court), and Marigold Roads and Jennifer Streets were generally the family of an architect. In London, you would usually get a Biko Street or Mandela Court, which the local Conservative councillors had made an election pledge to change to Thatcher Avenue. You would be mystified by stout surnames (Wiggins Parade) which were probably a forgotten alderman's tilt at immortality.

In a town like Milton Keynes, the only interest was to see

how quickly you could pick the designated theme for each district. Bolan Court. Musicians? Yes, here came Hendrix Drive, Orbison Court, and Lennon Drive. Now we turn on to Keaton Close. Comedians? Yes, there is Chaplin Grove. Now Caesar's Close. Easy, easy. See, it joins Hadrian's Drive and Octavian Drive. But at least this was more human than downtown, where V (Vertical) 8 met H (Horizontal) Z.

Each theme had been allotted a different housing style. There was the low-budget functional: grey crates and off-yellow boxes, brown oblongs, in long terraces on which an occasional door would be painted a different colour as a statement. The reproductive: a style called Bovis Tudor (the first name its builder), with pastiche thatch and black-oak lattice. There were three-bed detacheds in the style of a Roman villa, with colonnades and a roof beacon. There were aluminium roofs and red-brick bungalows, triple garages and swimming pools. The dream town tried to be all things to all budgets and tastes.

But in most important ways – and far beyond the triumph of the car – Milton Keynes had not worked out as its creators had intended. This showcase for state planning, created by a Labour government, was now fervently Conservative, returning verdicts for five more years of John Major in both of what, because of the town's growth, were now its two constituencies. Even so, neither of Milton Keynes's MPs could sensibly have used their seat as a demonstration of free-market policies. There had been so much subsidy, so many start-up grants for businesses, that it seemed unlikely that the town would ever repay its debt to the Treasury.

The social engineering had also blown a fuse. The town fathers had dreamed that low-income families would live alongside executives, the range of building styles providing for this. But the really rich, the local bosses, had opted for the properly old houses – the rectories and post offices – in God-made Buckinghamshire countryside like the original Milton Keynes. And the North Bucks slum clearance project had developed its own slums, of boarded doors, abandoned cars, admonitory Rottweilers.

And was the dream town happy? Was it safe? Happiness was

a difficult civic virtue to discern. But divorce rates were higher than the national average. You could argue that was because it was young pairs who uncoupled at the greatest rate and Milton Keynes attracted starters out. But there was other evidence of the place's tendency to desolate. Both Mormons and Jehovah's Witnesses had told me that new towns were particularly fertile ground for them. Someone I had known at college had moved to Milton Keynes, as a lapsed Catholic, and been a Mormon by the first Christmas. Jehovah's Witnesses were an unusual religion, building temples rapidly in weekends to meet local converts' demand. Milton Keynes had its temple.

A member of clergy of one of the Christian religions in Milton Keynes told me: 'A place like this – lots of newcomers, with no family roots – is always going to be vulnerable to what I call the door-to-door faiths, the hawkers and circulars religions. It might be the only knock on your door for months . . .'

As for safety, there was a high rate of car crime – theft from the parks, joy-riding on the estates – which was a direct consequence of the automopolis it was. There had also been a series of rapes and assaults on the Redways, which, local women felt, provided perfect cover for lurkers in their aesthetic dips and curves into the greenery. Dream town? Dream on.

Perhaps what Milton Keynes had learned – as had all the countries of the quiet world that year – was that there were no islands any more. John Major had promised a classless society, and had fulfilled it, at least to the extent that his economic policies were affecting Britons regardless of background or status.

The property-owning democracy looked as dodgy as the constitutional monarchy. You would have described the situation as a buyer's market, if there had been any buyers. The 'self-starters' of the 1980s now had a new uniting catchphrase: 'negative equity'. This meant that the mortgage you had got to buy your home, as an investment, when it was putting on value by the minute in the 1980s, was now substantially more than what you could sell the property for, as it lost value by the second in the 1990s.

Estate agents – buoyant cowboys of the previous decade,

playing off lines of buyers against each other – had started saying please and thank you. The unemployed, a club whose membership was within reach of three million again, fell behind with their mortgages, be they exorbitant or cautious, and handed over their homes to the building societies. The reservation in the *Telegraph* editorial about Milton Keynes in 1967 – 'Cathy's grandchildren have a better chance than she has of living in Milton Keynes' – had proved recklessly optimistic. Cathy's grandchildren were in cardboard boxes on the streets of London.

A British Conservative would have said that this distress was cyclical, that economic resurrection must eventually come. It was true that, from such a starting point, some kind of improvement was inevitable. But the real point was a different one. Milton Keynes had been the vision of a Britain which believed that the quality of life would incrementally improve. Would that view ever now revive? Lord Campbell of Eskan had been right about people having more leisure time, nearly right about the average working week for many people (he had said four hours). His only mistake had been to think that the trigger for this would be prosperity.

# PART FOUR

# SOMEWHERE

# CHAPTER NINE

# HELLO FROM LIMBO

## The Art of Static Travel

Even Switzerland isn't neutral enough for some travellers. It is still unmistakably foreign, the food tanged, the coins fiddly. So, as the first century of mass tourism moved to its end, the leisure movement invented the concept of Static Travel, in which, in a reversal of the usual process, the country came to you.

The first appeal of the Disney theme parks in the USA had been the possibility of meeting cartoon characters in the flesh, and making a journey, convincing enough for the childish mind at least, into the long gone or never been worlds of primitive kingdoms and fairy-tale castles to which no domestic airline flew. But a subsidiary attraction was always the chance to experience concrete foreign cultures without risking your own flesh. In a kind of trans-continental café at Disneyworld in Florida, you could move from country to country between courses of your meal.

Admittedly, the average modern city already offered the opportunity of vicariously dining in a different place each night – Athens today, Peking tomorrow, Hanoi the next, through tavernas and takeaways – but Disneyworld polished the promise. Not only could the exotic ingestion be conveniently compressed, but the fantasy kingdom's limbo status – the sense of being elsewhere already established – intensified the illusion of travel. There was also, perhaps, the tacit understanding that, there, the pseudo-native food had been prepared with American cleanliness.

As the Disney installations seeped around the globe – from California and Florida to Tokyo and Paris – another dimension of the pretence became apparent. Where the parks in the USA had brought other worlds to America, the satellite projects did the opposite. They offered the Japanese and Europeans an America on their own doorstep, a hologram continent, a consolidation of the presence already established there through movies, television, music, clothes, food, fizzy drinks, and political campaigning methods.

The phenomenon spread. All travel meant being somewhere else; but, now, some travel meant being somewhere other than the place where you had gone. One aspect was the defeat of national weather. At an establishment called Center Parcs, in the damp heart of drizzly England, pale and sniffly Britons were permitted the fantasy of a tropical holiday in a sealed dome, which covered a snaking azure swimming pool flanked by imported sand and palm trees. But the phenomenon also involved the compression of distance and time. An event like an Expo – the world trade shows, in which a glimpse and taste of every country in the world was distilled on a single site – was surely part of the same attempt to create the illusion of significant distance and difference for small effort.

It seemed fitting that my journey to all the safe places should end on this new cosseted continent of Somewhere, a territory of limbo cities and consensus cultures. I would begin with a voyage around the Disneys, America's globally spread empire of sentiment.

# CHAPTER TEN

# WISH YOU WERE THERE

*Disneyland and EuroDisney*

It was a smoggy Los Angeles dusk when I checked in to the squat concrete hotel opposite the gates of Disneyland. The fantasy world was rooted in the all too drably pragmatic Los Angeles suburb of Anaheim. The Rodney King riots had never reached there – although cultural historians must have prayed daily for that most resonant of American conflagrations – but the territory had escaped few of America's other present tensions. Disneyland printed its own jokey banknotes, with the heads of cartoon characters where Lincoln loomed on real greenbacks, but its currency was still subject to exchange rates with the proper dollar. With the real stuff from the US Treasury increasingly seeming to be Mickey Mouse money, takings at Disneyland were reportedly well down that year.

The hotel was about as pretty as the Watergate Building, with the difference that no one would want to break in to this one. The whorehouse corridors, on which the jaded doors waited forlornly in lines for a client, were deserted. But, as I sat on the edge of the musky bed, trying to raise faces on the apparently dead television, I realized that it was a loaded silence, like the latest UN-engineered ceasefire in a civil war. Soon, from above and below, I heard fast feet and squeals, like rats in a rackety farmhouse.

Finally noticing that the failure of the channel-changer might be connected with the absence of the battery flap and the empty cavity exposed by the missing plastic, I tried working on the set direct. As I did, the underground and overhead sounds expanded and clarified to reveal falsetto stroppiness, soprano alarm, unintelligible distress. Suddenly, I understood what had happened to the television.

The channel-switcher had buckled and split while doubling as a Mutant Ninja Turtle's zapper in some Munchkin improvisation. The knobs on the set had been twisted off by tiny, chubby fingers. The inevitable antechamber to the kiddie heaven of Disneyworld was the dormitory from hell. In the real world, hotels boasted in brochures 'Children welcome'. Here, it was the other way round: 'Adults tolerated'. I was doomed to spend a night in that shadowy region of the leisure industry where half the sheets were plastic and all the ducks were rubber.

Here was the temple of the Family, the capital city of the would-be America which tele-evangelists dreamed up in their speeches. Looking out from the window, across the lots of identical hotels, I saw that even the local Chinese restaurant was tot-enticingly called 'Panda City'. Everywhere, neon advertised 'Family Rooms'. Mine had as many beds as a hospital side-ward. It was the first hotel on my journey since Timaru to have no come-on candy on the coverlet. This was not only economy, but in line with a hotel décor which encouraged nothing bulkless enough to be experimentally enveloped in a small and forming mouth.

As for the items encouraged to be chewed, all around the room were flyers, posters, and pamphlets advertising more-for-less meals. The promise was junk in bulk. A drum of twenty-eight Kentucky Fried Chicken pieces, with a side-bucket of fries. A plastic pail of battered shrimp, with a jug of sweet 'n sour sauce. A family pan of spaghetti with meat sauce, serves four or serves eight, with complimentary loaf of garlic bread. A pizza as big as a trash-can lid, for many competing hands to tear at.

When I finally teased the TV to life, with one point of a pair of nail clippers, President Bush was on CNN, waving the phrases 'family values' and 'the American family' from the stump once again in a last attempt to save himself in Campaign '92. As the scuttling and squealing began to build in volume around me, the illusory curfew of bedtime now shattered by premature juvenile anticipation of the morning, I fantasized about a constitutional amendment requiring all politicians who used any campaign phrases about 'the Family' – and, in particular, 'I care about family values while my opponent, uh, just doesn't seem to' – to spend two weeks in solitary confinement in this hotel, allowed out only with a day pass to Disneyland.

At breakfast next morning, the *Los Angeles Times* reported that Bush was running twenty poll points behind Clinton in California, double the Democrat's lead elsewhere.

The exceptional contempt for Bush on the west coast was, as elsewhere, a commentary on his economics. California had seen ruinous job losses, particularly among the new technology businesses. There was also anger for his late and lazy response to the Los Angeles riots. Finally flying into the street-war zones for a mercy inspection, he had remarked that he was coming down to the west coast to do some campaigning, so this trip had 'kind of fitted in nicely'. This was typical of the president's in-bred patrician langour which, particularly during a recession, produced so negative a response from theoretically working people that it decisively challenged the decade-long repetition of the cruel untruth that there is no class war in America.

But Bush's other Californian handicap was to have backed the wrong horse, or horseman of the apocalypse, in the religious war. The president's cowardly espousal of an official Republican platform which called for a constitutional amendment outlawing all abortion had seemed at the time a safe enough sop to established national intolerance. So had his cheerfully cynical (as he hoped) admission to the party convention of rhetoric taunting homosexuality and single parenthood as abhorrent. This would – it seemed – play in Peoria.

Liberals who tuned in judged these tactics sick but slick and prepared, in yet another election, to be better but to be second. Yet now there were unlikely signs of a liberal miracle. The Republicans seemed to have got their cynical sums – so clinically correct in the 1988 race – wrong. Winning few votes anywhere outside of the rock-head west, this demonology of lifestyle options had played so poorly in vote-rich California, where difference is a convention, that Bush had more or less stopped campaigning there. It was less that America had matured morally than that the minorities had expanded to the levels where they statistically matched the majority. But, in America, an accidental benevolence sometimes had to do. And it was fitting that a Republican president's cynically Puritan pitch should have proved especially disastrous in the Disney state, because Bush had fallen for a cartoon vision of human relationships: Mickey Mouse sociology.

In Millie's Kitchen, my Disneyland hotel restaurant, surrounded by blaring children and dented parents, I raised an optimistic cup of coffee to the possible death of the Family as a US campaign weapon.

'Jesus, some of those heads weigh thirty pounds,' said a young man at a nearby table. It was a perplexing comment, and I wondered for a moment if he was an American hairdresser, lamenting the size of his clients, but then I realized that he must be a Disney animal, a costumed steward, de-anthropomorphized for the morning into jeans and T-shirt.

I girded my soul with an internal humming of 'Heigh ho, heigh ho, it's off to work we go', from *Snow White and the Seven Dwarfs*, and headed off, heigh ho, heigh ho, to catch the van to the gates of the magic kingdom.


In the van, I was getting strange looks. There dawned the realization, stupidly delayed, that my carefully cultivated disguise – the single man travelling alone – was useless, even ruinous, here. Solo in the capital of the Family, what might you be *except* a travel writer, or a pederast, or some sad fuck denied access to his children by divorce, who now wandered the juvenile resorts of the world, in search of a surrogate buzz.

For me, I had to admit, it was more of a bug than a buzz. The van was jammed with a few museum-display versions of what George Bush called the American Family – wide-hipped Mom and Pop, kids with metal-fenced teeth – but a majority of the visitors looked to be on what you might call guilt-trips: solitary adults pulling dollars from their pockets to satisfy the whim of children on whom they spent money more than time.

On my left was a frayed-eyed mom, a single parent I suspected, who had won the right to access of little Stephanie. Make that, more likely, lost the toss of a coin for little Stephanie.

Squirming and bouncing in her seat as if it were covered in porcupine skin, the child had become over-excited at, eavesdropping established, the prospect of seeing the video of Spielberg's *Hook*, a later item in the guilt trip.

'When am I seeing Captain Hook, Mom?'

'In two sleeps' time, Stephanie.'

'Why is Captain Hook called Captain Hook, Mom?'

'Because . . .' Mom scanned the van, checking carefully for any digit-disadvantaged or limb-challenged individual who might take offence. 'Because of his, uh, hand, Stephanie . . . Now sit back in your seat, honey . . .'

Instead, Stephanie made an ambitious attempt at the *pas de deux* in *Coppelia* from a sitting position.

'Honey, sit back in your seat . . .'

'Why, Mom . . .?'

Because, I thought, if you go through that window, you might have on your neck what Captain Hook has on his wrist.

'Why, Mom . . .?'

'Because, Stephanie, if the van crashes . . .'

Mom sounded more sanguine about the prospect than a mother might. But, with Stephanie bouncily intact, we arrived, swapped our Treasury dollars for the other Mickey Mouse money, and time-slipped on to Main Street, USA.


This initial parade of shops and food concessions – with which all the Disney parks started – was a vision of American living so supernaturally cute that it made Norman Rockwell look like Magritte. It was a journey to the safe places of the American imagination. Buxom girls in lacey bustiers presided over big glass jars of rainbow-shaded candy. Barbers, willing to croon unaccompanied in fours on request, brandished razors the envy of any Los Angeles street gang and painted visitors' chins with shaving foam as frothy as a milk-shake.

Given that children were not normally programmed for nostalgia, this street seemed to pander more to adult prejudices than those of children. It was a USA which existed only in the opportunistic rhetoric of Republican presidential candidates and their hopeful voters. One of its stalls was even called Carefree

Corner. The only whiff of reality was the dung dropped from the horse-drawn streetcars. Even Disney hadn't found a way of faking horse shit yet. (After the Los Angeles riots, several newspapers used the headline, above a picture of an armed national guardsman warily patrolling a rubbled shop front, MAIN STREET, USA. *Touché*, Walt Disney and George Bush.)

I turned left at the Duck County Jail and the Duckburg Courthouse. These were hardboard reproductions of old-fashioned judicial buildings, in which children could pose for photographs, jokily pretending imprisonment, or parents could cathartically imagine their offspring behind bars. Depicting a small American town in which – after some blip of democracy on the Perot model – all the senior legislative positions were held by Donald Duck and his relatives, it was a small example of Disneyland's attempt to imbue values through cuteness. This was a mallard morality tale: the duck justice a reminder that no one could duck justice.

But, if Disneyland was the capital of the family, it was also the Mecca for the safe traveller. The park's promise was to offer the illusion of danger – of transport across cultures and histories – in a protected environment. The attentiveness of the staff was partly a corporate fetish, but also a legal precaution. Every 'Mind how you go!' and 'Need a hand there?' was another personal-liability waiver. The visitor could be reasonably sure that the company's terror of being sued ruled out any need for the visitor to fear being hurt. Most attractions imposed bans on some travellers. After a few samples, you realized that definitions of riskiness were conservatively worked out. The rides barring merely the wheel-chair bound were a breeze. Those closed to cardiac patients were genuinely frisky, but only those refusing the wheelchaired, the heart-weak, and the heavily pregnant were serious pulse-raisers.

The rides at Disneyland divided between three historical periods, two past, one future, but all of them chronologies of optimism. The first were loving recreations of the way Americans liked to think their nation once had been and might yet be again – Main Street, USA, Critter Country ('Teddi Barra's Swingin' Arcade – Get your change ready for frontier-themed fun and games'), and Frontierland ('Big Thunder Ranch (Petting Barnyard Closes At Dusk)'). If this level of pretence involved making old

movies flesh, the second did the same with cartoons. In Fantasy-
land, you could ride a fibre-glass Dumbo, experience Snow
White's Scary Adventures ('Heigh ho, heigh ho, it's off to the
Wicked Witch's castle we go') or join Pinocchio's Daring Journey
('Pinocchio finds Pleasure Island isn't so pleasurable').

The third circle of Disneyland, Tomorrowland – the newest,
smartest part of the park – concentrated on projections of future
travel methods. There was a choice of Rocket Jets ('Take off on a
soaring adventure'), PeopleMover ('Move gently through rooftop
views . . .'), and Space Mountain ('A warp-speed adventure
. . .'). Oddly possessing a more concrete connection with reality
than those attractions fradulently calling up the past, Tomorrowland even held the park's one representation of a real person or,
anyway, Michael Jackson, who, uncannily captured in pale plastic, presided over the entrance to the rides.

Torn between the two never-never lands and the one maybe-
maybe, I called in first at Space Mountain in Tomorrowland.
Walt Disney – like his protegée, Tinkerbell – had understood the
importance of believing. At their best, the Disney attractions had
an exactitude, a design pedantry, which aided faith, especially of
the childish kind. On Space Mountain, objectively a warehouse
wallpapered with tin-foil, the jargon and hardware were persuas-
ively correct: true, at least, to the movie version of the future.

You walked across long gantries, past flashing panels, to a
launch pad where an electronically authoritative voice crackled
commands about crews and fuel and boosters. Strapped in to
what was, objectively, a grey-painted fibreglass crate with a
cinema screen pretending to be a window, you were rocked so
violently in your seat, and shown images of such speed on the
screen, that a child might plausibly have imagined themselves an
astronaut. Vicariously hurtling down dark passages, an adult
could pass the time by imagining themselves a sperm.

Or, let us be honest, an astronaut, for one of the incidental
clevernesses of Disneyland was that it licensed adults to experience
a second childhood, disguised as guides for their young. In
Tomorrowland Autopia – a vaguely sci-fi go-kart track – I
jammed my foot down on the pedal, which allowed mild influence on speed though not direction, and bumped and parped the
dumb slow-coaches in front like a naughty boy. It would be silly

even to pretend that the second circuit I rapidly went back for was prompted by my diligence as a travel writer.

Perhaps it was not merely research either which sustained me through a forty-minute wait in midday Californian scorch to descend beneath a fake lagoon in a plastic submarine. Here, again, the surface looked and sounded right, with voices crying, 'Close the bridge, captain . . . ready to dive!' so authentically that those children who had not already wet themselves now nearly did.

Beneath the ocean, objectively an enlarged bath, there were fibreglass fish and coral, as real through the glass as those you saw through a viewing porthole at the Barrier Reef, and even bubbles spiralling above us to suggest descent. But, then, our submerged imaginations were hi-jacked by images from undisputed fantasy. A coquettish ceramic mermaid and a plastic sea serpent with hug flirtatious eyes and mechanically-flapping lashes loomed out of the bubbles beside our craft. The laughter broke the spell established by the pretend technology. This easy pull of sentiment was always the drawback with Disney, an artist who had sold his bile duct to the devil in exchange for fame.

For lunch, I toyed with the Blue Bayou Restaurant, in New Orleans Square, where it was reportedly possible to 'enjoy moonlit dining all day in this nonsmoking restaurant', a symptomatic Disneyland promise, the cigarette ban emphasizing how far you were from the real New Orleans, the twenty-four-hour moonlight indicating how far you were from the real world. My stomach, seconded by my ear, voted against Orville Redenbacher Gourmet Popping Corn. I hovered outside Tahitian Terrace ('Enjoy Polynesian specialties . . .') and Village Haus Restaurant, Hosted by Minute Maid ('Enjoy a *storybook* selection of burgers . . .').

But then I chickened, or strictly cheesed out, and ate bread and Camembert and a half-bottle (yes, I know, I know, real travel writers would have ordered two) of cold west coast Chardonnay in something called the California Wine Cellar. There were only three other people in it. Perhaps the rest of the visitors all thought they could get enough of that kind of thing in California. Or they were in Tahitian Terrace, thinking it meant they had sort of been to Polynesia.

Fraying in the heat – Disneyland that day burned orange for

80s *Fahrenheit* on the *USA Today* full-colour weather map, while Barrow, Alaska, I noticed, was already bruised purple for below 10 – I liked the sound of Splash Mountain. Strapped into a swollen metal shoe, you were rushed around a humpbacked track which was regularly interrupted by waterfalls. The circuit was seriously vertiginous. On the upward rush, you clapped your hands to your pocket to save your change and key-rings, with the result that, on the downward plunge, you lost your sunglasses.

But, even here, the consequences of Disney's pact with the devil were apparent. The interludes between the buckings and drenchings were used for a corn cabaret of cuddly toys. Consequently, the ride was like attempting three-in-a-bed sex with a sadist and a softy. At one moment, you were being thrown at high speed through curtains of cold water; at the next, you were being serenaded by banjo-playing plastic alligators performing 'Zip-ah-dee-doo-dah!' Solo among quartets, trios, and duos, I had been placed in the toe of my six-person shoe. Looking around during the saccharine gaps, I realized that the trick was to use a spouse or child as a water-break. Alone, I was soaked, and then endured twenty minutes of other visitors giving me spot-the-incontinent looks.

It seemed proper to this project to end the day in Disney's answer to the United Nations. Called 'It's A Small World!' this entertainment promised 'a flavour of every country of the world, with the underlying message of cultural harmony and peace'. Within a pastel-coloured gothic castle – the cutesy design of which would have made you throw up if it had been a birthday cake and throw bricks if it had been a hotel – you boarded a small boat in the shape of a swan and floated round a snaking river circuit.

On the banks were placed national tableaux, interspersed with a puppet choir – the faces of the singers painted alternately white, pink, brown, and yellow – singing, in different languages, a ditty with the chrous: 'It's a small world after all!' It was like watching a Eurovision Song Contest for midgets. The ballad was clearly intended as an anthem of tranquillity – we were invited to imagine a world in which the warring peoples were united by this tune, a choir abhorring violence – but it seemed to me, forced to listen to it, that its greater potential would be as a deterrent. The warring nations of the world could threaten to sing the song to each other, if any other country contravened international law. Perfectly meeting the requirements of the balance of terror theory – that only a madman could reasonably contemplate the weapon's release – the tune was ideally suited to a no-first-use agreement.

Trapped, however, in a dystopia in which the song had been foolishly used by one nation, and others had been remorselessly drawn into a rendition as retaliation, I contemplated the grottos allotted to each country. Despite the pan-cultural ambitions of the entertainment, the displays betrayed American attitudes. There was, for example, no Cuba, and Canada was, even by the advertised parameters of a small world, microscopic, its history represented only by a fibre-glass Mountie saluting from his horse.

New Zealand was two Kiwis (birds, not fruits) and a grinning mannequin of a Maori. Australia was a kangaroo and a midget Aborigine about to throw a boomerang. You got the impression that the research on this project had been mainly instinctive. Africa was cuddly toy lions and grinning black dolls banging drums. Japan was geishas flapping paper fans. It struck you that geishas waving dollars or US Treasury bonds might have been closer to the truth, if also closer to the American bone. But then this was an idealized universe. Baghdad was mosques and flying carpets, rather than flying Scud missiles. My own nation was a red double-decker bus and a Beefeater, rather than a jobless miner and a puppet in a grey suit and glasses looking as if he was unsure what to do.

The exposition ended with a top-volume rendition by a globally representative doll choir – Mountie beside geisha, Beefeater beside Aborigine, fakir beside kiwi bird – singing 'It's a small world after all!' The balance of terror had failed and this was the holocaust of soppiness. Reaching daylight and clambering unsteadily out of my swan, I made for the main gate – refusing the brand on the hand which allowed you to return for free later on – and caught the next van back to the hotel.

Then I lay on the bed and blacked out, from a combination of jet lag and reality lapse. I was woken two hours later by the scampering of small feet, but also by a more ominous sound. Above and below and around, small voices could be discerned singing: 'It's a small world after all . . . It's a small world after all . . .' Walt Disney would have wanted to believe that this repetition meant that the children had bought the message of the song – and were now less certain to murder each other or their parents – but it seemed more likely that a catchy song had simply caught. The unpopularity of Bush's family tactics in California now seemed quite logical. How could you spend a day at Disneyland and not come out believing in abortion?

But, despite the contraceptive attempts of cultural nationalists, Disneyland had successfully reproduced. As if to prove that it really was a small world, after all, the sentimental revolutionaries had now invaded Europe. It was in the mid-cultural limbos of my native continent that my journey through the quiet world would end. I landed at Orly Airport in Paris, and followed the bright signs for the EuroDisney connection.

It has to be said that the prospect of the French running Disneyland sounded at first like one of those jokey 'Trading Places' competitions run by magazines (John McEnroe to run a charm school, suggests F. K. of Surrey; Warren Beatty to be a monk for a day, says J. P. of Edinburgh).

The French to run Disneyland, suggests M. L. of London. Imagine. An unsuspecting American girl skips up to Mickey Mouse amid the pastel clapboard frontages of Main Street, USA. 'Hi, Mickey, my name's Euphoria and I'm from South Dakota . . .' Mickey holds up one finger, snarls *'Tais-toi, enfant!'* leans against the wall, and drags on his cigarette. Around him, uniformed attendants roam the park, advising attendants: 'Have a *bad* day, huh!'

These were, I knew, racial stereotypes but it had to be allowed that, compared to Americans, the French were, to use the evasions of the age, differently polite, perhaps even manner-challenged. Such was their legitimate free expression, but why the fuck had they agreed to host a Disneyland? The work ethic of the Japanese – the only previous un-Americans permitted to host a Disney spin-off – coincided, across cultures, with that of the USA. The European attempt, though, was a transfusion using different blood groups.

The difficulties of a culture transplant, of establishing an America-on-the-Seine, had become apparent in transit. The baggage claim area at Orly Airport reeked of dead fish and, although a van was on hand to shuttle you direct from France to the enchanted kingdom, the Disney dream machine could not magic away the two-hour Parisian traffic jam ahead.

But, as soon as you reached the site, the intensity of the pretence became clear. While the entertainment complex seemed, from the brochure, to be a simple reproduction of the American ventures, EuroDisney sold a trickier subsidiary fantasy. The hotels offered quarantine from Europe, immersion in a transferred USA. My lodging in Anaheim had been functionally American; my accommodation in Paris was strenuously, nudgingly so.

I checked in to the Newport Bay Club. A cream and blue eight-storey clapboard mansion backing on to an artificial lake, this was intended as a Parisian simulacrum of Rhode Island. Perhaps this was the easiest look to fake – New England architecture, with its roots in timber, tended, anyway, towards a twee artificiality – but the effect was outwardly convincing. And the mood in reception was all too gruesomely authentic; chillingly Disney, if not necessarily New English, with young children sitting on the floor, or skidding across it, while singing 'It's a small world after all!' or 'Zip-ah-dee-doo-dah!'

As I carried my cases towards the lift, forgive me, elevator, one chubby boy closed his eyes, extended his arms like aeroplane wings and spinning on the spot, all the while Zip-ah-dee-doo-dah-ing, accidentally left the spot because of the slippery parquet and cannoned in to me. 'Watch it,' I hissed. 'Fuck you, mister,' he shot back. You had to admit it. They were faking America very well.

The safety chain on my door was broken, and I merely shrugged, which you would not have done in the nation simulated. But the room had white walls, a bed with a white wooden headboard and a deep blue coverlet: a passable mass-market version of an east coast sea-view inn. I found CNN on the television and, drinking coffee in front of a bay-view window which held a vista of mist and yachts, I thought: Yes, you could trick yourself, at this moment, that you were in America. But my sensations held a complication. I had holidayed in New England so that, in this hotel, I projected my memories on to the imitations and thus intensified them. It was what you might call dildo tourism, inflatable doll holidays.

It was a pleasurable enough substitute. But I would not have paid money for that feeling, or even sought it, except for this project. What was the market for this make-believe? Some of those in the hotel were obviously Americans. But were they expatriates formerly denied their Disney birthrights, or tourists from the US, seeking brief refuge from the European experience, a fix of home comforts? Was it plausible that Europeans would be drawn here rather than attempt to travel to the true America? Because of the operation of an informal airline cabal in Europe, the cost of reaching EuroDisney was not decisively lower than that for Disneyland or Disneyworld. As an example of the relative expenses, I was paying at the Newport Bay Club a room rate which would have bought a suite at the originators of the establishments being aped.

And a Paris suburb would always lack the weather of California or Florida. My impostor's Rhode Island was lashed by a late autumn storm. Peering through it, I postponed my walk around the lake to the skyscrapers of New York, the tranquil, scented forests of the national parks, or, more distantly on this compacted map of the States, the deserts and cacti of New Mexico. California, maybe ten minutes away, was too much of a pain in this rain. I had been forewarned that some of the places might not be open, because of the recession, but this, too, could be taken as an uncannily accurate representation of the real America.

Waiting for the weather to achieve its own required counterfeiting of an east coast summer, I read Christopher Hope's novel *Serenity House*, in which the Florida Disneyworld was equated with – or, anyway, placed ironically alongside – the Nazi concentration camps. In the final chapter, a fugitive war criminal, finding refuge from British justice, drew warm historical comparisons with the Magic Kingdom's steely herding of human cargo through fake railway stations.

This, it seemed to me, risked designer irony – the contrast was more startling than it was morally illuminating – but the book was not the first such Disney fiction. A few years before, I had read Stanley Elkins's *The Magic Kingdom*, a dark comedy about a party of disabled children at Disneyworld. There was not yet enough material for a thesis on Disney in fiction but these books reflected a perception of something creepy behind the Disney cleanliness, not just because it was innocence icily enacted for commercial gain, but because it represented an increasingly bogus hopefulness, a false whitewash of the world's problems.

Outside my window, it was clear that the energetic pretence was still being wrecked by the weather. I considered a wet walk to New York or California for dinner, but finally decided to stay indoors on Rhode Island, eating at the Yacht Club, allegedly a New England fish restaurant. It was decorated with wooden panels and so many ship's wheels and telescopes that you feared for the future of maritime navigation. Nets, maps, buoys, and identification charts for Atlantic fish added their weight to the sham atmosphere. If they had been used in a film, as west coast approximations of the east coast, the set designer would have won good reviews, but, in this context, the proof was in the eating.

At my window table, looking out on to the boiling lake, I ordered clam chowder, followed by baked salmon, deliberately selecting dishes I had eaten in the original location. Waiting – reading, for added realism, that date's *USA Today*, sold at the hotel shop – I realized the drawback of EuroDisney's movie-set approach to tourism. The joy of such restaurants in New England was the understanding, advertised or tacit, that the fish was fresh from the Atlantic. Here, there was the nagging suspicion that it was flown (at best, from where England's south-west coast was lapped by the Atlantic) or frozen. The stink of dead fish at Orly Airport came back to me.

The clam chowder was a lukewarm fraud. In a demonstration of the problems of French chefs working grudgingly to American recipes, the chowder had become a delicate soup rather than the pseudo-stew it should be. The salmon was passable. Served it in America, you might have blamed a bad catch or hack chefs. Presented with it in a Paris suburb, you had suspicious visions of crates being bundled on and off planes. Only the wine was a perfect pretence: the single essence of a nation's tastes which could be trapped and exported without deterioration. I enjoyed a Californian Chardonnay which I might have drunk at Long Beach. But this was a small triumph for static travel. I had bought the same wine round the corner from my house in south-west London. Unfortunately, there were no half bottles, but irritations have to be borne in the course of travel writing. I sank a whole one.

This perhaps aided the suspension of my disbelief, but the staff weakened it. They were French but apparently the unwilling recipients of a crash course in American. Two tables away were a couple who had loudly announced – alarmingly for the experiment – that they were from Boston. After man and wife had resorted to watch-consultation so elaborate and slow that it brought to mind Marcel Marceau miming the drinking of tea, the male Bostonian called over the *maître d'*. 'We ordered two Planter's Punches twenty minutes ago and we're still waiting . . .' he explained. At the American Disney parks, the waiter would have bent down, changed into running shoes and threatened Carl Lewis's Olympic records as he made for the bar. At the Japanese Disney park, the waiter would have pulled from his apron a ceremonial sword, and fallen on it.

At EuroDisney, though, the waiter gave a Gallic shrug so hammy that it looked as if he had sat on a cow-prod. Then, tracked by the disbelieving eyes of the Bostonians, he wandered around the restaurant, rearranging the napkins on five or six tables. Finally, he walked – at a speed which suggested the simultaneous pain of massive suppurating blisters, athlete's foot, and a recent knee ligament operation – towards the bar. Eventually, he returned. 'Zere cummin',' he revealed. Scarcely mollified, the Bostonian later sent back his salmon: 'I like my food *hot* . . .' As I left, he was refusing to pay the bill. 'If you do not pay the bill, sir, I will call the police,' said the *maître d'*. The Bostonian started quoting Food and Drug Administration consumer rights legislation, but the unworried face of the employee said: I think you'll find you're in *France*.

This was the way it was at EuroDisney. The staff kept intruding Brechtian alienation effects into the proscenium-arch realism of the fake USA.

Next morning, I felt too weak to face something called a 'character breakfast'. This, apparently, involved your coffee and croissants being served by a 'Disney favourite', which was to say, I supposed, a surly Parisian in a plastic head. How did people keep their character breakfast down?

Rain becoming hail was sweeping New England as I left after breakfast to walk around the lake to New York. The skyline was a neatly compressed sketch of the familiar Manhattan jag shape. The Hotel New York was divided between five towers, each evoking either skyscrapers or brownstones. But the character of New York was a product of human energy as much as architecture and, because of the weather and the recession, this reproduction lacked the injection.

The mock-up Rockefeller Plaze in front of the eye-trick tower blocks was deserted, the ice-rink a dry shell, tented over. In the echoing lobby of the Hotel New York, Gershwin played to jog the imagination and, in the shop, genuine New York souvenirs – Empire State mugs, I Love NY tea-towels, World Trade Centre pens – were available. The possibility of buying authentic New York souvenirs in an ersatz Manhattan was, even for Disney, a dizzying level of unreality.

A memento more associated with EuroDisney than with its brother parks in other countries was the big yellow raincoat with a Mickey Mouse logo on the back. While I had been in New York, an electrical storm had begun over New England and now – in a minutely compressed version of the actual American climate – had enveloped Manhattan before heading west to California. Huddled inside my character waterproof, I followed the clumps of tourists similarly dressed towards the other American clone zones in the accommodation area of the park.

Over in the national parks, the Hotel Sequoia Lodge was like a penitentiary: low, flat-roofed, anonymous cabins. Reeboks leaden from the flooded ground, I headed for New Mexico. Lashed by rain, the cactuses looked drab as marrows. The desert was threatening to become cement. The Hotel Santa Fe itself was a scattering of dun-coloured boxes, which resembled bunkers, but which the brochure called *pueblos*. The leaflet also showed that the hotel's rooms were fitted with ceiling fans. It seemed a lunatic self-deception. What did they do for two-thirds of the year? Jam the thermostat?

Chilled by the New Mexican climate, I quickened my pace

towards the Hotel Cheyenne. In contrast to the other parts of the accommodation park, this was a historical spoof rather than a geographical one – a meticulous Western movie set, with wagons and wigwams, swing-door saloons and sheriff's offices – but this licence gave it no more protection from the European winter climate. It looked to be the first Wild West town in which you could imagine a high noon shoot-out being rained off.

I flagged down a van heading to the Hotel Disneyland, the last and most ghastly residence, but one which had the advantage of leading in to the park proper. Although its restaurants were broadly Californian, the Hotel Disneyland represented no state except that of Walt Disney's imagination. Supposedly a magic castle, it most resembled a strawberry blancmange with a door in it.

Slightly dried off by paper towels, I swapped my francs for Mickey Mouse dollars and dripped through the turnstile. Purely in the interests of comparative research, I visited the reproductions of Space Mountain. Then – safe travel writing being, as has been stressed, not without its dangers – I took in 'It's A Small World'. Disproving any theories of cultural compromise as the empire spread, France was represented here, as at Anaheim, by a miniature Eiffel tower and a pile of onions and cheeses.

Splash Mountain seemed, somehow, redundant. Back on Rhode Island, wrapped in blankets and bingeing hot drinks against pneumonia, I reflected on the risks of this fool-you tourism. Just before I had left the site, there had been an announcement that the Flying Dumbos – a cute centrifuge in which the customers sat in fibreglass versions of the Disney elephant – had been grounded, owing to dangerous weather conditions. It was hard not to see this as symbolic of the problems of EuroDisney.

# CHAPTER ELEVEN

# NEW WORLD ORDERS

---

*Expo '92*

On the flight from Paris to Seville, I had the aisle, sandwiching, in the inside seats, two pinstriped businessmen whom I took to be Chinese. A certain nervousness was in the air. We had just been shown, as part of the in-flight entertainment, the only news bulletin in the world that day which failed to mention that an El Al cargo jet had landed on an Amsterdam apartment block, compressing its tenants. Media companies with a contract to provide news videos for airlines had a clause insisting on the omission of plane crash pictures, however big the story. This was, surely, more a superstition than a sensitivity, for did they really imagine that every passenger on a post-crash plane would not have that footage spooling through their heads?

The solidarity of unspoken fear, and need for diversion, encouraged conversation. Abandoning the man-made chicken breast of our coach-class lunch, we had one of those hand gesture and mispronounced proper noun conversations: me striking out into French, they courageously scaling English. It emerged that they were Koreans (unless *career* was one of the English words they knew, in which case they were Chinese, and ambitious).

'What you do? . . . er . . . er . . . *L'occupation?*'

'Journalist . . . *Ecrivain pour les journeaux* . . .!'

They telegraphed incomprehension with head-shake, half-smile, and fluttering hands. The serious travel writers, I knew, learned the language of their destinations. This was admirable, if swottish. Had I read something about Theroux, or was it Thubron, and *dialects* of Mandarin? I had been lucky so far. You could just about get by with English in Australia, New Zealand, Canada, and America. And EuroDisney was a spoken no man's

264

land. Now I had been found out. But surely even Theroux and Thubron could not learn the langugaes of any nationality they might meet by chance in flight?

On an instinct, I pulled out my latest piece of reading material from the seat-pocket. It was the new Anita Brookner, which I was reading for review purposes and had finished on the first part of the flight. A spinster went missing, prompting police concern. But there was a happy ending. She was later discovered to have been nursing a headache in a darkened room. I held up the slim volume with one hand, and mimed, with the other, the movement of a pen across a page, then turned that hand towards myself and pointed.

The Koreans – or career-conscious Chinese – beamed. The one nearest to me took the novel from my hands and showed it to the other. Then the first man turned the book over, took in the jacket snap of ascetic, angular Anita, and held it up alongside my face. He pointed, both men giggled, and then, as they both bowed to me, the first man handed back my – a possessive they now, it was clear, took more deeply than they should – book.

I fantasized about the moment at a future Seoul cocktail party when one of these men would say: 'You know this Anita Brookner, who writes these elegant books about ladies with migraines? Do you know that she is, in fact, a huge bearded man? Yes, yes, this is true. We met her, which is to say him, on a flight to Seville . . .'

'And you,' I said slowly. 'What do you do?'

They spoke briefly in their own language, and laughed. I supposed it was something like: Oh, our lives are not as exciting as yours, writing these romantic novels under your other name of Anita.

'Pipes,' the man nearest to me said. 'We make pipes . . .'

I did a quick mime of Sherlock Holmes smoking. They shook their heads, then put both their hands out in front of them, palms facing inward a yard apart, and moved them up and down, like a juggernaut driver's on his wide wheel.

'Big pipes,' the self-elected spokesman explained. 'Pipes. *Grand* pipes. Long. To Middle East. We work – last week – Libya . . .'

Big pipes, long pipes, to the Middle East, to Libya. I was

suddenly glad that they were under the impression that I was Anita Brookner, rather than a journalist. I supposed, though, that I would feel mildly guilty if I ever read in the newspaper that the author of *Hotel du Lac* had been dropped to the bottom of the Thames in concrete slippers because of her inadvertent knowledge of the international arms trade.

'At Expo, you show your pipes?' I enquired.

'We see . . . people. You . . .?'

He pointed at Anita Brookner's *Fraud*, which peeped from the seat-pocket. I made an ambiguous inclination of the head, hoping that the Korean long-pipe salesmen would conclude that it was the policy of British industry to send transexually pseudonymous romantic novelists to universal trade expositions.


An Expo, as universal trade expositions were known in the logo age, was, essentially, an Olympics for businessmen – a source, to paraphrase George Bush, of new world orders – though with the significant difference from the athletic version that the participants were under the influence of drink rather than drugs. Most nations of the world – the publicity Jesuitically liked to suggest *every* – took a stand on which they advertised their culture, industries, and visitability. In the Canada chapter, we passed by the site of the last such global blow-out in Vancouver in 1986, a significant stop, as the world had learned in 1992, on the marital *via dolorosa* of the Prince and Princess of Wales.

But, as well as being trade showcases, Expos, as they had become more ambitious, had increasingly promised vicarious travel: the opportunity of flicking, as if with a tourist channel-changer, through a hundred nations in a day. Like an animated atlas, the Expo held the promise of a universal exposition of world culture, a voyage from a standing start. So what was, objectively, a glorified business convention had become a huge tourist pull. It was another aspect of static travel. An Expo was an adult version of Disney's 'It's A Small World!'

If, though, an Expo gave a country the short-term boost of a huge influx of tourists, you got, when the show was over, the long-term problem of a ludicrously large exhibition centre around which your national associations of fishmongers and astrophysicists would echo and rattle at annual conventions previously held in church halls. Impressive and expensive but with limited secondary applications, Expo sites were the architectural equivalent of a wedding dress.

This time, the building of the industrial stage-set had fallen to Spain. 1992 – being the five hundredth anniversary of Columbus's discovery/exploitation/racist claim to (choose your cultural poison) the New World – had brought lucrative spin-offs to Spain. Barcelona hosted the Olympics. Expo '92 went to Seville, coincidentally the birthplace of the Spanish Prime Minister, Felipe Gonzalez. It was at Seville – on La Isla de la Cartuja, Expo's home – that the corpse of Columbus was said to have been first interred. (If a place was really stuck for a traveller-magnet, it was always worth inspecting the hotel registers and church records to find a celebrity who lay there, however briefly, in death or in rest.)

An air-traffic predictor programme, run through the computer by European aviation regulators, had predicted a mile-high traffic jam – planes hovering nose to tail above Spain – for the weekend when Expo overlapped with the opening of the Olympics. This stratospheric congestion threatened to become a symbol of the way in which human greed, the absolutism of usage which the species always showed, had extended to travel. But either the computer was a pessimist, or schedules were adjusted, because Spanish air-traffic controllers got everything up and down with no more than the usual delays.

Bowing goodbye to the Koreans at Seville airport, I headed for my hotel, the name of which optimistically translated as the Gates of Heaven. On the pillow in my room was a wrapped boiled sweet: the Mediterranean climate's compromise for chocolate.

I walked through the wide, dusty streets of Seville. It was a city as thick with basilicas, churches, and chapels as Peoria and Normal, but these, being relics of a time of piety rather than contemporary reflections of one, were places of history and beauty, objects of secular tourist devotion. Their magnificence was a sad reproach to the grimy, crimey city Seville had become. The city had been given Expo, with its accompanying intrastructure, investment, and tourist loot, as a goad to improvement.

Seville's half of the bargain was not being taken for granted.

There was a policeman or a soldier every few metres. It was a reliable guide to safe travel that the best time to visit a European city was when the forces of law and order have been unofficially co-opted by the tourism minister (the worst time to visit a European city being, by extension, when the forces of law and order had unofficially co-opted the prime minister).

The Expo brochure boasted that La Isla de la Cartuja was 'formerly a dirt strip, which has now become a city'. To be accurate, what it had become was an Olympic village, for no one except athletes and characters in science-fiction stories would have lived in these settlements of white shells and spangly pavilions.

Once through the turnstile, as busy as the gate at an Australian one-day cricket match, I crossed the 'perimeter road'. Much of the English-language Expo brochure had, to the ears of the speakers it was aimed at, a distressing tinge of the penitentiary. Even more ominously, other aspects of the terminology seemed to be drawn from warfare. Between the national pavilions were something called 'international zones', neutral areas holding shops, cafés, and bars.

The national sites were laid out in straight lines but exuberantly irregular designs, so that they resembled a psychedelic new town: a Milton Keynes with pop-art bungalows. With sardonic patriotism, I headed for the British site and, over a cup of tea in Lionheart's café, planned my viewing. I began with a cynical scan for absentees. Iraq seemed to have passed up the chance of exhibiting, perhaps because, at the time that building began, in 1991, Baghdad was, to adapt the language of the brochure, a city which had become a dirt strip. This was a pity, as it would have been intriguing to see the ways in which the Iraq pavilion described its major industries without alerting the United Nations weapons inspectorate ('New Power Sources – Our scientists have pioneered a type of generator which is long and conical and pointing at Tel Aviv . . .'). There was, however, a pavilion still called Yugoslavia, and apparently still open, despite the absence of a nation of that name.

Given more advance warning by history, the Russian republics had clubbed together on one site. Between Thailand and the

Solomon Islands, I was surprised to find Rank Xerox, a country new to me. I wondered if some Western democracies were now so bankrupt that they had turned to sponsorship, replacing their historical designations with the names of their financial backers. (Later, an Expo spokesman explained that the show's main industrial funders had been permitted to build a pavilion. *To treat a company as if it were a country*: an expert piece of flattery by the Spanish organizers.)

Rank Xerox was also, of course, a logical sponsor. An Expo offered cultural reproduction, a microcosmic photocopy of a nation. Conscientiously keen to check the case made by those countries visited for this project, I began in New Zealand. The pavilion was a large mock rock, its door presided over by wooden kiwis. A sign advertised 'Maori performances'. (At the first Expo of the epoch of political correctness, most nations were showing respect, in their displays, to first settlers, although, perhaps revealingly, such involvement usually took the form of colourful dance turns or ethnic music.) The doors slid back – at hourly intervals, designed to control the throng, an unnecessary precaution, on this morning at least – to reveal a circular vestibule, at the dead centre of which was a spinning suspended bronze globe.

'Wilcome,' boomed a vowel-vice voice, 'to the lind of the ling white cloud.'

Clouds, unarguably white and probably pretty long, were superimposed on the roof. 'Millions if yirs igo, there was nithing here,' the voice explained. The seasoned visitor to New Zealand had to suppress the thought that, millions of years later, there wasn't all that much more, but such cynicism was inappropriate at Expo. Suddenly, the dome filled with the flute of birdsong and the drum of rocks colliding. This was the birth of New Zealand, the beginning of the topographical and mystical process which would culminate, millennia later, in the All Blacks, Kiri Te Kanawa, and the kiwi fruit. The long white clouds gave way to waves of the same colour and measurements, and the voice said: 'Ind the sea wiz ir gift, ind ir heart would become a ship.' Given the national accent, it was impossible to tell whether the hearts of the early dwellers had become a ship or a sheep. My own prejudice was for the latter.

In the walls of the dome, doors slipped back and we were

ushered through to a second chamber. Fibreglass rocks framed a cinema screen. 'Wilcome to part two if the story if the foundation if Ni Zilland,' a blushing blonde usher said. 'This sigment riflicts the ipportunities iffered by midern Ni Zilland.' An obviously Australian voice shouted from the back: 'Oh, that'll be *short* then . . .' The screen filled with sea and sails. So far, a completely uninformed viewer might have got the impression that New Zealand was the world's oldest established yacht club. You also wondered if there had not, perhaps, been, in the presentation so far, a rather suicidal emphasis on the methods of getting away from the place.

A voice sang: 'Simply by sailing in a new direction / You could enlarge the world . . .' It was Kiri Te Kanawa, the inevitable ambassadress. It was not the most lyrical of lyrics, but she padded it out in the operatic fashion, so that the word 'enlarge', for example, had as many syllables as a Welsh village. As Kiri exploded from the speakers, the screen filled with images of people collecting driftwood on a beach, either a representation of the early dwellers or of modern New Zealanders passing the time. Suddenly, from the orchestra pit, there rose white Perspex triangles, which might have been sharks' fins, but which, given the shape of the story so far, were almost certainly sails. 'Simply by sailing in a new direction / You could enlarge the world,' Kiri reiterated.

The waves faded and, still backed by the soprano testament to the possibilities of yachts, mixed to images of modern national treasures. 'To the commitment of the old was added the pulse of the new,' said a voice. An All Black touched down, a steak sizzled at a beach barbecue, a stream of Chardonnay broke and scattered on the side of a glass like a golden wave. And, yes, a Kiwi fruit was sliced. 'Simply by sailing in a new direction / You could enlarge the world,' Kiri concluded.

The screen emptied and more doors slid back. One of the accidental achievements of modern technology, and incidental lessons of Expo, was that people of all genders and ranks could have doors held open for them. In the lobby, a selection of native merchandise was on sail, I mean sale. New Zealand's commercial dependency on its hairy fruit was disturbingly apparent. There was a Kiwi fruit soft drink, and a boxed presentation gift-set of

Kiwi fruits, with the furry ovals cossetted in green crinkly paper like expensive soap. There was also, however, Marlborough Chardonnay by the glass, and I sank one while, in the closest a tourist gets to being a tyrant, deciding which country to grab next.

I opted to take America. The USA pavilion was, even by Expo standards, an unusually scrupulous reflection of the country's condition. Delayed by furious debate about who would pay for it, the presentation was finally forced – in symbolic thrift and consciousness of the federal deficit – to recycle two geodesic domes from previous trade shows. In the eighties, an American exhibit abroad would have been self-advertisingly expensive and technologically extravagant, with all the screw-you wondrousness of Hollywood and NASA. In the recession election year of 1992, though, all you got was a screening of a video about the Constitution and the Bill of Rights and then an exhibition of the scarred parchment of one of the surviving copies of the Bill.

Rhetoric, however, was cheap, and so the Americans had resonantly titled their display 'Where Liberty Dwells – There Is My Country'. As we queued outside the first dome, each visitor was handed a free pocket-sized copy of the American Constitution. The stern introductory preface, I noticed, was by the statesman Warren E. Burger. It had always been one of my regrets, given the centrality of the grilled meat meal to the American image, that this politician had never reached the White House. President Burger would, it seemed to me, have made a wonderfully fitting late twentieth-century leader.

We were shown a video on which young Americans of all backgrounds, read, in calculatedly winsome singsong voices, the first ten amendments to the constitution, words which in turn formed – a Reagan soundalike had just explained upfront – the Bill of Rights. 'Nor shall any person be subject for the same offence to be twice put in jeopardy of life or limb . . .' lisped a WASP tot. 'Nor be deprived of life, liberty, or property, without due process of law,' added a mulatto one. 'Nor shall private property be taken for public use without just compensation,' declared a small African-American.

It was, in the nineties, increasingly hard to read or hear the Constitution – especially in this trilling of innocents – without feeling almost tearful about the gulf between template and current design. Eventually, these young children would learn that the small exclusion clause 'without due process of law' excused, in large parts of the United States, the deprivation of life through a death penalty. And these were state executions which, in most cases now, no longer pretended to be the execution of moral justice but were simple revenge.

Soon, too, the African-American would learn that a guarantee against the taking of his private property for public use would be small comfort given that he was unlikely to have, demographics suggested, much private property. Only once did the tape admit reality, when an adult contributor reminded us that 'the pursuit of happiness is only possible with a functioning economy . . .' Well, yes. But this, it turned out, was a rebuke to Communism rather than an admission of American difficulties.

Flanking the domes was a side exhibit called the American Spirit Home. Built of white-painted wood, with enough bedrooms to house the offspring of even the keenest Republican pro-lifer, it combined the anciently tasteful (carved hearths, four-poster beds) with the modishly slick (outdoor whirlpool, cinema-sized television screen). This was the face shown to the world by a nation in which 10 per cent of the population was on food stamps.

'Is this really typical?' I asked one of the spookily even-teethed hostesses, each of whom wore a two-piece suit in the colours of Old Glory. 'Typical but not average . . .' she grinned. 'It's typical in being made of wood. Timber remains a key fabric in the building of American homes. I can give you a leaflet, sir, if you're interested . . .' I declined, persisting: 'But surely not many Americans live like this . . .?' Her smile lost several watts. 'Well, yes, sir, this would certainly be an upper middle-class residence. The intention of the exhibit is essentially to demonstrate the flexibility of wood as a building material . . .'

The truth, I supposed, was that it was the timber industry which had put in money to the American Expo effort, and therefore this was the representative residence. If an ice company had come up trumps, an igloo would have been presented as the rule. But, as an American domestic residence, this white house was about as average as *the* White House. I hoped that not too many of the huddled masses passing through Expo were led to emigrate by this façade.

Opposite the American pavilion was a shop which supposedly sold genuine US souvenirs. I wandered around. Even here, there was a sense of making do. For example, a sizeable display was given over to something called Wild Cherry Spoons from Illinois, although I seemed to have avoided spooning any wild cherries, or even tame ones, in either Peoria or Normal. Space was also allotted to bottles labelled San Francisco Bath Oils. As used, you assumed, in the bath houses of San Francisco.

I had lunch at a café, in an international zone between Africa and Malaysia, which promised: 'Your own selection of salads for 900 pesetas.' Impromptu entertainment was provided by the many American visitors who arrived at the till carrying trays laden with as many plates as a juggler doing the crockery trick. At this point, the news would be broken to them: Your own selection of salads, *on one plate*, for 900 pesetas. Niobe, all tears, was back on her feet again quicker than were these Americans after this revelation. Their dismay was so fantastic that it was tempting to check my pocket-size Constitution for a forgotten amendment: 'And the right of the people to enormous portions shall not be curtailed.'

In the afternoon, I considered doing Australia, Canada, and my mother country, but the lines outside all were defeatingly deep. The attraction of Australia I could understand. The country had a fun image: warmth, water, body fluids, booze, cricket, rugby, swearing, oddly shaped animals. Its single tourist draw-back was distance. Alert to its selling points, the Australian pavilion employed white sails, reminiscent of that well-known concert venue, blinding primary colours on all the promotional material, and strategically placed fake kangaroos overlooking the queue routes. The winding lines outside the British tent I attributed to residual historical interest. But *Canada*. The word was that this was the place with the greatest wait. There were rumours of two-hour queues, of people being passed back over the heads when they swooned.

Heat and impatience overtaking me at these pavilions, I headed for the less patronized sites. The Vatican stand was a box of tinted glass, subtly reminiscent of the shades worn by monsignors around Rome. With the Vatican as bankrupt as America, the main attraction was, apparently, the daily celebration of mass.

Luxembourg's pitch consisted of six dial-a-subject video screens, with translation headphones, and a small café. This was commendably honest. No one could seriously claim to have been misled if they went there after seeing this. When I selected the programme called *The Royal Family*, the screen filled with footage of Grand Duke Jean in khaki shorts. 'Grand Duke Jean is also the official leader of the nation's Boy Scouts,' my translation explained. Visitors from less idyllic monarchies could only marvel. The way things were going, it could not be long before it was reported that one of Britain's royals did it with the nation's Boy Scouts.

It was Switzerland, always an individualistic country, which had the gall to be extraordinary. The pavilion was approached up a teetering flight of wide pine steps. These were dotted with hundreds of mouse-traps, half painted white, the rest red. Veil-like screen prints were suspended above the steps. One showed a grainy close-up of a knee, another a mouth. Although the timber pavilion itself might just have been taken as a futuristic chalet – and the numerous mouse-traps as a subtextual reference to cheese-making – the Swiss display was remarkable for daring to break the Expo convention of providing a slice of national life.

The easiest option would have been to mount a sort of *Heidi-Hi!*, an exhibition of cow bells and red crosses and Toblerone moulds. Instead, the Swiss had given over the space to young artists. Gathering in the pavilion cinema, almost certainly expecting a travelogue of snow-caps and yodelling, visitors witnessed a short movie in which a lump of snow melted – in real time. The icy liquid dripped into a bowl. Eventually, the weight of the receptacle knocked a chair forward, causing a burning taper to ignite a rope. At last, the rope broke, releasing a tube of ball-bearings into a dish, which rolled round a table. Ultimately, the bowl fell off. It was like an industrial variation of the old saying about the thigh bone being connected to the hip bone.

Leaving the building, stepping forward carefully across the mouse-traps, I reflected that Switzerland was the first country to manage a surprise at Expo, to venture beyond its international pigeon-hole, its unique tourist selling-points. It was true that potential travellers might have left with the impression that Switzerland was a nation full of experimental performance artists and rodents, but the exhibits at least showed a refreshing independence.

I had walked past the site signposted 'Yugoslavia' several times, fastidiousness defeating curiosity. The pavilion was crowded, but it was obviously Expo's equivalent of the crowds which gather around car and plane crashes. I went inside. The exhibition began with a glass case containing an eight-thousand-year-old warhead found on the banks of the Danube. It was small and chipped, like a stone molar. On a magazine rack were paperback editions of books by Danilo Kis and a note about the proud history of the nation's literature.

The remainder of the display consisted of large colour photographs on a wall. One showed young men leaping and heaving in a chlorinated pool. 'The water-polo players of Yugoslavia are among the best in the world,' a caption explained. Next to it was a shot of a mosque. 'Four religions live peacefully together on Yugoslav territory,' claimed the description, a peace of paper as forlornly hopeful as Neville Chamberlain's. People stood in front of the picture, giggling as they read this canard in four languages. The Yugoslav stewards ignored them. They knew that the pavilion was a fib, an anachronism. But what would you have done? Gone to the organizers and said: 'Obviously, now that there is no country called Yugoslavia, it is right that we should close up this pavilion and go home'? The lie might be saving their lives.

Back late to the Gates of Heaven, I just made last orders in the restaurant. Half-way through a Spanish omelette which threatened to bounce if dropped, a grimy youth appeared beside my table. He goldfish-opened his mouth, pointing a finger inside it each time it gaped. My memory bank rattled. Was it possible that they had sign-language rent boys in Seville as well as Seattle? Would he soon place a card on the table, saying, in Spanish, 'Te Amo'?

Then he began to rub his tummy, and I realized that he was a beggar. I was shovelling pesetas at him as the head waiter bundled him out. Soon, the server reappeared, said 'Sorry, sir,' and handed back the notes I had given the boy. I shrugged and began to put them away. The waiter remained by the table, looking straight at me. I suffered my second belated realization in a few moments and split the notes between us. He beamed and glided away. It was a sharp lesson in the economics of hotel residence.

In the morning, I was back early at Expo, but Australia and Canada were still two-hour waits, so I joined the line waiting for admission to Britain. If Christopher Hope thought that Disney parks resembled concentration camps, then I supposed that Expo – with its angry jostling queues, and barriers crashing down to deny admission to the choiciest countries – was, to that analogy, a pseudo-refugee camp.

Outside the British pavilion, there was a clash of queue culture. French, Italians, Spanish, and Germans were insolently merging, through feet and shoulders, at the front of the line. The British, hanging back from social habit, were doing that thing the British do in queues: exchanging pointed glances, and admonitory coughs, behind the backs of those cheating the system, too ruined by manners actually to do or say anything. The Americans, less held back by conditioning, yelled objections but were ignored and sympathetically shook their heads in time with their special relations.

The British site had a vast flat Perspex front, down which water coursed, collecting in a pond at the bottom. This was impressive, if not particularly representative. In thirty years' residence, I had never thought Britain particularly associated with waterfalls. Then it came to me. I had been wrong to accuse my compatriots of dishonest depiction. The design of vertically mobile water was a tacit admission that, in Britain, it rained all the time.

After an hour of minimal shuffling progress in the leaping heat, a second conceptual breakthrough came to me. This huge queue was part of the demonstration of British culture, for the art of the orderly influx was one of the few things in which my mother country still led the world. The swell of people was diluted through half-hourly intakes, and, eventually, I was allowed into a room lined with long black leather benches, like a leisure centre changing room, but with terraces of television monitors where the lockers would be. Two late-teenagers with microphones, dressed like airline stewardesses, promised 'a journey of discovery to a country you may think you know very well'.

A blizzard of images filled the screens. The expected pictures included the large red oblongs and smaller black boxes of London's traditional transport methods; the even smaller red boxes of its traditional communications centres; the navy blue domes of its traditional law-enforcement headgear. A train raced through the countryside, running so fast that it must have been late. There was an extract from *The Archers* and the opening titles of the BBC evening news. To soft rock music, Gary Lineker kicked a football and John Major waved from in front of the door of Number 10. British Airways had generously loaned a lengthy stretch from one of its television commercials, presumably from a desire to showcase the skills of the British advertising industry.

The Queen and the Queen Mother – selected, you suspected, as the only two members of the Royal family now able to appear in public without strain – did that clever sideways movement of the wrist for which they were paid several million pounds a year. In non-celebrity segments, ordinary Britons were shown about their daily tasks – digging, sparking, welding, banging, steering – in scenes disturbingly reminiscent for the British visitor of those honest artisans in Tory party broadcasts the previous April, who would all allegedly have been demotivatingly taxed under Labour.

The video over, we were elaborately formed into another queue, a tacit confirmation of the exhibition's subtext, and ushered on to escalators. At the top of the pavilion was a theatre, in which a clever rock-laser-and-video show was performed on the theme of modern communications methods. An actor, limbed and lit to resemble a robot, gyrated and crackle-spoke through a series of telephone and computer conversations, the links indicated through lasers or chains of light.

Perfect for this event, because the purely visual was automatically multilingual, it was undoubtedly a smart piece of art. But it was here that I most appreciated the improbability, though also the brilliance, of the Expo trick. When you thought about it, the project conned torrents of people (the final attendance figure for Seville was put at twenty-seven million) into queueing for hours for an experience of a foreign culture which was, in the end, no more intense than that offered by a television documentary.

Indeed, a majority of the pavilions contained only a video travelogue: an exact replica of the static travel standard on a television holiday show. Some authentic tastes were on offer, it was true, but, again, ones no more vivid than those available in restaurants and wine shops in most modern high streets. That Expo was tenable at all, in its present form, was evidence of the deep human desire for easy experience of other cultures.

I was not so homesick that I could be lured by the Traditional Steak 'n Kidney Pud in Lionheart's Restaurant in the British pavilion. But I lingered in the shop selling 'traditional British souvenirs'. These included *Diana*, 'a delightful illustrated account of the life of the fairy-tale princess'. So an Expo was, then, just a Disneyland for grown-ups, a magic kingdom in which no nation listed arms manufacture among its industries or social unrest among its problems, monarchies had no problems, and Yugoslavia was a country in which four different religions lived peacefully together.

And in which, it might be added, people battled to get into Canada. I queued for ninety minutes outside the maple leaf pavilion on my last afternoon, but, in the end, low expectation overcame patience. I never did discover how Canada was packing them in – a sneak preview of Madonna's *Sex* book? A large sign reading 'Drinks on us'? – but I was unable to shake off my conviction that there were some things even the travel business could not fake.

# CHAPTER TWELVE

# NO PLACE LIKE DOME

### Center Parcs

The heat, the heat. I shifted my feet on the baking promenade, glad of the protection of a palm tree, but envious of the travellers who had reached the waterside early enough for a sun umbrella. Through the heat haze, I could make out banana plants and cacti. I dropped my book and plunged into the seductive deep blue water. My hope had been to be cooled, but the water was warm. That was the problem – if a small one – with the tropical climate. I splashed towards the small island bar with its coconut-matting roof.

It was deep English winter at the dog end of the year. The country was its usual winter germ circuit of sniffles and bugs and shivering to work. My train had been delayed by a bomb scare. Eight months after his election triumph, you could get sensible bets at the turf accountant's on how long John Major might survive in office. There was every motivation to get away from it all, restore yourself in a warm climate. Once, Britons would have had to take a plane: to Spain, Italy, Miami. Now, however, they could drive or take the train.

I was in a tropical corner of Nottingham. Center Parcs – spelled in American, but an Amsterdam invention – was the most mainstream manifestation of the genre of static travel: the *trompe l'œil* holiday. Tourism's weakness was its dependence on the weather. Always true of Northern Europe, this was increasingly the case elsewhere, because of the realignments of climate caused by the environmental tremors. Center Parc's promise, and marketing appeal, was the defeat of the elements. Swimming and sunbathing were possible every day of the year.

This was achieved through a huge sealed dome, which

maintained a steady jungle heat. It was a cross between a swimming pool and a solarium, in a space the size of a shopping mall. The obvious objection was that the essence of a country consists of more than its climate, and that – beyond the meticulous and genuine imported vegetation – there was no recreation of a Caribbean or tropical culture. But this, at least for mass audience travel, was the genius of Center Parcs. All that a majority of travellers sought from abroad was its weather. They didn't want the germs, or monuments, or people.

Cunningly, then, Center Parcs delivered Mediterranean climate in the midst of English countryside: you stayed in a villa with underfloor heating (two more fingers to the winter), among four hundred acres of trees and deer, birds and flowers; cooked your own food from an on-site supermarket or chose from one of the multi-cuisine restaurants in the complex, and then took a brisk shivery stroll each morning to the beach. As a piece of attempted social engineering – a reorganization of British life – it was to play what Milton Keynes had been to work. But, here, so far, the truth remained close to the blueprint.

From James Cook to Thomas Cook to static travel: three ages of exploration. One day, the currently still virgin science of Virtual Reality – a three-dimensional stimulation of the senses – would allow a far more spectacular form of static travel. Strapped into their wrap-around televisions and headsets, visitors would feel the lap of the waves, the pat of the sun, and the scrape of the sand without ever leaving their own damp home. Trip in the hippy sense and trip in the travel agent sense would become combined. You would go places in your head. Perhaps some subscribers would even take out the New Zealand cassette and hear the authentic bleating of the sheep and twang and occasional snap of the bungee-jumpers.

But, with technology as it existed, I had been forced actually to travel to all these places, assisted by science only at Center Parcs. I looked at my bags in the corner of the villa. At each airport I had passed through on the project, a brightly coloured tag had been attached to them, with an abbreviation of the destination city on it: LAX, LHR, ZUR, ANCH, AUK, SYD. At each subsequent airport, the label had been torn back by a check-in clerk, to prevent confusion with the new one, leaving a small coloured stub still tied to the handles. There were so many of them now that they looked like popped party balloons. It was an appropriate enough image, for I had been, among other things, to a party in Timaru. But now I was going to the place and to the word which seemed to me the only one which could properly end this project. Home.

# LAST BULLETINS

## *From the Quiet World*

In reaction to the author's passionate dissertation on the slowness of the elevators at the Delta Place Hotel in Vancouver, Canada – delivered on the guest comments questionnaire – the General Manager of the hotel, Grant McCurdy, wrote: 'I was very disappointed to read your comments that this will probably be the last time you will stay at a Delta Hotel due to our elevators and consequently being late for your meeting. We are currently discussing ways to improve the speed of our elevators with Montgomery Kone, our elevator contractors . . . Mr Lawson, we at Delta Place pride ourselves on our customer service excellence and our continual goal of striving to exceed our customer's expectations. It is only by receiving direct customer feedback and comments that we are in a position to endeavour to improve our product and our services . . . [I] trust that you will not exclude all Delta Hotels from your travel choices based on your perceptions of the elevators at Delta Place . . .' However, no compensation or incentive to stay again was offered.

Following the author's father's written complaint about the quality of the food at the Hotel Monopole in Lucerne and the Royal St Georges in Interlaken, he received a letter from Carol M. Stebbings of the Customer Services Department of Thomson Holidays. Addressing the author's father throughout as 'Mrs Lawson', Ms Stebbings advised him/her that 'we do at all times monitor food services provided for our customers' and 'can advise you that there would seem to have been some improvement'. However, in the circumstances, she believed that 'an *ex gratia* payment would be applicable'. The letter enclosed a cheque for

£100, made out to the author. He decided to let the matter rest.


In the US presidential election, on November 5th, 1992, the majority of electors in Peoria and Normal, Illinois, voted either for the incumbent, George Bush, or for the peculiar tycoon Ross Perot. Barrow, Alaska, the northernmost point of the Union, voted handsomely for Bill Clinton. The extremity proved more representative than the bell-wethers, and Bill Clinton was elected forty-second President of the United States.

This was despite George Bush's continuing attempts to impute sinister motives to Clinton's student holiday in the Soviet Union in 1968. The decision of Gennifer Flowers – who claimed to have had a twelve-year affair with the candidate – to pose naked in the election edition of *Playboy* also made no fatal impact. Optimists read in Clinton's victory – against the formerly insuperable odds of a negative Republican campaign and exploding biographical bimbos offstage – a new maturity in the USA with regard to political and sexual smears against candidates. Pessimists concluded that the electorate's unusual moral generosity was an aberration, a product of the economic emergency.

Paradoxically, an electorate which had seemed all year volcanically hostile to the existing system had sent to the White House the most dedicated and cunning career politician (a five-term governor) to gain the presidency for decades. But it was wrong to see the seismic uncertainties of America in 1992 as completely appeased by this outcome. The movement which put Ross Perot on the ballot in all fifty states reflected a genuine hunger for deliverance from America's plight. In the election, Perot's 18 per cent of the vote was an extraordinary score for a third candidate and was an ominous shadow across the victor's mandate.

The conventional system had apparently been vindicated. But if the economic chaos did not abate, a still, small, whiny voice would be heard from Texas: 'Ah told 'm.' Perot had left himself the excuse, the ego-salve, that the people simply did not dare take the risk they needed to. The unnerving burden on President Clinton was to restore democratic equilibrium – and confidence in the conventional ballot box – or America might yet be the territory for a populist, anti-political, sinister Mr Fixit.

After Clinton's victory, it was admitted by the Bush administration that the State Department had permitted searches of the passport files of Clinton and his elderly mother in pursuit of a rumour that the candidate had once unpatriotically sought to change nationality. An official resigned in contrition. Three weeks before leaving office, President George Bush used the tradition of Christmas Eve pardons to clear from prosecution officials expected to testify against Bush in forthcoming hearings on the Iran–Contra illegal arms case. Planned to twist historians' arms in his favour, this action seemed rather to have bunched their fingers into fists against him.

The USA's latest hit non-fiction book was – for students of anthropology through bestseller lists – *Sell Yourself – The Complete Guide to Selling Your Organs, Body Fluids, Bodily Functions and Being a Human Guinea Pig*. Previously, the rent, mortgaging, and sale of living body parts had been a Third World phenomenon.

In Britain, the year's literary hit was Andrew Morton's *Diana: Her True Story*. In November, the Queen agreed that she would in future pay taxes, subjecting herself to the same obligations as her citizens. Her Majesty would also now support the majority of her expanding family from her own purse, they having been previously bank-rolled by the tax-payer. These moves were widely seen as a public relations response to the increasing public scepticism about the British Royal Family's moral and symbolic function. Two weeks later, it was announced that the Prince of Wales ('Fred' to his friends) and the Princess of Wales ('Squidgy' to hers) were to separate. The Prime Minister insisted that there was no constitutional complication. Others wondered whether a coronation in which the King and Queen approached the abbey from separate directions – perhaps even knelt in different abbeys – would have the proper *gravitas*.

The commissions of inquiry into the morality of John Major's closure of the coal mines – and into the propriety of his government's dealings with the sales of arms to Iraq – opened their investigations as the year closed. The Prime Minister was also faced with the difficulty of persuading his party – and, by extension, his nation – to ratify the Maastricht Treaty, giving Britain closer economic bonds with Europe.

In New Zealand, the Bolger administration ended the right of its citizens to free hospital treatment. It was estimated that one in three of school-leavers went immediately on to the dole.

As the year ended, unemployment in Australia stood at 11 per cent. Like other countries in the First World, the economy was flinching from the red bills on the mat. The national debt was £68.25 billion. This represented 39 per cent of Gross National Product, an extraordinary blow-out for a sparsely populated country with no direct involvement in the arms race.

In an end-of-year address, the Prime Minister, Paul Keating, predicted that Australia would be a republic by the year 2000. His espousal of republicanism substantially raised his previously poor poll rating.

Following falling ratings for all the recession-hit Australian television stations, evening news bulletins introduced Bingo promotions between the headlines to attract viewers. Count the dead Bosnians and win a Lamborgini!

The new Sydney Harbour Tunnel opened. A local radio station announced a competition with a prize for the first couple to achieve sexual intercourse while negotiating the thoroughfare. Public officials angrily protested that any such attempts would pose a safety risk to other drivers.

And Melbourne's reputation for alarming calm went the way of those of other celebrated oases in that strange year for the quiet world. In early November, one hundred thousand people marched through the city in protest against the free-market economic policies – as previously seen in the USA and Britain – of the state government. This public anger was another curious example of the political instability which had begun to grip the fabled stable places of the globe. The demonstration came only a few weeks after the ruling party, making little secret of its economic policies, had won a landslide in state elections.

In a national referendum, the people of Canada rejected the new constitutional package proposed by Brian Mulroney and the provincial prime ministers. Confusion over the next step was intense. Support for Preston Manning's Reform Party increased.

On January 1st, 1993, it became illegal for road signs in Montreal requesting cars to cease moving to feature the word *Stop*. In future, they must bear the single word *Arret*. The replacement of eleven thousand signs cost the city of Montreal an estimated $600,000.

In December, Switzerland voted, in a referendum, against membership of the EEA (European Economic Area), an interim step towards membership of the European Community, which would have created a free-trade zone comprising Switzerland, Liechtenstein, Iceland, Norway, Sweden, Finland, and Austria and containing nearly four hundred million customers, between the Mediterranean and the Arctic Circle. The result was another of the year's European racial divides, though more peaceful than most, with Francophone Swiss generally voting in favour and the German-speakers, the majority population, saying no. 'You would have to say that the Swiss have voted for isolation,' said the External Relations Commissioner of the European Community.

*Et tu*, Belgium? In December, the Belgian riot police were called out in force on to the streets of Brussels. The nation's farmers had blocked the city's main intersections with tractors, and then grouped menacingly outside the building where EC foreign ministers were meeting to discuss the GATT treaty. Order, however, was restored and no deaths or serious injuries were reported.

The first annual operating profits for EuroDisney showed a much lower volume of visitors than had been predicted and a larger financial loss than expected. Accordingly, the annual contribution which the park had been scheduled to make to its American parent company was waived.


In the last part of the year, an anecdote began to be widely circulated in Europe, particularly among new mothers. It concerned a family that took a weekend break at EuroDisney. On the first afternoon, so the tale unfolded, the mother looked around and realized that one of her children was missing. She found a security guard, who barked into his walkie-talkie, 'Lock all the gates!' and rushed the mother to a room stacked with closed-circuit television monitors. The woman began to babble a description of her child's blonde hair and clothes. 'Madame,' interrupted the security guard, 'look at the children on those monitors but look *only* at the face.'

Frantically staring at the screens, she eventually recognized her child's nose, mouth and eyes on a black-haired child, being led away from the park hand-in-hand with Mickey Mouse. The security guards pounced and there was a joyous reunion, removal of hair-dye, and arrest of the bogus Mickey Mouse. British mothers shivered at this story. Cynical journalists, however, spotted another specimen of that interesting literary form: the urban legend.

Further research matched the EuroDisney anecdotes with similar relay tales that had attended the opening of the American parks. There seemed to be something particularly resonant about the collision of innocence and evil, of scariness and fairy tale, culminating in the abductor being, of all non-people, Mickey Mouse. Yet America was a culture in which so many children disappeared that their pictures were printed on milk cartons. The new prevalence of the legend in Britain – a related tale featured abducted kids grabbed back by their parents as their hair was dyed in London supermarket lavatories – reflected a gathering perception of an American level of threat to the young.

In Milton Keynes, in late November, an eleven-year-old girl was raped – in broad daylight, at eight thirty in the morning – on her way to school. She had been walking alone on the Redway. Residents publicly – and the local police privately – attributed the vulnerability of pedestrians to such attacks to the idealistic *trompe l'œil* landscaping of Central Milton Keynes.

Throughout 1992, Australia was disturbed by what appeared to be a trend towards mass shootings and violent seiges. The volumes of assaults, rapes, and robberies had all doubled in the previous ten years. The government cited a breakdown in home and classroom discipline. Evangelists blamed Satan. Liberals pointed to a sense of grievance instilled by the lengthy recession and to one of Australia's most significant Americanizations: the fact that one in four Australians now owned a fire-arm.

New Zealand suffered another mass slaying, when a disturbed grandfather picked off his family one by one on their farm. A

British tourist was stabbed to death on a beach in North Island. In the capital, Wellington, a seventy-two-year-old woman was raped in her house. On the South Island, an eight-year-old girl was raped while walking home.

So what conclusions could a traveller draw from a year spent in the quiet world? Only a fool or a neurotic would deny that it was still better to be born in any of these destinations than in Bosnia, Somalia, Beirut, or one of the other horror spots that kept CNN and the UN in business. But it was equally apparent that the borders of the safe zones were receding. There were no islands any more. There was no easy opt-out anywhere from poverty, joblessness, or – and this most strikingly – some variety of violence.

On the latter topic, I had spent years appearing at seminars and on media discussions rejecting the easy connection made by the censorious right between the invention of television and video and the extension of social violence. In fact, secretly I half agreed with them, except that they identified the wrong material. The stuff, in my opinion, which might subliminally disturb was not the war films and the gun-and-punch police series but the commercials and the soppy love stories, the profiles of the famous, the documentaries on the lifestyles of the rich. One effect of television was to give the disadvantaged and disgruntled a greater sense of social inequity, of their own helplessness in the wider scheme.

Other factors, which perhaps also contributed to increasing violence, linked the constituent nations of the quiet world. In many of them – Britain and the antipodes particularly – a money-saving scheme euphemistically called 'Care in the Community' had released on to the streets patients who perhaps ideally needed psychiatric care and confinement. But this decision was merely a symptom of another problem common to these regions: the crisis of financial provision. The prevalent political idea of reduction of the personal tax burden had left these countries struggling to fund the lifestyles to which electorates had become accustomed.

Maybe, then, it was no coincidence that, in each of these former oases of stasis, there was also a crisis of belief in leaders.

In the period of a year, in nearly every nation of the quiet world, a leader – be they president, prime minister, or queen – had been retired by their colleagues, rejected in a referendum or election, or in some way humbled in the eyes of the public. The only exception was Australia, in which a political leader cannily consolidated his position by directing public discontent against the unelected, absentee head of state.

After the fall of the Berlin Wall in 1989, an American academic called Francis Fukuyama had become rich and famous with a thesis called *The End of History*, which boasted that capitalism had triumphed unequivocally in the century's conflict of ideas. We were all, he had said, free marketeers now. It was now increasingly clear that he had held the party too soon. History didn't end anywhere, not even at the borders of the boring world.

So you could conclude, if you wished, that the quiet world had lost its innocence and its citizens their awe. Or you could argue that, when the money came back, the rest would follow. But perhaps people had lost their innocence about that too. The most obvious conclusion was this: that the bomb ticking under every democracy is its economy.


While completing this book, the author became involved in lengthy correspondence with a British insurance company over a policy which he was seeking to take out to guarantee an endowment mortgage. The company argued that – because of the author's primary employment as a journalist – he might be liable to pay an extra war and riot risks insurance premium. The author replied that this proposal was a complete misunderstanding of his career and beliefs. In evidence, he directed the risk assessors towards his published articles, the testimony of his colleagues to his extreme and diligent cowardice, and the manuscript of this book. The additional premium was withdrawn.

# ACKNOWLEDGEMENTS

A small portion of the text – around 5 per cent, mainly that concerned with the progress of the 1992 American election and some of the observations on the antipodes – previously appeared in a different form in the *Independent Magazine* and the *Independent*. I am grateful to Andreas Whittam Smith, editor-in-chief of the *Independent*, for permission to rework the material here and to him, Alexander Chancellor and Lucy Tuck for their generosity about time off.

I am grateful to Faber & Faber for permission to quote from Philip Larkin's 'The Whitsun Weddings'. Throughout the journeys, I used the excellent Fodor's range of guidebooks, in the 1992 editions, for logistical information. Other books consulted included *The Penguin History of Canada* (Penguin, 1988) and – as specified in the Canada chapter – *The Will of a Nation* by George Radwanski and Julia Luttrell (Stoddart, 1992); *Oh Canada! Oh Quebec!* by Mordecai Richler (Penguin, 1992) and *The Betrayal of Canada* by Mel Hurtig (Stoddart, 1992). The information on world travel danger zones in the Prologue comes from the December 1992 edition of *Business Traveller* magazine.

I would like to thank the following for hospitality and assistance overseas: 'Jessica', 'Gemma', 'Cousin Claire', and their relatives and friends in New Zealand; Carrie Mishima and Sally Payne. I am grateful to Peter Straus and Cat Ledger for advice and support; to Susan Feldman for research and travel arrangements; to Frank Lawson, for research and company in Switzerland; and to Sarah and William Lawson, for many things, including, in the case of the latter, agreeing to sleep at night during the critical stages of composition.

Mark Lawson, January 1993

# picador.com

blog
videos
interviews
extracts